First World War
and Army of Occupation
War Diary
France, Belgium and Germany

66 DIVISION
197 Infantry Brigade
Lancashire Fusiliers
3/5th (T) Battalion
28 February 1917 - 13 February 1918

WO95/3137/2

The Naval & Military Press Ltd
www.nmarchive.com
Published in association with The National Archives

Published by

The Naval & Military Press Ltd

Unit 10 Ridgewood Industrial Park,

Uckfield, East Sussex,

TN22 5QE England

Tel: +44 (0) 1825 749494

www.naval-military-press.com

www.nmarchive.com

This diary has been reprinted in facsimile from the original. Any imperfections are inevitably reproduced and the quality may fall short of modern type and cartographic standards.

© Crown Copyright
Images reproduced by permission of The National Archives, London, England, 2015.

Contents

Document type	Place/Title	Date From	Date To
Heading	WO95/3137/2		
Heading	197th Brigade 66th Division Disembarked Havre 1.3.17. 3/5th Battalion Lancashire Fusiliers 28th February To 31st March 1917		
War Diary	Colchester	28/02/1917	28/02/1917
War Diary	Havre	01/03/1917	02/03/1917
War Diary	Wittes Ref. Map Hazebrouck 5 A	03/03/1917	05/03/1917
War Diary	Les Lobes	08/03/1917	09/03/1917
War Diary	Beuvry	10/03/1917	19/03/1917
War Diary	Gorre	22/03/1917	23/03/1917
War Diary	Givenchy Left Sub-Sector	24/03/1917	31/03/1917
Miscellaneous	The following copy of a Telegram is forwarded for your information with reference to this Office Number M/175 of 4.2.17. Appendix I	08/02/1917	08/02/1917
Miscellaneous	Special Order By Lieut-Col A.S. Bates D.S.O. Commanding 3/5th Batt Lancashire Fusiliers Goojerat Barracks Colchester	26/02/1917	26/02/1917
Miscellaneous	Move. Order Lieut-Colonel A.S. Bates. D.S.O. Commanding 3/5th Batt Lancashire Fusiliers Goojerat Barracks Colchester	26/02/1917	26/02/1917
Miscellaneous	Appendix 3	31/01/1917	31/01/1917
Miscellaneous	3/5th Battn. Lancashire Fusiliers. Casualty Report For Month Of March 1917. Appendix 4	31/03/1917	31/03/1917
Heading	197th Brigade 66th Division 3/5 Battalion Lancashire Fusiliers April 1917		
War Diary	Givenchy Left Sub Sector	02/04/1917	30/04/1917
Miscellaneous	The following figures of men reporting sick for the month of April are forwarded for your information. Appendix I.	04/05/1917	04/05/1917
Miscellaneous	3/5th Bn. Lancashire Fusiliers List Of Casualties For Month of April 1917.	01/05/1917	01/05/1917
Heading	197th Brigade 66th Division 3/5th Battalion Lancashire Fusiliers May 1917		
Miscellaneous	Appendix 2	03/05/1917	03/05/1917
Diagram etc	Diagram		
Operation(al) Order(s)	Special Brigade Order No. 4.	11/05/1917	11/05/1917
Miscellaneous	Casualties During Month of May 1917	01/06/1917	01/06/1917
Miscellaneous	The following figures of men in the Brigade reporting Sick and Admitted to Hospital during month of May are forwarded for information.	31/05/1917	31/05/1917
War Diary	Givenchy Left Sub-Sector Refce Trench Map La Bassee Edition 8a 1/10000	01/05/1917	18/05/1917
Heading	197th Brigade 66th Division 3/5 Battalion Lancashire Fusiliers June 1917.		
War Diary	Givenchy Left Sub-Sector	01/06/1917	20/06/1917
War Diary	Bellerive (Bethune Combined Sheet N 12 B)	24/06/1917	30/06/1917
Miscellaneous	Instructions For Coast Defences-Dunkirk Area	29/06/1917	29/06/1917
Miscellaneous	Amendment No 1. Operation Order No. 1	01/07/1917	01/07/1917

Miscellaneous	Operation Order No. 1 by Lieut Colonel A.S. Bates D.S.O. Commanding Zuydcoote Sub-sector & 3/5th Bn Lan	30/06/1917	30/06/1917
Miscellaneous	Appendix "A"		
Miscellaneous	Casualties For Month of June 1917 3/5th Battn. Lancashire Fusiliers	01/07/1917	01/07/1917
Diagram etc	Diagram To Accompany Alarm Operation Orders No.1.		
Miscellaneous	3/5 Battn. Lancashire Fusiliers	01/07/1917	01/07/1917
Heading	197th Brigade 66th Division 3/5th Battalion Lancashire Fusiliers July 1917		
Heading	War Diary of 3/5th Battn. Lancashire Fusiliers From:- 1st July 1917 To:- 31st July 1917 Volume 6		
War Diary	Malo Terminus	01/07/1917	01/07/1917
War Diary	Malo-Les-Bains Dunkerque 1a Belgium 1/100,000	03/07/1917	12/07/1917
War Diary	Coxyde Bains (Map Ref. Dunkerque Belgium 1/100000)	13/07/1917	16/07/1917
War Diary	Nieuport Bains (Dunkerque Belgium 1/100000)	16/07/1917	29/07/1917
War Diary	Coxhyde Bains (Map. Ref. Dunkerque Belgium 1/100000)	30/07/1917	31/07/1917
Miscellaneous	2nd Division No. G.S. 1215	28/06/1917	28/06/1917
Miscellaneous	Operation Order No. 2. by Lieut Colonel A.S. Bates D.S.O. 3/5th Lan Fus Commanding Zuydcoote Sub-sector	08/07/1917	08/07/1917
Miscellaneous	Coast Defence Scheme Zuydcoote Sub-Sector	20/06/1917	20/06/1917
Miscellaneous	Operation Order No. 2 by Lieut Colonel A.S. Bates D.S.O. Commanding 3/5th Bn Lancashire Fusiliers	09/07/1917	09/07/1917
Miscellaneous	Appendix "A"	09/07/1917	09/07/1917
Miscellaneous	Appendix "C". S.A.A. & Grenade Reserve.		
Miscellaneous	Subject:- Practice Alarm.	10/07/1917	10/07/1917
Miscellaneous	Subject:- Practice Alarm.	11/07/1917	11/07/1917
Miscellaneous	Subject. Alarm on night July 10/11th.1917.	11/07/1917	11/07/1917
Miscellaneous	Situation on Corps Front	11/07/1917	11/07/1917
Heading	197th Brigade 66th Division 3/5th Battalion Lancashire Fusiliers August 1917		
Heading	War Diary of 3/5th Bn. Lancashire Fusiliers From 1/8/17 To 31/8/17 Volume 7.		
War Diary	Coxyde Bains (Dunkerque Ia Belgium 1/100000)	01/08/1917	28/08/1917
War Diary	Oost Dunkerque Bains (Dunkeque IA Belgium 1/100000)	28/08/1917	31/08/1917
Miscellaneous	Special Order Of The Day By Lieut. Col. A.S. Bates, D.S.O. Commanding 3/5th. Lan. Fus.	01/09/1917	01/09/1917
Operation(al) Order(s)	Administrative Operation Order No. 1	30/07/1917	30/07/1917
Operation(al) Order(s)	Administrative Operation Order No. 2.	01/08/1917	01/08/1917
Operation(al) Order(s)	Operation Order No. 1by Lieut Colonel A.S. Bates D.S.O. 3/5th Lan Fus	01/08/1917	01/08/1917
Operation(al) Order(s)	Operation Order No. 2 By Commanding	03/08/1917	03/08/1917
Operation(al) Order(s)	Operation Order No. 3 By Commanding	04/08/1917	04/08/1917
Operation(al) Order(s)	Operation Order No. 4 by Lieut Col A.S. Bates D.S.O. commanding 3/5th Battn Lan Fus	05/08/1917	05/08/1917
Miscellaneous	Index To Orders Etc.	05/08/1917	05/08/1917
Miscellaneous	Appendix "A"		
Miscellaneous	3/5th Battn. Lancashire Fusiliers Casualties For Month of August, 1917.	31/08/1917	31/08/1917
Heading	197th Brigade 66th Division 3/5th Battalion Lancashire Fusiliers September 1917.		

Type	Description	Date From	Date To
Heading	War Diary Of 3/5th Battalion Lancashire Fusiliers From:- 1/9/17 To 30/9/17 Volume 8.		
War Diary	La Panne Dunkerque 1A Belgium 1/10000	03/09/1917	24/09/1917
War Diary	Zuydcoote Dunkerque 1 A Belgium 1.10,000	24/09/1917	30/09/1917
Miscellaneous	Preliminary Coast Defence Scheme 3/5th Bn. Lan. Fus.	02/09/1917	02/09/1917
Miscellaneous	Headquarters 197th Infantry Brigade	16/09/1917	16/09/1917
Miscellaneous	Amendments To Preliminary Coast Defence Scheme 3/5th Bn. Lan. Fus.	10/09/1917	10/09/1917
Miscellaneous	Coast Defence Orders La Panne Section.	14/09/1917	14/09/1917
Miscellaneous	La Panne Section Coast Defence		
Diagram etc	La Panne Section Coast Defence		
Miscellaneous	Orders For Sentries		
Diagram etc	Diagram		
Miscellaneous	Report On Defences		
Map	Training Area		
Operation(al) Order(s)	Coast Defence Orders No.1	24/08/1917	24/08/1917
Miscellaneous	Appendix "A". S.A.A. and Grenade Reserve.		
Operation(al) Order(s)	Addition To Coast Defence Orders No.1	25/09/1917	25/09/1917
Miscellaneous	Appendix "B". Barrage details so for as Battalion posts are concerned.		
Miscellaneous	3/5th Battalion Lancashire Fusiliers	30/09/1917	30/09/1917
Heading	197th Brigade 66th Division 3/5th Battalion Lancashire Fusiliers October 1917		
Heading	War Diary of 3/5th Battn. Lancashire Fusiliers From 1/10/17 To 31/10/17 Volume 9		
War Diary	Eecke (Hazebrouck 5A) Belgium 1/1000000	03/10/1917	03/10/1917
War Diary	Winnizeele J.4.b.	04/10/1917	04/10/1917
War Diary	Frezenberg Ridge	05/10/1917	10/10/1917
War Diary	Winnizeele	11/10/1917	19/10/1917
War Diary	Campagne	20/10/1917	31/10/1917
Miscellaneous	Appendices To War Diary For October 1917		
Miscellaneous	Battle Standing Orders	03/10/1917	03/10/1917
Miscellaneous	Officers. The following Officers accompanied the Battalion into action.	09/10/1917	09/10/1917
Miscellaneous	Detail Camp Narrative	05/10/1917	05/10/1917
Miscellaneous	Diary Of Message Sent And Received To And From Brigade Headquarters Unless Otherwise Stated-From 081017 To 101017	08/10/1917	08/10/1917
Miscellaneous	Message Sent	08/10/1917	08/10/1917
Operation(al) Order(s)	197th Infantry Brigade Operation Order No. 54	08/10/1917	08/10/1917
Miscellaneous	4 Battalions	08/10/1917	08/10/1917
Miscellaneous	Operation Orders Issued To Company Commanders	08/10/1917	08/10/1917
Miscellaneous	Subject. Action of October 9th-11th. 1917. Appendix 8	14/10/1917	14/10/1917
Miscellaneous	Medical Officers Report		
Operation(al) Order(s)	Operation Order No. 55	10/10/1917	10/10/1917
Miscellaneous	List Of Names Of Officers And Other Ranks Submitted To Brigade For Gallantry And Good Conduct During The Operations. Appendix 11		
Miscellaneous	Battle Casualties By companies and ranks	16/10/1917	16/10/1917
Miscellaneous	Casualties In The Brigade	13/10/1917	13/10/1917
Miscellaneous	Congratulatory Telegrams	15/10/1917	15/10/1917
Miscellaneous	Special Order By Lt Col A.S. Gates D.S.O. Commanding 3/5th Lan Fus	18/10/1917	18/10/1917
Miscellaneous	Gallant Conduct	16/10/1917	16/10/1917
Miscellaneous	Honours and Awards	20/10/1917	20/10/1917
Miscellaneous	Honours and Awards	22/10/1917	22/10/1917

Miscellaneous	Honours and Awards	27/10/1917	27/10/1917
Miscellaneous	3/5th. Lan. Fus. Appendix 20	18/10/1917	18/10/1917
Miscellaneous	Casualty Report Of Officers Of This Unit For The Month of October, 1917	31/10/1917	31/10/1917
Miscellaneous	3/5th Battalion Lancashire Fusiliers	09/10/1917	09/10/1917
Miscellaneous	3/5th Battalion Lancashire Fusiliers	31/10/1917	31/10/1917
Heading	197th Brigade 66th Division 3/5th Battalion Lancashire Fusiliers November 1917		
Heading	War Diary of 3/5th Battalion Lancashire Fusiliers From:- 1st November, 1917 To 30th November, 1917. Volume 10		
War Diary	Campagne	01/11/1917	08/11/1917
War Diary	Westoutre	09/11/1917	09/11/1917
War Diary	Ypres	10/11/1917	22/11/1917
War Diary	Berthen	23/11/1917	23/11/1917
War Diary	Staple	24/11/1917	30/11/1917
Miscellaneous	Brigade Tactical Exercise No 5	05/11/1917	05/11/1917
Operation(al) Order(s)	3/5th Bn. Lancashire Fusiliers Operation Order No. 23.	07/11/1917	07/11/1917
Miscellaneous	Cow Operation Order	09/11/1917	09/11/1917
Miscellaneous	Distribution of officers	10/11/1917	10/11/1917
Miscellaneous	Cow Operation Orders	20/11/1917	20/11/1917
Miscellaneous	Appendix Casualties 10/11/17-19/11/17 3/5 Battalion Lancashire Fusiliers. Appx V	10/11/1917	10/11/1917
Miscellaneous	Appendix Distribution Of Officers Referred To In Appendix As At 21/11/17. Appx VI	21/11/1917	21/11/1917
Operation(al) Order(s)	Cow Operation Order No. 23	21/11/1917	21/11/1917
Miscellaneous	Routine Orders By Lieutenant-General Sir A.J. Godley K.C.B. K.C.M.C. Commanding 2nd Anzac Corps	26/11/1917	26/11/1917
Miscellaneous	Cow Operation Order-G.24	22/11/1917	22/11/1917
Miscellaneous	Subj:- Immediate Honours & Awards. Appendix IX	21/11/1917	21/11/1917
Miscellaneous	Nominal Roll of Officers	30/11/1917	30/11/1917
Heading	197th Brigade 66th Division 3/5th Battalion Lancashire Fusiliers December 1917		
Heading	War Diary of 3/5th Battalion, Lancashire Fusiliers From:- 1.12.17 To:- 31.12.17 Volume 10		
War Diary	Staple	05/12/1917	30/12/1917
War Diary	Busseboom	31/05/1917	31/05/1917
Operation(al) Order(s)	Operation Order G.30	29/12/1917	29/12/1917
Operation(al) Order(s)	Operation Order G.31	30/12/1917	30/12/1917
Heading	War Diary of 3/5th Battalion Lancashire Fusiliers From:- 1.1.18 To:- 31.1.18 Volume 11		
War Diary	Busseboom (Ref. Belgium And France Sheet 28 Edition3 G.22.b.8.6)	01/01/1918	02/01/1918
War Diary	Busseboom	03/01/1918	10/01/1918
War Diary	Halifax Camp (H.14.C.3.5)	11/01/1918	15/01/1918
War Diary	Line H.Q.D.16d.8.2. Line	16/01/1918	17/01/1918
War Diary	Halifax Camp	18/01/1918	18/01/1918
War Diary	Line	20/01/1918	21/01/1918
War Diary	Support J.3.a.4.2.	22/01/1918	27/01/1918
War Diary	Halifax Camp	28/01/1918	31/01/1918
Miscellaneous	Work On Corps Line. Appendix 1	03/01/1918	03/01/1918
Miscellaneous	Work On Corps Line. Appendix II	02/01/1918	02/01/1918
Miscellaneous	Instructions for Working Parties In case of attack	03/01/1918	03/01/1918
Miscellaneous	Appendix IV	08/01/1918	08/01/1918
Operation(al) Order(s)	3/5th Battn. Lancashire Fusiliers Operation Order No. G.32	11/01/1918	11/01/1918

Miscellaneous	Administrative Instructions Issued with Reference To 3/5th Bn. Lancashire Fusiliers	11/01/1918	11/01/1918
Miscellaneous	Warning Order	13/01/1918	13/01/1918
Miscellaneous	Administrative Instructions Issued With Reference To Operation Order	15/01/1918	15/01/1918
Operation(al) Order(s)	3/5th Battn. Lancashire Fusiliers Operation Order G.33	15/01/1918	15/01/1918
Operation(al) Order(s)	3/5th Battn. Lancashire Fusiliers Operation Order G.35	21/01/1918	21/01/1918
Miscellaneous	Instructions Re Gum-Boots-Vide O.O.35.	22/01/1918	22/01/1918
Operation(al) Order(s)	3/5th Bn Lancashire Fusiliers Operation Order No. 36	27/01/1918	27/01/1918
Miscellaneous	Notes To Accompany Operation Orders No.36	27/01/1918	27/01/1918
Miscellaneous	3/5th Battalion Lancashire Fusiliers	31/01/1916	31/01/1916
Heading	War Diary Of 3/5th Battn. Lancashire Fusiliers February 1st-February 13th Volume 12		
War Diary	Halifax Camp Line	01/02/1918	08/02/1918
War Diary	St-Jan-Ter-Bizen	09/02/1918	13/02/1918
Operation(al) Order(s)	3/5th Bn. Lancashire Fusiliers Operation Order G.37.	02/02/1918	02/02/1918
Operation(al) Order(s)	3/5th Bn. Lancashire Fusiliers Operation Order G.38.	07/02/1918	07/02/1918
Operation(al) Order(s)	3/5th Bn. Lancashire Fusiliers Operation Order G.39.	09/02/1918	09/02/1918

WO 95/3137/2

197th Brigade.

66th Division.

Disembarked HAVRE 1.3.17.

3/5th BATTALION LANCASHIRE FUSILIERS

28th FEBRUARY to 31st MARCH 1917.

Army Form C. 2118.

WAR DIARY
or
INTELLIGENCE SUMMARY

(Erase heading not required.) 3/5th Battn LANCASHIRE FUSILIERS   Vol 19

Place	Date	Hour	Summary of Events and Information	Remarks and references to Appendices
COLCHESTER	1917 Feby 28		The Battalion less Advance Party (Appendix I) proceeded to entrain for Southampton. The first train consisting of the C.O., Adjutant, "A" "B" Coys with half the Transport left at 12.8 p.m. The Second train consisting of 2nd in Command, Transport Officer, 2 M.G's him consisting of "C" "D" Coys and remainder of Transport left at 2.40 a.m. (see Appendix 2) First train arrived at SOUTHAMPTON at 7.20 a.m. the second one at 9.40 a.m. The Battalion embarked as follows:- The first boat THE QUEEN ALEXANDRA containing the C.O. Adjutant 12 M 18 other officers and 562 other ranks left for HAVRE at 5.55 p.m. The Havre over The Second Boat MANCHESTER IMPORTER containing 2nd in Command 70 other officers and 295 other ranks together with the whole of the Transport leaving at 6.0 p.m.	Appendix 1. Appendix 2.
HAVRE	March 1st		First boat arrived at 11.30 p.m. disembarking next morning at 8.0 a.m. and proceeded to REST CAMP No 2. Second boat neared the tide at HAVRE by half an hour and remained outside the harbour until 1.0 p.m. disembarkation was completed by 5.0 p.m. and the party then proceeded to the DOCKS REST CAMP	1. I Herewith
	2nd		Battalion entrained at the Gare Dept. GARE des VOYAGEURS in two trains the first consisting of CAPT HASTINGS 5 other officers and 250 other ranks left POINT I about 8-30 a.m.	

Army Form C. 2118.

W.W.

WAR DIARY
or
INTELLIGENCE SUMMARY

3/5th BATTA (Erase heading not required) SHIRE FUSILIERS

Instructions regarding War Diaries and Intelligence Summaries are contained in F.S. Regs., Part II. and the Staff Manual respectively. Title Pages will be prepared in manuscript.

Place	Date	Hour	Summary of Events and Information	Remarks and references to Appendices
HAVRE	1917. March 2nd		The Advance Party, consisting of the C.O. 19 other officers and other ranks, Sergeant Cook, the O.R. Sergt being left behind to proceed to ROUEN at O.R. Sergt attached to 3rd Echelon. After numerous delays on the journey, the Battn arrived	
WITTES	3rd		at THIENNES at 5.15 pm some 12 hours late, the first train having arrived about 3 hours earlier. The Battalion was congratulated by several R.T.O's both on its entraining and detraining. The C.O. being personally congratulated by the Brigadier on this latter. The C.O. being personally congratulated on the behaviour of all ranks whilst leaving COLCHESTER and at all parts of the journey was excellent. The Battalion marched from THIENNES 16 WITTES, 4½ miles away. The billets very scattered and mostly barns and hay lofts had been provided for them by the Advance Party.	
do	4th		Sunday spent in cleaning up the arrangement of billets and thereby settling down. The C.O. inspected all billets and the M.O. all sanitary arrangements.	
do	5th		Training was carried out under Company arrangements (see Appendix 1) 2 officers and N.C.O's 2nd Company left at 8.30am for GIRRE Chateau (Ref Map HAZEBROUCK 5A) for a 48 hours tour of duty in the trenches.	Appendices (see Appendix 2) (Coy details & training programme). Appendix 3

WAR DIARY or INTELLIGENCE SUMMARY

Army Form C. 2118.

3/5 Bath Lancashire Fusiliers

Place	Date	Hour	Summary of Events and Information	Remarks and references to Appendices
WITTES	May 7th		The Battalion left at 8.0 am for fresh billets at les LOBES near LOCON (map ref HAZEBROUCK), via THIENNES and ST VENANT a distance of over 20 miles arriving there at 5.40 pm. The weather was fine but a very strong cold East wind made the march very trying. The CO and 9 other officers left the Battn at ROBECQUE to attend a lecture at LOCON Chateau by Lieut General Sir R.C.B HAKING KCB Comm of XI ARMY CORPS at 5.0 pm.	
les LOBES	8th		The CO & other officers and a platoon from each Company left at 9.50 am for GORRE Chateau for 48 hour instructional duty in the trenches. The weather was still bitterly cold and there was a good deal of snow.	
do	9th		The Battalion left for BEUVRY (ref Map HAZEBROUCK 5A) at 9.0 am arriving at 11.30 pm and went into billets	
BEUVRY	10th		The 2nd in Command Adjutant and 5 other officers and 1 Platoon from each Company left at 10.30 am for GORRE Chateau for 48 hours and to proceed from there to the trenches for 48 hours instructional duty.	

WAR DIARY
INTELLIGENCE SUMMARY

Army Form C. 2118.

3/5th Batt. Lancashire Fusiliers

Place	Date	Hour	Summary of Events and Information	Remarks and references to Appendices
BEUVRY	March 12th		A further H. Officers and 4 Platoons from the Battn. left at 10-15 am for 48 hours instructional duty in the trenches.	
	15th		Took over trenches GIVENCHY Left Sub Section S22c 45.00 on the North to A3 on the South from the 1/4th WARWICKSHIRE REGT. Strength of Battn. in trenches 22 Officers 681 other ranks. The 2/7th LANCASHIRE FUSILIERS on the right flank and the 1/4th WEST RIDING REGT. on the left flank. Length of line was 1800 yards. 3 Companys holding the front line and one close support, 1 Company in reserve line together north of the support. 1 Company from the Batt. in the VILLAGE was placed at the disposal of the C.O and also occupying the reserve line.	
	17th		Owing to the illness of the Brigadier, General BANON, LIEUT-COLONEL GUGGISBERG CRE took over command of the Brigade. Batts on the left was this day relieved by the 1/5th WEST RIDING REGT.	
	19th		Batt was relieved by the 2/6th Battn LAN FUS and went into rest billets at GORRE. During the tour in the trenches the weather was fine. The trenches were all breast works there were only had communication trenches in the sub sector another one SHETLAND ROAD on the sector on the left was at the disposal of the Batt. but was not much used, only very small parties being allowed up or down it.	

2449 Wt. W14957/M90 750,000 1/16 J.B.C. & A. Forms/C.2118/12.

WAR DIARY or INTELLIGENCE SUMMARY

Army Form C. 2118.

1/5th Battalion (Erase heading not required) Seaforth Highlanders

Place	Date	Hour	Summary of Events and Information	Remarks and references to Appendices
GORRE	March 22nd		The Battalion billets 3 Companies in the left round the Courtyard of the CHATEAU, and 1 Company on a farm adjoining. C.O. 2nd in Command, Adjutant M.O. and Sgt. Officers billeted in the Chateau. From about 10 am until 6.0 pm the FESTUBERT ROAD close to the Chateau was shelled by 4.5" and 6" Howitzers. At 11-30 pm any more shells were sent over. One dropping in the Court yard and wounding 4 men. Both in the afternoon and at 11-30 pm the Companies were got out of the Chateau and farm adjoining into fields some 300 to 400 yards in rear of Chateau quickly and without commotion.	
do	23rd		At 8-30 am Chateau again shelled. One direct hit being made no casualties. Most of the men had left for the trenches before this hour.	
BINCHY LEFT SUB-SECTOR	24th		4-50 a.m. attempted bombing raid by 12.6.15 Germans on CANADIAN ORCHARD one German killed on our wire (brought in some night) another taken prisoner very badly wounded, died soon after being got down to Dressing Station.	

Army Form C. 2118.

WAR DIARY
INTELLIGENCE SUMMARY

3/5th Battn: London Regiment

Place	Date	Hour	Summary of Events and Information	Remarks and references to Appendices
GIVENCHY LEFT SUB-SECTOR	March 26th	10.30 a.m.	the Divl. Commander General Heton Sir H.A. LAWRENCE. K.C.B. accompanied by the Brigadier General inspected the trenches in the Centre and the Left sub sectors viz: RICHMOND TERRACE, COVER TRENCH and CANADIAN ORCHARD.	
do (WINDY CORNER)	March 27th		Battalion relieved by the 2/6th Lan. Fus. and went into Billets in the VILLAGE LINE. During the four days the Battn. had in the trenches the weather was very cold and wet. Increased enemy activity on the part of the enemy from Minen Werfer and Rifle Grenades especially on the 1/BRINTON TRENCHES, COVER TRENCH and CANADIAN ORCHARD. LIEUTS STEVENS and GODDARD Two new officers reported for duty.	
	29th			
GIVENCHY LEFT SUB-SECTOR	31st		Battalion returned to the trenches for six days tour. At 12 o'clock midnight a German "Minen-Werfer" dropped exploded in "D" Company's ammunition dumps in COVER TRENCH causing it to catch fire. CAPT. LAUGHLIN and 2/LIEUT REID and a few men were successful in putting out the fire by means of great quantities of sand bags. List of Casualties for the month as Appendix 11	Appendices G Casualties List.

Army Form C. 2118.

WAR DIARY
or
INTELLIGENCE SUMMARY

(Erase heading not required)

3/5th Battalion LANCASHIRE FUSILIERS

Instructions regarding War Diaries and Intelligence Summaries are contained in F.S. Regs., Part II. and the Staff Manual respectively. Title Pages will be prepared in manuscript.

Place	Date	Hour	Summary of Events and Information	Remarks and references to Appendices
GIVENCHY LEFT SUB-SECTOR	1917 March 31st		The question of boots for the men had been very difficult during this month. The men had not had new boots or been able to get their old ones mended since February 17th. Numerous applications were made for new boots and leather but it was not until March 29th that a fresh supply was received. Whale oil was procurable and great care was taken that the men thoroughly rubbed their feet before returning to the very wet trenches and the fact that notwithstanding the Battn had no cases of trench feet.	

SECRET   Bde. Min. M/175.

To:- O.C.
    3/5th L. Lan. Fus.,

    The following copy of a Telegram is forwarded for your information with reference to this Office Number M/175 of 4.2.17.

" (Secret) 66th East Lancs Divn. Colchester.
"Q.105 Feb. 6th aaa Your wire S.R. 203/a dated 3rd inst
"the advance party personnel 66th Division less personnel
"of divisional artillery headquarters and that of Artillery
"Brigades and batteries will be embarked for France 11th
"instantaaa Train times later aaa Addressed 66th Division
"repeated Southarmy."   Practician, London"

                Captain. F. M. Bentley.
                  ..   G. Gall.
                Lieut.   F. D. Unger
                  ..   F. H. Crouch.
                2/Lt.   S. T. Collins.
                  ..   J. W. Pickett.

                                        (sgd) D.A.F. NEEDHAM.
                                                Captain,
                                             Staff Captain,
Colchester   197th Infantry Brigade
    8.2.17.

SPECIAL ORDER
by
LIEUT.-COL. A. S. BATES D.S.O
Commanding 3/5th Batt. Lancashire Fusiliers
Goojerat Barracks, Colchester   26. 2. 1917.

On the Eve of embarking for overseas the Commanding Officer wishes to draw the special attention of all Officers & N.C.O's to the following extract from a German document whose wording he cannot improve, in connection with normal trench warfare, which is likely to be the Battalions first task.

"The most important preparation for successfully
"repelling an attack consists in fostering and
"constantly maintaining a healthy and active
"offensive spirit amongst the troops. By careful
"instruction in all methods of close fighting,
"each individual man must be trained to fit and
"know himself superior to the enemy, in order that
"the penetration into our position of an hostile
"attack must involve its annihilation.

In the same connection he would call the attention of all ranks to the concluding paragraph:-

"The united efforts and energies of the troops
"holding a defensive position in face of the enemy
"must be devoted to preparation for the final
"victory. It is not a question of merely repelling
"the enemy's attack; the object should be to
"annihilate them"

The above sentiments are admirable and the Commanding Officer knows that the British soldier, not only feels himself better than a German, but undoubtedly is so.
He is proud to take the Battalion overseas in the sure knowledge that it will create its own honour, and consequently enhance the glorious ones won in the past by the XXth Foot and in the present Campaign by The Lancashire Fusiliers and its Territorial and New Army Battalions.

(SD)R.SPENCER ASHWORTH Capt.
Adjt. 3/5th Lan.Fus.

MOVE ORDERS
by A S BATES. DSO.
LIEUT-COLONEL T. L. BROWN T.D.
Commanding 3/5th Batt. Lancashire Fusiliers
Goojerat Barracks, Colchester   26th Feb.1917
PART 1

(1) PARADE.

The Battalion will entrain at Colchester (St.Botolphs) Station on the morning of 28.2.17 in 2 trains; the 1st leaving at 12.15 a.m. and the 2nd at 02.50 arriving 07.15 and 09.40. Dress:- Full marching order - Greatcoats worn.

22.30 (27.2.17) "A" & "B" Cos. & H.Q.Sigs. parade in mass facing N.

01.00 (28.2.17) "C" & "D" Cos. parade in mass facing N.

(2) COMPOSITION OF TRAINS.

1st train:-   C.O.
                 Adjutant
                 H.Q.Signallers
                 "A" & "B" Cos.
                 R.S.M.
                 R.Q.M.S.
                 Transport Sgt.
     Transport:- 31 horses
                 2 baggage waggons
                 "A" & "B" Cos. Field Kitchens
                 5 G.S. Limbers
                 2 Water Carts.
                 9 bicycles.

The R.S.M. will detail a bugler to travel as near the C.O. as possible.

2nd train:-   2nd in Command
                 Lt. Rouse
                 "C" & "D" Cos.
                 T.O.
                 Q.M.
     Transport:- 32 horses
                 2 supply waggons.
                 "C" & "D" Cos. Field Kitchens
                 5 G.S.Limbers
                 1 Maltese Cart
                 1 Mess Cart.

C.S.M.Doodson will act as R.S.M. to this train, and will detail a bugler as for the 1st train.

(3) FATIGUE PARTIES.

(a) O.C."A" Co. will detail 1 platoon to entrain vehicles and horses on 1st train. This party will act under the instructions of the T.O.

O.C."C" Co. will detail a similar party to load horses and vehicles on the 2nd train.

The T.O. will take all necessary steps to ensure that no friction arises with the Railway authorities.

(b) O.C."B" Co. will detail 1 Officer and 20 men to report to the R.T.O. when the train arrives at the Port of Embarkation. This party will entrain together in carriages next to the waggons to be unloaded and will unload the train as quickly as possible. After unloading they will direct the vehicles to the cranes detailed by the Embarkation Staff and assist in slinging.

(c) O.C. "D" Co. will detail a similar party to act similarly with regard to vehicles on the 2nd train.

(d) O.C. "B" Co. will detail 2 parties each of 1 N.C.O. and 5 men who will travel with the unloading party. This party will report to the Embarkation Staff Officer for duty in the holds assisting stevedores.

O.C."D" Co. will detail similar parties for the 2nd train.

(e) O.C.Cos. will roll blankets in bundles of 20 lengthwise. Accomodation for these blankets will be provided on the trains. These bundles must be tightly packed and consist of not more and not less than 20 blankets. Nothing whatever will be carried inside these blankets.

1.

O.C.Cos. will detail on instructions from the Q.M. the necessary fatigue parties to roll, load and unload these blankets.
The R.S.M. will detail a Guard for the blankets on the 1st and 2nd trains.

(4) TRANSPORT.

All horses, transport and bicycles will be at the entraining station 2 hours before the train is due to start. Capt.Gowland together with 2 markers from each of "A" & "B" Cos. 2 markers for H.Q.Sigs, & 2 markers for fatigue parties detailed in para. 3 to travel with 1st train. will proceed to Colchester (St.Botolphs) by 11.15 and allot the carriages.
Lt.Morley together with 2 markers from each of "C" & "D" Cos. and 2 markers detailed for fatigue parties detailed in para. 3 to travel with 2nd train will proceed to Colchester (St.Botolphs) at 01.50 on 28.2.17 for a similar purpose. Nothing of any description is to be chalked on the trains.

(5) BLANKETS.

Blankets will be conveyed to the entraining station, Colchester (St.Botolphs) so as to arrive there 6 hours before the departure of the train on which they will proceed. They will be dumped in a place which will be pointed out by the Railway Authorities.

(6) REFRESHMENT BARS.

Refreshment bars will be open and men will be able to purchase hot coffee &c. and something to eat. They will be marched into the Refreshment Rooms under a N.C.O. in parties of not more than 15 so as to avoid congestion.

(7) HOT MEALS.

A hot meal for "A" & "B" Cos. and H.Q.Sigs. will be served at 20.30 and for "C" & "D" Cos. at 22.30

(8) LEAVING TRAIN

Once troops have been put into trains no N.C.O. or man will leave the train without the authority of an Officer.

(9) OFFICERS.

Cos. will render to Headquarters by 09.00 tomorrow a nominal roll of Officers proceeding with the Batt. These rolls will shew all Officers on the strength of the Unit and if not proceeding with the Batt. an explanation will be given in the remarks column. Full particulars as regards substantive, temporary and acting rank, also Regiment, will be shewn.

(10) SICK.

On arrival at Port of Embarkation sick men, if any, with their accoutrements will be taken to the 1st Aid Dressing Station by a N.C.O. after reporting to the Embarkation Staff Officer on duty.

(11) FIRE & COLLISION STATIONS.

As soon as possible after the troops have embarked fire and collision stations will be practised. The C.O. will issue the necessary orders.

(12) COOKING &c.

(a) There will be no arrangements for cooking on board ship other than the provision of boiling water for making hot tea.
(b) An extra ration will be issued to all ranks regimentally, who are advised not on any account to touch it, until the Unit has arrived in France and then to retain same as long as possible as the duration of the journey is uncertain.

(12) LIGHTS & NOISE.

The passage across the channel is to be treated in all respects like a night march and no lights or noise are to be permitted, particularly no smoking on deck, if the voyage is by night.

(13) SANITATION

After disembarkation the Batt. may be sent to a Rest Camp. Each Co. will pay the strictest attention to the Sanitary arrangements and leave the camp clean.

(14) ORDERLIES.

If in camp the R.S.M. will detail 2 Orderlies to stay at Camp Headquarters ready to take messages to B.H.Q.

(15) CORRESPONDENCE.

No indication of the locality occupied by the Unit is to be mentioned in private correspondence.

(16) MUSIC.
   The band will not play from the Port of Disembarkation to the Rest Camp without direct orders from the C.O.

(17) ENEMY AGENTS.
   Every N.C.O. and man is particularly warned against enemy agents. On being asked for information by a stranger whether soldier or civilian, the correct procedure for all ranks is to reply that they do not know even the name of their own Battalion, or anyone connected with it, and to take the person asking the question to their Company Officer.

(18) CAPACITY AND METHOD OF LOADING ROLLING STOCK.
   (a) 3rd Class Coaches - It is unlikely that these will be available for the conveyance of troops. When provided, they will accomodate eight men per compartment.
   (b) Goods waggons are usually provided for the accomodation of the troops. They each hold 40 men. Sometimes seats are provided, sometimes straw to lie on. Spaces at each end of the waggon should be left clear for rifles and accoutrements, the rifles being secured by an improvised rack made with screw rings and a strap or sling.
   (c) Horse waggons - Hold eight horses in two rows of four, facing each other. A rope is tied from side to side of the wagon breast high in front of each row, which must be provided by the Unit concerned, to a big ring on an overhead bar. The central space between doors is used for saddlery, forage and the two men who travel in each waggon.
   (d) Vehicle tracks - Usually accomodate three axles, but sometimes four. The system of loading vehicles is almost entirely that of side-loading, with the aid of ramps from ground level or platforms 1 foot high. The system of securing is the same as that on British railways. Assistance in loading is usually given by the French railway staff.
   Vehicles must not be loaded to a greater height than 9 feet 10 inches from the floor of the truck.

(19) REFRESHMENT HALTS.
   All instructions and orders received from the R.T.O. at the station where the halt is made for refreshments must be most carefully adhered to.

(20) DETRAINMENT.
   A R.T.O. will be at the detraining station and will give orders as to the detrainment. As a rule, platforms will be of the ordinary continental type, i.e. about 1 foot high and 300 yards long, unpaved. Movable ramps will be available for detraining horses and vehicles.

(21) PARADE STATES.
   Cos. will render to Headquarters by 11.00 tomorrow parade states as follows:-
   Officers, W.O's, Sgts. Cpls. Ptes.
   The T.O. will render at above hour parade states for each train, under horses as follows:- Riding, Draft, Pack, Mules, and in Limbers and other vehicles as follows:- Horsed, 4 wheeled, 2 wheeled.
   Lt. Holdsworth will render parade state at above hour for H.Q. Signallers, shewing Sgts. Cpls. O.Ranks.

(22) CASUALTIES.
   Cos. will render to the Adjutant immediately they occur a nominal roll of any casualties.

(SD) R. SPENCER ASHWORTH Capt.
Adjt. 3/5th Lan. Fus.

SECRET

Edc. Min. M/216 d/d
31.1.17.

To:- O.C.
3/5th Bn. Lan. Fus.,

    It has been notified that the 66th Division will be required to commence its embarkation on the 1st March, and for this move it is hoped to adopt a 6 days programme.
    In This connection it is also notified that the Division will remain at its present station until its embarkation, as it is not now possible to concentrate it for 2 months in a training area before its departure to France.

(sgd) C. J. GASSON. Captain.
Brigade Major.
197th Infantry Brigade

Colchester,
31.1.17.

Appendix 4

3/5TH BATTN. LANCASHIRE FUSILIERS.

CASUALTY REPORT FOR MONTH OF MARCH 1917. APPENDIX.

Day	WOUNDED Names of OFFICERS	Numbers of O.R.	KILLED Names of Officers	O.R.	(x)DIED OF WOUNDS Names of Officers	O.R.
16.3.17		2				
17.3.17		6				
18.3.17		6		202444 Pte BENJAMIN		
19.3.17						202240 Pte KERNS. 202436 Pte KAY
23.3.17		4				
24.3.17	1	5	1		1	
25.3.17	1	1	1		1	
26.3.17	2		2	203626 Pte KELLY	2	
27.3.17		1		202644 Pte GILBERT 203623 Pte HEYWOOD		
31.3.17				202460 Pte BENNETT.		

(x) These are also included in the return of wounded

197th Brigade.

66th Division.

3/5th BATTALION LANCASHIRE FUSILIERS APRIL 1917.

WAR DIARY or INTELLIGENCE SUMMARY

3/5 Bat FUS¹ʳˢ

Army Form C. 2118

Place	Date	Hour	Summary of Events and Information	Remarks and references to Appendices
GIVENCHY LEFT SUB SECTOR	1917 April 2		Lieut. J. POUSE having been appointed Adjutant vice Capt. R.S. ASHWORTH (the latter assuming command of "C" Co.) authority A 6/337 and two other medical officers from Ent. & I.Q. reporting. Lieut. C.H. TYE, W. CHESHIRE REGT reported for duty.	
	6		Batt. left trenches for GORRE on our way to our billets. Special N.C.O.s and 51 men who were left behind as the 3/8ᵗʰ in GIVENCHY RIGHT SUB-SECTOR is where rich in trench mortars will if the trenches for official training for a field.	
	8		EASTER SUNDAY. Church Parades	
	9		News received from Bde. of success of 1ˢᵗ & 3ʳᵈ Army on VIMY RIDGE and ARRAS.	
	12		Battn. returns to trenches. The front line being held by "A" Coy on left. "C" Coy in the Centre and "B" Coy on the right. "D" Coy in reserve in the OLD BRITISH LINE.	
			On the night of 11ᵗʰ/12ᵗʰ in consequence of a heavy barrage of GERMANS, attempts up Kraigt trench CANADIAN ORCHARD early this morn line has been engaged & each 3 O.R. were wounded which S.O. kept up sniping one man wounded. At midnight one man wounded all from the 2 after 8000 rounds of trench mortars.	
	16		Enemy Trench Mortars much the active but two artillery fires increasingly over new Battn. Headquarters before occasion in a short thing over the OLD BRITISH LINE. Between QUINQUE RUE and SUNKEN ROAD. Portion of the old H.Q. and advanced H.Q. being vacated.	
	18			

Vol 3

Army Form C. 2118.

WAR DIARY
or
INTELLIGENCE SUMMARY

35TH BATTALION N.E. FUSILIERS

Place	Date	Hour	Summary of Events and Information	Remarks and references to Appendices
GIVENCHY LEFT SUB SECTOR	1917 April 19th	10ᵃ	Battalion in support in VILLAGE LINE at WINDY CORNER (Map LA BASSEE 36.c.NW1. 8a.1.10,000. 80.84) Enemy artillery fire much increased	
	27th		Battn. returns to front line trenches and french Mortars also active. Weather fine much drier	
	28th		At 10 P.M. a/c received R.E. Party, fired 130 lethal shells and 480 lachrymating shells from this sector on enemys support line. Battn. & Regimental H.Q. in front of our 20/65. Enemy retaliation small. No Casualties.	
	30th		Battalion was relieved. Relief complete by 1 A.m. on relief Battn. moved into Reserve at GORRE. Casualties during month see Appendix I	Appendix 1

A. K. Stubbs M.
5/1/17

Appendix I

To:- 3/5th Bn. Lan. Fus.   Bde. Ref. S.C. 775/A.

The following figures of men reporting sick for the month of April are forwarded for your information.

Unit	Reporting sick.	Admitted to Hospital.
3/5th Lan. Fus.	196	28
2/6th	335	43
2/7th	279	46
2/8th	328	32
202 M.G. Coy	42	5
197th L.T.M. Batty	53	2
Total	1233	156.

(sgd) F.H. LIDDELL
Captn.
Staff Captain
197th Infantry Bde.

B.H.Q.
4-5-17.

3/5th Bn. LANCASHIRE FUSILIERS

LIST OF CASUALTIES FOR MONTH OF APRIL 1917.

Date	WOUNDED Officers	Other Ranks.	KILLED. Officers	Other Ranks.
1.4.17.		202401 Cpl SMITH.T.		
2.4.17.				202586 Pte CHATTERTON.
3.4.17.		202690 Pte MULLEN.J.		202590 .. TATTERSALL.
4.4.17.		202564 .. WALLWORK.J.		
		202691 Cpl NIGHTINGALE (acc. gas.)		
8.4.17.		203026 Pte BLAND		
13.4.17.		3/5987 L/C BAKER.J.		
		201303 Pte BRIDGE.T.		
16.4.17.				(x) 4/29804 Pte RATCLIFFE.H.
				(x) 203243 .. WALKER.F.
19.4.17.		9/24079 .. BOWLEY.C.		
20.4.17.		203573 .. GRIFFIN.J.		202678 Pte ADSHEAD.J.
		202425 .. SIMMONS.G. (slightly)		202431 .. CRABTREE.G.
21.4.17.		202526 .. GREENLEES.W.		
		203601 .. HILLIER.G.		
		202449 .. WALTON.G.		
25.4.17.		202523 .. CARR.H.		
		203681 .. LIVESEY.W.		
26.4.17.	2/Lt.S.T. COLLINS. (died of wounds 29.4.17.)	202017 Sgt KEEBLE.J.		2/9534 Pte McINTYRE.J.
28.4.17.		10/4194 Pte NAUGHTON.J.		
		203633 .. SHAW.E. (slightly.)		

MISSING

2.4.17.	203153 Pte SWIFT.T.	Missing (Buried, believed killed.)	
	203167 .. MURPHY.H.V.	.. (buried, believed killed.)	
13.4.17.	203227 L/C REECE.A.D.	Missing, believed Prisoners of War.	
	13/13468 Pte APPLETON.E.	Missing, believed Prisoners of War.	
	13/26752 .. BOULTON.A.	Missing, believed Prisoners of War.	
	202676 .. ADDIS.H.	Missing, believed Prisoners of War.	
	203128 .. MACGILL.J.	Missing, believed Prisoners of War.	

Deceased men marked (x) are buried at BETHUNE: all others are buried at BROWN'S CEMETERY, GORRE.

In the Field.
1.5.17.

Lieut.-Col.
Commdg 3/5th Bn.Lan. Fus.

197th Brigade.
66th Division.

3/5th BATTALION LANCASHIRE FUSILIERS MAY 1917.

Appendix E

SECRET:-
Copy No. 8

SUGGESTED OPERATIONS BY "ARCH" ON THE NIGHT OF MAY ―― 1917.

Reference Trench Map LA BASSEE, Edition 8a 1/10,000, Aeroplane photograph 10.A.B. 63 and Sketch Map attached.

1. INTENTION:- A raid will be carried out on the night of May "z" 1917, the exact date will be circulated later to all concerned. The operation will always be referred to as "ANTHEAP".

2. OBJECTS:-
   (a) To ascertain if the enemy trench is held.
   (b) To kill Germans.
   (c) To capture Germans and obtain identifications.
   (d) To lower enemy's morale.

3. STRENGTH:- 2 Officers, 7 NCO's and 30 men "ARCH".

3(a) EQUIPMENT:- See appendix E.

4. POINT OF ENTRY:- A.3.b.35.05 (see also sketch attached.)

5. DURATION:- 4 minutes in enemy trench.

6. ARTILLERY:- See programme in Appendix "A".

7. STOKES MORTARS:- See programme in Appendix "B".

8. MACHINE GUNS:- See programme in appendix "C".

9. SPECIAL R.E.:- See programme in Appendix "D".

10. ZERO HOUR:- Will be notified later to all concerned. It will be the hour at which the first action detailed in Appendix "D" takes place.

11. PARTIES & ACTION:- The raiding parties will be divided into 4 parties as under. They will form up in NO MAN'S LAND prior to Zero Hour as close to the enemy's wire as advised by the Special R.E.- in the following order:-

         ø "A"

         ø "B"

        ø ø "C"

         ø "D"

O.C. "A" will lay a white tape which will lead back to the gap in our wire.
At zero, they will at once rush forward.

(a) Party "A":- 1 Officer, 2 NCOs and 8 men. Of these latter
    2 men are for identification searchers (see para. 15)
    2 are rifle men.
    2 are bombers.
    2 are carriers.
On reaching the point of entry they will proceed along the communication trench as far as A.3.b.42.08 and form a bombing block numbered 1 on sketch.

(b) Party "B":- Strength and composition as for Party "A", will follow Party "A" and then go down the communication trench running East as far as the dugout at A.3.b.43.07 marked "X" on sketch. If this is occupied and the inmates will not come out, "P" bombs will be thrown in. Efforts will, however, be made to enter it as it is expected to be an M.G. or L.T.M. emplacement. Any

-2-

11.(b)(Cont.)		weapon inside should, if possible, be brought out.
11.(c)	PARTY "C":-	will form 2 bombing blocks of 1 NCO and 4 men each, these latter will be divided into 1 rifleman, 1 bomber and 2 carriers. These 2 parties will form bombing blocks 5 yards North and South of the point of entry in the front line.
(d)	PARTY "D":-	will form a covering party and will remain outside the enemy trench - strength 1 NCO and 6 men. The latter divided into 2 checkers being riflemen (one will carry a light ladder and both will accompany Party "A" up to the front parapet), 1 Bomber, 1 Carrier and 2 riflemen. Its duties will be:-

      (i)- To check the number of Officers & O.R. who actually enter the German trench.
      (ii)- While the raiders are in the German trench to enlarge the gap, if necessary, in the wire to facilitate withdrawal.
      (iii)- To count the number of Officers & O.R. who return from the German trench and if all are not present, to assist in the search, if possible, for any missing, and to assist in the withdrawal.
      (iv)- Receive and escort prisoners across NO MAN'S LAND.
      (v)- Bring in the white tape.

12. DETECTION:- If the parties moving out are detected and the enemy open fire, they will lie down at once where they are and wait for zero.

13. WITHDRAWAL:- (a) The signal will be 2 mortar signals, colours will be notified later to all concerned, sent up from WARWICK NORTH. O.C. "D" Coy will detail an officer to superintend these. They will be sent up 5 minutes after Zero.
(b) As soon as the signals are sent up Party "B" will at once withdraw to the point of entry. As soon as Party "B" is clear of the point A.3.b.43.07, Party "A" will commence withdrawing to the point of entry. As soon as the last man of Party "A" is clear of the enemy trench, Party "C" will withdraw.
(c) The Officer or NCO in charge of each party must report to the NCO i/c Party "D" that his party is correct or otherwise, but such reports will not absolve the checkers from counting as laid down in para 11.(d) (i)

14. ALL CLEAR:- To inform all concerned that the whole of the parties are back in our own trenches, the senior officer of the Raiding parties or the Officer detailed in para.13 (a) will order 2 mortar signals to be sent up from WARWICK NORTH. Colours will be notified later to all concerned.

15. IDENTIFICATION:- Parties "A" & "B" will each detail 2 men whose sole object, unless attacked, will be to obtain identifications of the enemy. All papers, letters, books &c found will be brought back in sandbags carried for the purpose and sent at once to Battalion Headquarters.

16. PRISONERS:- As alive Germans are of incalculably greater value than any documents as a rule, any prisoners taken will at once be taken to the exit and handed over to Party "D" whose duty it will be to escort them across

-3-

NO MAN'S LAND. Prisoners will be sent at once under escort to Battalion Headquarters.

17. GAP IN OUR WIRE:- O.C. Raiders will arrange to cut the necessary gaps in our own wire 2 nights before "Z" night. These must be carefully concealed.

18. NOMINAL ROLL:- A complete nominal roll of the Raiding Party will be handed in to Battalion H.Q. by 8 p.m. "Z" night.

19. WATCHES:- Correct time will be issued at Battalion Headquarters at 3 p.m. and 6 p.m. on "Z" day. O.C. Raiders will arrange for all watches to be at Battalion Headquarters at these hours.

20. ADVANCED BATTN. HEADQRS. will be at BARNTON TEE.

21. COMMUNICATIONS:- The signalling officer will arrange telephonic communication between WARWICK NORTH and BARNTON TEE HEADQUARTERS.

22. MEDICAL ARRANGEMENTS:- see Appendix F.

23. CODE WORDS:- See Appendix G.

24. COUNTERSIGN:- will be issued only to those directly concerned. It will be different from the Battalion password and must not be used North of BARNTON SOUTH.

25. ABANDONMENT:- The operation can be abandoned at Advanced Battn. H.Q. O.C. Raiders or the Special R.E. Officer, if, in the opinion of the Officer so deciding, there is any unforeseen circumstances which would militate against the success of the raid. This decision need not be arrived at before leaving our line, but must be come to prior to the action to be taken by the Special R.E. at zero and in time to stop such action. The earliest opportunity must be taken to advise Battalion H.Q. in order to stop the artillery firing.

26. REPORTS:-
(a) On his return O.C. Raiders will report to the C.O. at Battalion H.Q.
(b) The NCO i/c Adv. R.A.P. will report to the C.O. at Battalion H. Qrs on his return.
(c) The Adjutant, "~~Marine will be asked to~~ send a runner to the R.A.P. at Zero plus 30 minutes and thereafter hourly till counterordered who will bring back the total number of casualties which have passed through the post up to time of report.

Arthur W Sates
Lieut.-Col.
Commanding "ARCH".

DISTRIBUTION:- Copy 1. C.O. with code
2. LAUNDRY " "
3. Adv. Bn H.Q." "
4. O.C. Raiders" "
5. Adjt & War Diary
6. War Diary.
7. Spare.

Necessary extracts to:-
YOUTH
PLOW with code
202 M.G Co. " "
Special R.E " "
M.O.
Signalling Off.
O.C."C" Coy
.. "D" ..

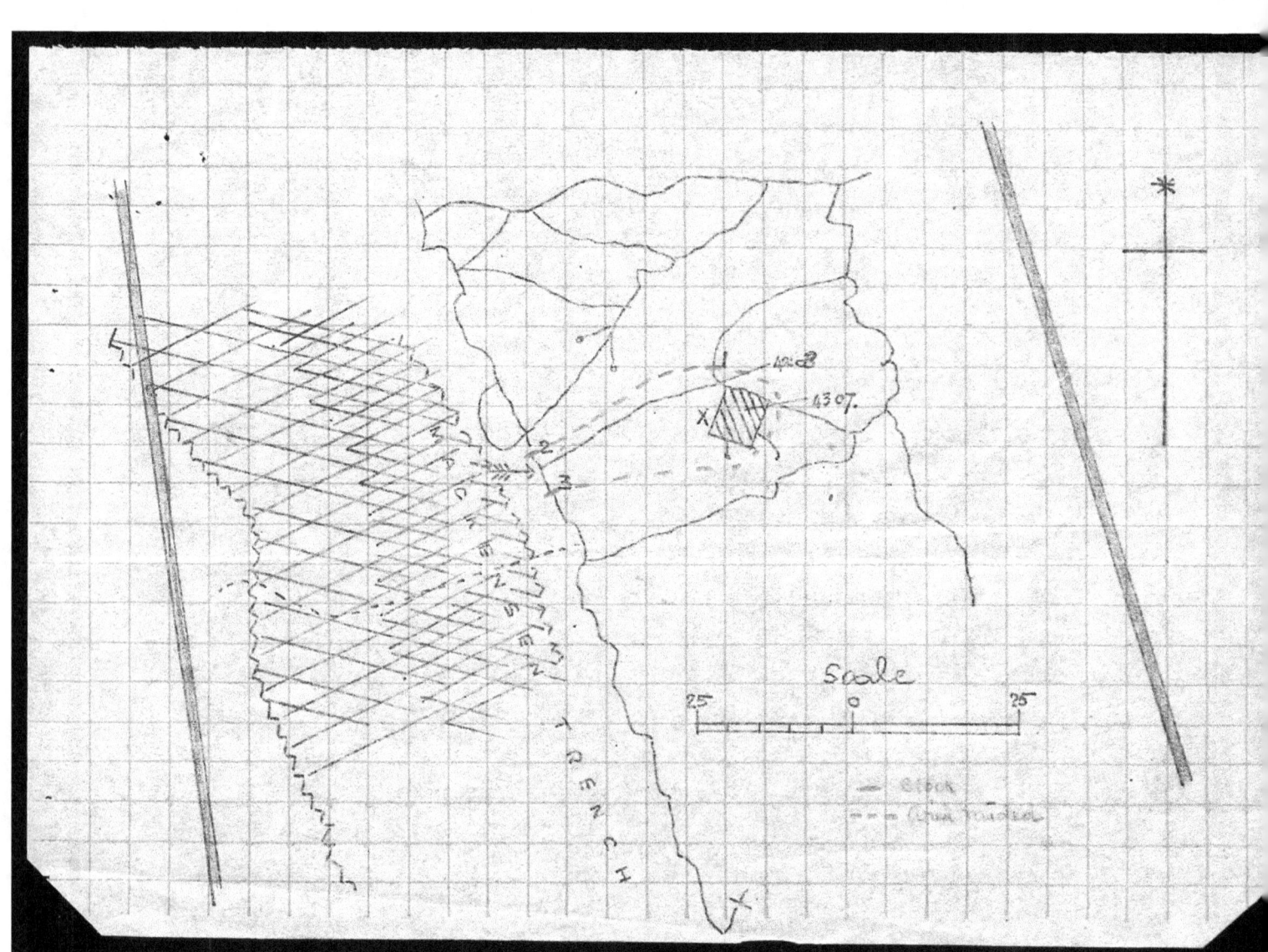

Copy No.1.

197th INFANTRY BRIGADE.

SPECIAL BRIGADE ORDER No. 4.

1. The Brigadier congratulates Lieut. Colonel BATES, D.S.O. and the 3/5th Battn. Lancashire Fusiliers on the success of the raid on the night of the 9th/10th May, 1917 which resulted in important identifications.
He wishes to record his appreciation of the good work of Lieuts. CROUCH 3/5th Bn. Lan. Fus. and 2/Lieut. GRAY 2/6th Lan. Fus. (Brigade Intelligence Officer) in a close reconnaissance of the enemy wire during a recent bright night, of Lieut. KENDALL and men of the 430th Field Coy R.E. who placed and exploded the Bangalore Torpedo which opened a way for the raiding party.   This last consisted of Lieyts. CROUCH - REID and PICKETT and 39 other ranks of "D" Coy 3/5th Lan. Fus.,
He wishes to thank Lieut. ELLIOT and the men of "F" Coy Special R.E. for their valuable co-operation, and Lieut. Colonel MURRAY and the Left Group Artillery for the rapidity and effectiveness of their barrage fire, and to the N.C.O's and men of the Light T.M. Battery, and 202nd M.G. Coy who also co-operated.
The Artillery of the Division on our left gave valuable assistance by placing a false barrage on the "PARABOLA".
Both the Corps and Divisional Commander personally expressed to the Brigadier their approval of the way the raid was carried through.

2. The following telegrams are published and the Brigadier feels confident that the results of the appreciation of their Divisional and Corps Commanders will encourage every unit in the Brigade to further offensive action.

(a) Following received from XI Corps aaa G92aaa The Corps Commander wishes his satisfaction with the arrangements for last nights successful raid to be conveyed to the 197th Infantry Brigade aaa. He also wishes his congratulations to be given to the detatchment 3/5th Lan. Fus who carried out the raid aaa Message ends aaa 66th Div.

(b) 66th Div.
Your G92 of 10th aaa Kindly forward following to XI Corps aaa 197th Infantry Brigade thank the Corps Commander for his kind message which has been passed to the 3/5th Lancashire Fusiliers aaa The Corps Commander's approval will be an incentive to further offensive action on thepart of all Battalions of the Brigade and the affiliated R.E. Company who prepared the way for the raiding party by blowing up the wire and for the Artillery who assisted the operation aaa   197th Infantry Brigade.
    197th Infantry Brigade.
(c) I am directed by the Divisional Commander to request that you convey to the 3/5th Bn. Lan. Fus. his appreciation of the work done by their raiding party, and the troops attached for the purpose on the night of 9th/10th, 1917 and his congratulations on bringing the first offensive action of the Division to a successful issue.

(sgd) B.C.B. TOWER. Capt.
G.S. 66th Div.
(sgd) C.J. GASSON. Capt.
Brigade Major.
197th Infantry Brigade.

B.H.Q. 11.5.17.

Copies to:- No.1 3/5th Lan.Fus.   No.7 Left Art Group
          2 2/6th   "   "   8 430th Fld Coy R.E.
          3 2/7th   "   "   9 "F" Coy Special R.E.
          4 2/8th   "   "   10)
          5 197th L.T.M.B.   11) War Diary.
          6 202nd M.G. Coy   12 File

Appendix 3

CASUALTIES DURING MONTH OF MAY 1917.

Date	OFFICERS Killed	OFFICERS Wounded	OTHER RANKS Killed	OTHER RANKS Wounded
May. 4th				201174 Sgt HOWARTH.R.
8th				203247 Pte ASHILL.D.
9th		Lt.F.H.CROUCH		202026 .. TOPPING.T.
				202626 .. ASHWORTH.R
				201382 .. ENTWISTLE R.
11th			202230 Pte MATHER.R.F.	203161 .. STUBBS.E.
				203281 .. JONES.W.I.
12th				203035 .. BEATTY.T.
				202552 .. SANDERSON.A.
13th			202604 Pte BLYTHE.E.	203143 .. THOMAS A.R
				201975 .. HARRISON.J
24th			203598 .. BAKER.W.J.	

1.6.17.

Lieut.-Col.
Commdg 3/5th Bn. Lan. Fus.,

To:- 3/5th Bn. Lan. Fus.,   Bde Min. S.C./1840/A.

Appendix 4

The following figures of men in the Brigade reporting Sick and Admitted to Hospital during month of May are forwarded for information.

UNIT	Reporting sick.	Admitted to Hospital.
3/5th Lan. Fus.	134	11.
2/6th --o--	141	16.
2/7th --o--	186	25.
2/8th --o--	264	37.
202 M.G.Coy	54	5.
197th L.T.M. Bty.	47	15.
Total.	826	109.

(sgd). R. SPENCER ASHWORTH, Captn
A/Staff Captain.
197th Infantry Brigade.

B.H.Q.
31.5.17.

Army Form C. 2118.

WAR DIARY or INTELLIGENCE SUMMARY

3/5TH BATT. LANCASHIRE FUS.RS

Place	Date	Hour	Summary of Events and Information	Remarks and references to Appendices
GIVENCHY LEFT SUB-SECTOR. TRENCH MAP REF. LABASSEE Edition 9a 1/10,000	1917 MAY 1st		Battn. in rest billets at GORRE. Battn. strength MAY 1st, 35 Officers and 824 other ranks. During his previous month 14 new officers joined the Battn. viz. 2/LT. C.H. TYE, 2/LTS S. BELCHER, A.E. JONES, J.C. BARLOW. 2/LT. ST. COLLINS was wounded, nil of our own band on APRIL 26th and died on APRIL 29th in hospital. At the Battn. during the previous month had been very calm & satisfactory. (ref: Appendix 1).	(to accompany Z (Hea Bn))
	6th		Battn. moved to WINDY CORNER from GORRE for one day. (6 guns of the RIGHT SUB-SECTOR of the BDE. Nº relieve 2/6th MANCH. REGIMENT in the LEFT SUB-SECTOR.	
	7th		Moved into front lines of same.	
	9th	11.23pm	LIEUT CROUCH & LT. REID ? PICKETT with 7 N.C.Os and 30 men of "D" Company and 2/Lt Hoyle raided the GERMAN front line. Important information was gained. See APPENDIX 2. for hand grenade and Stokes grenade boxes etc. Enemy retaliation very slight.	
	13th		Went into SUPPORT in VILLAGE LINE at WINDY CORNER only 2 Coys being left in the LEFT SUB-SECTOR and 1 Company as reserve. Being left in the LEFT SUB-SECTOR and 1 Company to strengthen the RIGHT SUB-SECTOR in the GIVENCHY KEEPS under BDE instructions.	
	16th		Enemy artillery fire much quieter, but more M.G. and rifle fire at night.	

3.I 11 sheets

Army Form C. 2118.

WAR DIARY
or
INTELLIGENCE SUMMARY

3/5th BATT.(Erase heading not required.) S. LANCS HIRE FUS.rs

Place	Date	Hour	Summary of Events and Information	Remarks and references to Appendices
GIVENCHY LEFT SUB-SECTOR	1917 May 18th		Battn. back in front line again for rifle & machine gun fire at night. Enemy transport heard behind their Support line and heavily fired upon by our artillery and machine guns on three nights under a code word arrangement. Enemy very quiet except	
	22nd		A Portugese Batt.n Staff came in on our LEFT relieving the Batt.n 1/49th Division (4th or 5th WEST RIDING REG.T)	
	24th		Back at rest billets in GORRE.	
	27th		Open air church service in field behind BRIGADE HQ at LOISNE (BETHUNE Combined Sheet). Div.al BAND in attendance.	
	30th		Left for one night and day at WINDY CORNER.	
	31st		Batt.n relieved 2/6th LAN. FUS. (normal) in front line LEFT SUB-SECTOR.	

Army Form C. 2118.

WAR DIARY
or
INTELLIGENCE SUMMARY

3/5th BATᴺ LAN. FUSʳˢ
(Erase heading not required.) IS HIRE FUS -

Place	Date	Hour	Summary of Events and Information	Remarks and references to Appendices
GIVENCHY LEFT SUB-SECTOR	1917. MAY 31ˢᵗ		Battle Strength: 36 Officers 803 other ranks. Trench strength. 27 Officers 594 other ranks. Three new officers reported for duty on the 28th YB:- 2/Lt E.H. BRIDGSTOCK R. HAMER. G.R. ALLEN, all from the 5th Reserve Battⁿ. 2/Lt H.R. TUCKER "sick on list" on leave (15/1/17 to 10/5/17) was struck off strength on instructions from ENGLAND. No 6552 A/RSM J. BYRNE left the Battalion on the 30th being granted a Permᵗ Comm as 2/Lt in the 10th Bn YORK & LANC REGT. Monthly Casualty list (see Appendix 3) Monthly sick report (see Appendix 4)	

Arthur Waber
Lᵗ. Col.
Comm'g 3/5th Batt. Lan. Fus.

197th Brigade.
66th Division.

3/5th BATTALION LANCASHIRE FUSILIERS JUNE 1917.

Army Form C. 2118.

WAR DIARY
or
INTELLIGENCE SUMMARY

3/5TH BATT. LANCASHIRE FUS.

Place	Date	Hour	Summary of Events and Information	Remarks and references to Appendices
GIVENCHY LEFT SUB-SECTOR	1917 June 1st		Battn. in front line trenches. Enemy artillery very quiet. Machine gun and rifle fire at nights moderate.	
	5th		C.O. (Lt.Col. BATES, D.S.O.) left for ENGLAND on 14 days leave. MAJOR W. WIKE acting C.O. and Capt. C.W. LAUGHLIN acting 2nd in Command	
	6th		Battn. instead of going into support as usual, days on the line to allow the 2/6th Batt. LANC. FUS. (2 Companies) to have general training for a raid. From now to the 12th our artillery and medium trench mortars very active on our front, cutting wire of enemy's 1st and 2nd line trenches.	
	9th		Our flank companies (B and C) relieved and go to GORRE, two companies of the 2/6th L.F. taking their places.	
	10?		Battn. cooperate in putting up a dummy barrage on enemy front line in order to assist a raid by the East Lancs Brigade on the CENTRE SECTOR of DIVSL FRONT. Bombers over 215 rifle grenades. Raid successful.	
	11th		Remainder of Battn. (less D Company under LIEUT GODDARD) relieved and go to GORRE.	

Army Form C. 2118.

No. 16

WAR DIARY
or
INTELLIGENCE SUMMARY

(Erase heading not required.) 3/5th BA HIRE FUSLRS

Instructions regarding War Diaries and Intelligence Summaries are contained in F. S. Regs., Part II. and the Staff Manual respectively. Title Pages will be prepared in manuscript.

Place	Date	Hour	Summary of Events and Information	Remarks and references to Appendices
GIVENCHY LEFT SUB-SECTOR	1917 Jan 12th		In the morning the No 13. B of 3.0 a.m. 8 officers and 200 men of the 2/6th BATT. LAN. FUS. made a raid on enemy's trenches. Many casualties were caused to him on withdrawing. D. Company of this Batt. rendered great assistance in bringing in wounded from NO MANS LAND. LIEUT GODDARD unfortunately being killed whilst assisting	
	13th		D. Co relieved by C. Company	
	15th		B. Company takes over PRINCES ISLAND & left sector by the Right Battn. to assist in enabling the 2/7th L. FUS. to withdraw from the trenches to repair for a moment of tremendous.	
	16th		Remainder of Battn. passes over the trenches. Only 1 Company in the BLINS owing to B. Co being away	
	18th		2/7th LAN. FUS. actions southward. B. Company returned to the OLD BRITISH LINE	
	20th		6/7th Division came out of the line being relieved by the 2nd Division Battn. relieved by the 17th MIDDLESEX REGT and go into Billets at BELLEVUE (BETHUNE.) (attached sheet) (Signed) ?????	

2449 Wt. W14957/Mgo 750,000 1/16 J.B.C. & A. Forms/C.2118/12.

Army Form C. 2118.

WAR DIARY
or
INTELLIGENCE SUMMARY

3/5TH BATT (Erase heading not required) R.E. FUSILIERS

Place	Date	Hour	Summary of Events and Information	Remarks and references to Appendices
BELLERIVE (BETHUNE Combined Sheet W12b)	1917 June 24th		Battn. entrained at CHOQUES for DUNKERQUE and go into billets there, about 1 mile South of the town, for training.	
	27th		50 shells fired into DUNKERQUE from a German Gun, reported to be a 12"7 (calibre). Several casualties caused to XV Corps Head-Quarters.	
	28th		Battn. leave for fresh billets. 3 miles E.N.E. of DUNKERQUE near the FORT des DUNES. With the 3/6 Lan Fus. East of them. Colonel Bates, O.C. 3/5th Lan Fus. in command of the two Battns. takes over the coast defences from under the French Command, with Battn. H.Q. in the FORT des DUNES (Map reference DUNKERQUE 1A BELGIUM 1/100,000) May Wilkie left Battn.	I. II. III. IV.
	29th/30th		At MALO TERMINUS - Instruction for Coast defences & operation orders for ZUYDCOOTE subsector & MIDDAS-BATES D.S.O Comdg the subsector attached - Casualties from 4th attached - plus the officers attached	

Arthur Winterbright Lt Col
Aug 3/5/17 Bn RE

Div. Ref 358/1G.

SECRET:-

54 G.

INSTRUCTIONS FOR COAST DEFENCES - DUNKIRK AREA

Reference attached Maps "A" & "B".

1. XV Corps will, in case of alarm, and on the requisition of the Governor of DUNKIRK, provide the troops necessary (in addition to certain permanent French machine gun and Coast Guard detachments) for the coast defence of the ZUYDCOOTE and MARDYCK sub-sectors of the Coast defences in the Region of DUNKIRK.

2. ZUYDCOOTE Sub-Sector   (see Map "A")

   Length of coast 10,500 yards.
   The defences consist of the following:-

   (i)   A continuous belt of high wire entanglement along the coast.
   (ii)   Infantry works close to the shore prepared for all round defence, as shown on Map "A".
   (iii) Machine gun positions permanently manned by French detachments.
   (iv)   Two searchlights manned by the French.
   (v)   Supporting points a few hundred yards in rear of the coast line, and dug-outs for supporting troops.

3. MARDYCK Sub-Sector   (see Map "B")

   Length of coast 6,500 yards.
   Defences:-

   (i)   Infantry works prepared for all-round defence.
   (ii)   Machine gun positions permanently occupied by French detachments.
   (iii) Supporting points and shelters for reserves.

4. Coast guard and look-out duties on the coast in both sub-sectors are carried out by night and day entirely by the permanent French detachments.

5. British troops as detailed below will be held in readiness to man the coast defences at two hours notice by day, and in immediate readiness by night or in foggy weather:-

   ZUYDCOOTE Sub-sector   ...   2 Battns of 66th Division.

   MARDYCK Sub-sector   ...   XV Corps Mounted Troops.
                                     (Corps Cavalry Regt, and
                                     Corps Cyclist Battn.)

6. COMMAND:-
   (a)   The chain of command in the coast defences is as follows:-

                        Governor of DUNKIRK

   Colonel (French)   Colonel (French)
   Commanding   Commanding
   Western Sector   Eastern Sector

   O.C. MARDYCK   ===   ===   O.C. ZUYDCOOTE
   Sub-sector   Sub-Sector.
   (Corps Mtd Troops)   (2 Battns 66th Div.)

- 2 -

(b) The senior Battalion Commander of the two Battalions detailed to the ZUYDCOOTE Sub-Sector will be the O.C. ZUYDCOOTE Sub-Sector.
   Headquarters will be as near to FORT DES DUNES as possible. Battle H.Q. will be in the fort.
   O.C. XV Corps Mounted Troops will be the O.C. MARDYCK Sub-sector.
   Headquarters - MARDYCK.

(c) French Interpreters will be allotted by the French Mission as follows:-
   In each sector -

   2 Interpreters at Sector H.Q.
   2   "   " " Sub-sector H.Q.
   1   "   for each flank of the British troops to maintain liason when the defences are manned.

   One interpreter will always be on duty at Sub-sector H.Q. to receive messages and orders. These interpreters will join their Sectors on 29th June.

(d) On the Alarm being given on the coast:-

   (i) The British troops allotted to the two Sub-sectors will come under the orders of the French Colonels Commanding the Sectors concerned.
   (ii) The permanent French detachments in the two Sub-sectors will come under the orders of the British Sub-sector Commanders.
   (iii) O.C's ZUYDCOOTE and MARDYCK Sub-sectors will report by telephone to the Colonels Commanding Sectors when their troops are in their battle positions.

NOTE:-
   (i) The Colonel Commanding the Eastern Sector is Colonel MILLOT. H.Q. at CHAPEAU- ROUGE (at intersection of the ROSENDAEL - TETEGHEM road and the DUNKIRK - FURNES Canal.)
   (ii) The Colonel Commanding the Western Sector is Colonel BARBET, Chief Engineer of the DUNKIRK defences. H.Q. (in normal times) at No. 27 RUE du SUD, DUNKIRK.
      Battle H.Q. of the Western Sector is at RUE du CRUYS BELLAERT, PETITE - SYNTHE (100 yards North of the MAIRIE).

7. The alarm will be passed as follows:-

(a) By the Governor of DUNKIRK to H.Q. XV Corps by means of:-

   (i) Telephone message to General Staff XV Corps.
   (ii) A message carried by an officer from the Governor of DUNKIRK'S H.Q. to XV Corps H.Q.

(b) By XV Corps to 66th Division and to Corps Mounted Troops by telegram.

(c) The above channel will be in addition to the passing of the alarm direct from Colonels Commanding Sectors to O.C's Sub-sectors.

8. In case of real or practise alarm, reports on the situation will be repeated to XV Corps H.Q. for information; in the case of MARDYCK Sub-sector direct; in the case of the ZUYDCOOTE Sub-sector through 66th Divisional H.Q.

9. The principles to be followed in the defence of the Coast by the British Troops will be:-

   (i) To occupy the defences with a portion of the force available, thus reinforcing the permanent French detachments.

   (ii) To hold the remainder of the force in reserve suitably disposed so as to be ready to counter-attack and drive into the sea any hostile troops who may effect a landing.

   (iii) In the MARDYCK Sub-sector, the Cyclist Battalion will be used to occupy the defences, and the Cavalry Regiment will form a mobile reserve.

10. 66th Division and Corps Mounted Troops will forward Defence Schemes for their Sub-sectors in duplicate to XV Corps H.Q.

11. This Defence Scheme will come into force at 12.00 noon on 30th June.

(sgd) P. NEAME, Major,
for Brigadier-General.
General Staff.

XV Corps.

29th June 1917.

Issued to:-

66th Division (2 copies)
Corps Mounted Troops (2 copies)
A.D.A.S. XV Corps.
French 36th Corps (3 copies for information)
Captn SEROT, French Mission.

Copy No. 12

AMENDMENT No.1 to OPERATION ORDER No.1.
by
Lieut.-Colonel A.S. BATES D.S.O.
Commanding ZUYDCOOTE Sub-sector & 3/5th LAN. FUS.,
--------o--------

1. For 2/8th Battalion Lancashire Fusiliers substitute throughout

2/7th Battalion Lancashire Fusiliers.

1/7/17.

Lieut.
Adjutant.,
For O.C. ZUYDCOOTE Sub-sector.

Distribution

As for Operation Order No.1.
dated 30.6.17.

SECRET

Copy No. 12

OPERATION ORDER No.1. by LIEUT. COLONEL A.S.BATES D.S.O.
Commanding ZUYDCOOTE Sub-sector & 3/5th Bn. Lan. Fus.,

Reference "BELGIUM & FRANCE" Sheet 19, Second Edition, 1/40,000 and diagram attached.

BATTALION SECTORS:-
1. (a) 3/5th Bn. LAN. FUS., will occupy the QUARTIER de MALO TERMINUS comprising centres of resistance 3 & 4 and the points d'appui "d" to "g" inclusive.
   (b) 2/8th Bn. LAN. FUS., will occupy the QUARTIER de SANITORIUM comprising centres of resistance 5 to 8 inclusive.
   Battalions will be held in readiness to take up their positions at two hours notice by day and in immediate readiness by night or in foggy weather.

GARRISONS:-
2. British - As per Appendix "A" attached.
   French - The 6 Mitrailleuse Sections, each of 2 guns, are situated as follows:-
      1 at the N.W. angle of ZUYDCOOTE Battery (points d'appui "f.1." on attached sketch.
      1 at the Centre of resistance No.4.
      1 at the point d'appui "g"
      1 at the centre of resistance 6
      1   "   "   "   "   7
      1 at a point 150 metres West of centre of resistance 8.

ACTION:-
3. Posts will be held at all costs. Should the enemy effect a landing, immediate counter attacks will be made by the nearest available troops to drive him back into the sea. Os.C. centres of resistance and points d'appui will make themselves acquainted with the gaps in the wire which could be used for counter strokes. In all cases the fullest information must be sent to Sub-sector Battle Headquarters.

S.A.A.
4. (a) 3/5th Lan. Fus.,
   (i) "A" Coy will take 1 S.A.A. limber superintended by the L.G. Officer, for centre of resistance No.3 and points d'appui "d".
   (ii) The 2½ platoons of "D" Coy in the points d'appui "e" and "f" will take 1 S.A.A. limber superintended by the Bombing Officer.
   (iii) "B" Coy will take 1 S.A.A. limber superintended by the Intelligence Officer for centre of resistance No.4 & point d'appui "f.1."
   (iv) The platoon of "D" Coy in point d'appui "g" will take 3 pack mules.
   The boxes will be distributed as per Appendix "A", carrying being done by garrisons.
   The 7 boxes remaining in the 2nd limber will be taken to the 3 platoons of "C" Coy in reserve.
   The above mentioned 3 superintending Officers will report completion of their task and distribution of the ammunition to the C.O. at Battle Headquarters.
   The remaining pack mules will go to the FORT.
   (b) The O.C. 2/8th Lan. Fus., will make the necessary arrangements to ensure a reserve of 100 rounds a man to be in his centres of resistance.

RESERVES:-
5. (a) 3/5th Lan. Fus.,
   3 platoons "C" Coy will be in reserve at C.15.d.7.4. and the O.C. Coy and the necessary runners will report to the C.O. at Battle Headquarters.
   (b) 2/8th Lan. Fus.,
   "C" Coy will be in reserve at C.11.c.9.2.
   "D" Coy will be in reserve at C.7.a.7.4.

-2-

BATTLE HEADQUARTERS:-
6. (a) Of the Sub-sector & 3/5th Lan. Fus., at the FORT DES DUNES.
   (b) Of the 2/8th Lan. Fus., at the Tower C.7.c.2.8.

RATIONS:-
7. All available rations will be issued and carried.

WATER:-
8. All water bottles will be filled.
   (a) 3/5th Lan. Fus.,   The water carts will take up the nearest possible positions to the 2 centres of resistance and the petrol tins will be distributed as per Appendix "A" Carrying will be done by garrisons.
   (b) 2/8th Lan. Fus.,   As ordered by the C.O.

LIASON:-
9. See footnote to Appendix "A". The O.C. point d'appui "g" will get into touch with the garrison of the centre of resistance 5.

COMMUNICATION:-
10. The signalling Officer will distribute the Battalion signallers so as best to assist in keeping the telephonic communications open

Runners from	are to know the best routes to
Garrisons on coast	posts on either flank & Battalion H.Qrs.
Reserves	All posts in their own sector and in the case of "C" Coy 2/8th Lan. Fus., the route to Centre of resistance No.4 & point d'appui "g"
Battalion H.Qrs	Other Battn. H.Qrs & all posts.

FORT DES DUNES:-
11. The following will accompany the C.O. 3/5th Lan. Fus., to the FORT. The Second in Command, Adjutant, Signalling Officer and all H.Q. runners.

MEDICAL ARRANGEMENTS:-
12. The M.Os will make the necessary arrangements for the establishment of regimental aid posts and will report action taken to the O.C. Sub-sector. When arrangements for evacuation have been made they will be notified to Battalion Commanders.

13. ACKNOWLEDGE.

                                                            Lieut.
                                                            Adjutant.
30.6.17.   for O.C. ZUYDCOOTE Sub-sector.
         Distribution
         Copy No. 1. Colonel MILLOT Cdt les Secteurs Est & Ouest,
              2. Lieut.-Col A.S.BATES D.S.O.   DUNKERQUE.
              3. O.C. 2/8th Lan. Fus.,
              4. O.C. "A" Coy 3/5th Lan. Fus.,
              5. O.C. "B"   ..   ..
              6. O.C. "C"   ..   ..
              7. O.C. "D"   ..   ..
              8. Second in Command, 3/5th Lan. Fus.,
              9. Adjutant, 3/5th Lan. Fus.,
             10. Medical Officer, 3/5th Lan. Fus.,
             11/13 War Diary.
             14. Interpreters.
             15. 66th Divn. for information.
             16. 197th Inf. Bde for information.
             17. H.Q. Officers, 3/5th Lan. Fus.,

APPENDIX "A"

Centres of Resistance.	Points d'appui	Garrison	Boxes of S.A.A.	Tins of Water.
		3/5th Lan. Fus.,		
3		"A" Coy ✱	20	22
	"d"	1 platoon "C"	6	6
	"e"	2 platoons "D"	10	12
	"f"	½ platoon "D"	9	3
	"f.1."	½ platoon "D"	6	3
4.		"B" Coy	20	23
	"g"	1 platoon "D"	6	6
		2/8th Lan. Fus.,		
5.		2 platoons "B"	As ordered by O.C.	
6.		1 platoon "B"	As ordered by O.C.	
7.		1 platoon "B"	As ordered by O.C.	
8.		"A" Coy ✱	As ordered by O.C.	

✱ An Interpreter (in the case of 3/5th Lan. Fus., M. ODDES) will accompany these Companies for liason with the Allied troops on the outer flanks.

CASUALTIES FOR MONTH OF JUNE 1917.

3/5th Battn. LANCASHIRE FUSILIERS

	OFFICERS			OTHER RANKS.	
Date	Killed	Wounded	Missing	Killed	Wounded	Missing
4th					203136 Pte SMITH.W.V.	
7th					202559 Pte ROBERTS.F.	
					203259 " " KNIGHT.T.	
					203637 " " THORNTON.J.W.	
					203230 " " THORNLEY.E.	
8th				202555 Pte HARDMAN.J.T.	201271 Cpl NORTH.R.	
					201179 Pte HOWARTH.J.W.	
					202409 " " SIMONS.J.	
13th	Lieut. W.N. GOBBARD.				202568 " " BIRKS.H. (posted 197th L.T.M.Battery)	
					203563 Pte CLAYS.A.	
					202607 " " WESTWELL.J.	
					203570 L/Sgt HIGGS.T.	
					204429 Pte SMETHURST.W.	
					202638 " " EARNSHAW.A.	
					203667 " " FOX.H.	
					204351 " " AYLIFFE.W.G.	
					203648 " " EVANS.T.	
					204443 " " FLOOD.E.M.	
					204472 " " SMITH.A.	
					202642 " " FROST.B.	
					204179 " " HOPKINS.E.	

Captain S.F.H. MACKAY (2/5th East Lancashire Regt) attached 3/5th Bn. Lancashire Fusiliers--Missing 13/6/17.

1.7.1917.

Lieut.-Col.
Commanding 3/5th Battn. Lan. Fus.;

DIAGRAM TO ACCOMPANY
ALARM OPERATION ORDERS No.1.
dated 30/6/1917.

| FRENCH ZONE. | QUARTIER DE MALO TERMINUS 3/5th Lan. Fus. | QUARTIER DE SANATORIUM 2/8th Lan. Fus. | BELGIAN ZONE. |

1 Coy.
Malo Terminus — 1 platoon
2 platoons
½ platoon
Batterie de Zuydcoote. — ½ platoon
1 Coy.
½ platoon
1 platoon
2 platoons
1 platoon
Sanatorium. — 1 platoon
1 Coy.

3 Platoons in Reserve.

2 Coys in Reserve.

Centres of resistance shewn thus :—
Points d'appui shewn thus :—

3/5th BATTN. LANCASHIRE FUSILIERS

OFFICERS JOINING AND LEAVING THE BATTALION
DURING JUNE 1917.

Temp. Captain S.F.H. MACKAY attached for duty 8/6/17, from
2/5th EAST LANCASHIRE REGIMENT.

2/Lieut. HALL.W.   joined 20/6/1917.

2/Lieut. WILSON.E.J.   joined 20/6/1917.

2/Lieut. YAPP.G.H.   joined 26/6/1917.

Temp. Captain S.F.H. MACKAY   Missing   13/6/17.

Lieutenant   W.N GODDARD.   Killed.   13/6/17.

1/7/1917.

Lieut.-Col.
Commanding 3/5th Bn. Lan. Fus.

197th Brigade.

66th Division.

3/5th BATTALION LANCASHIRE FUSILIERS JULY 1917.

C O N F I D E N T I A L

WAR   DIARY

OF

3/5th BATTN. LANCASHIRE FUSILIERS.

From:- 1st July, 1917   To:- 31st July 1917.

(VOLUME. 6)

-o-o-o-o-o-o-o-o-o-o-o-o-o-o-o

Army Form C. 2118.

WAR DIARY
or
INTELLIGENCE SUMMARY

3/5th BAT (Erase heading not required) LANCASHIRE FUSILIERS

Place	Date	Hour	Summary of Events and Information	Remarks and references to Appendices
MALO TERMINUS	1917 July 1st		Congratulatory message from 2ND DIVISION which relieved 66th received. During 1st 2nd Battn. continued Fatigues with the exception when engaged on Coast Defence work, until it moved on 13th of July to COXYDE.	WW XX
MALO LES BAINS	3rd		COAST DEFENCE. The ZUYDCOOTE Sub Right. Which consisting of 2 QUARTIERS viz. ZUYD TERMINUS on the West and the SANATORIUM on the EAST were manned. Until the manning of the QUARTIER BRAY DUNES - on its date. 2/6 MANCHESTERS occupied this under Major HORTON D.S.O. the QUARTIER of Rebec'd right	
DUNKERQUE			up to the BELGIAN FRONTIER	
BELGIUM 13.000	10		By 10 the Belgian sector has come under the command of Colonel Millot the French Army. He was under the command & responsible to the General of Division COUTANCEAU the Governor of DUNKIRK. 2/7 A LAN. FUS (LtCol HOBBINS) had relieved the 2/8 LAN FUS on the SANATORIUM QUARTIER. This Battalion was suddenly relieved by the 1/10 MANCHESTERS (the rest. slipping to the 90th army) which was now transferred on the BRAY DUNES QUARTIER by the 2/5 th EAST LANCASHIRES (LtCol WHITEHEAD)	
	12th		Subsection. Operation Order No 2. dated and duly attacked. Marked I. Also Divisional Scheme of Defence dated 6th July, which was incorporated in abbre 00 No 2. attached and marked II. Battalion Operation Order No 2. dated July 9th attached marked III.	
		5	On July 10th a post colonne was held. Battalion report to O/C SANT. Q.R. marked IV. Report from O.C ZUYDCOOTE Subsector to the French authorities att. marked V. Report from O.C. ZUYDCOOTE Subsector to the French Authorities on the same date. on the night 10th/11th fire attacked target III. The Battalion was relieved on front & defence on July 13 by 2/9 MANCHESTERS. (C/Col THORNEYCROFT D.S.O) Hay C.O relieving was Lt Col BATES D.S.O 3/5 LAN FUS in Command of the sub sector.	

Army Form C. 2118.

WAR DIARY
or
INTELLIGENCE SUMMARY

(Erase heading not required.)

3.5TH BATT FUS.

W.W.

Place	Date	Hour	Summary of Events and Information	Remarks and references to Appendices
MALO TERMINUS Malo-Les-Bains DUNKERQUE BELGIUM (100.000)	1917 July 10th 11th 12th	10A 11A 12A	Germans attacked XVth Corps front. See summary attached marked VII. This was received by 66th Division to the C.O. as O.C. ZUYDCOOTE Sub sector. MAJOR WIKE expired of wounds. Battalion moved in Ranges to FURNES then by Lorry to COXYDE (W6C.3.3) Sheet II SE where it bivouacked (36 tents being available only) and was at 1 hours notice to move. General information - MALO TERMINUS was seat of 4th ARMY H.Q. (General RAWLINSON) The move from the South took place while the Batt was at MALO TERMINUS. See Battery was enjoyed daily by all ranks. A.M. the King visited BRAY DUNES and LA PANNE where the King & the Belgians were staying during this period. On two or three occasions the enemy aeroplanes bombed the neighbourhood but no damage was done in the vicinity. Billets for the Batt. were small and very scattered & therefore were not bad. Extract from 108th Infy Bde Order No.31 attached and marked VIII.	

Army Form C. 2118.

WAR DIARY
or
INTELLIGENCE SUMMARY

3/5th Batt. N C S FUSILIERS

Place	Date	Hour	Summary of Events and Information	Remarks and references to Appendices
COXYDE	1917 July 13		Orders were received that the 66th Division would take over the line from the 1st Division.	
DUNKERQUE 1A BELGIUM (1/100,000)		4 pm	Col Bates DSO OC 3/5th Lan. Fus. Major Wike & 2 Coy Commanders proceeded to the line to inspect the Left Sub. Sector.	
		10 pm	The Batt. took over the trenches from the 1st Oxf & North Lancs (Lt. Phillips Comdg) Relief commenced at 10.30 pm and was completed by 4.30 am (17th). The line held was from the sand-dunes Nieuport Bains to a point M14 a 54 55 Ref. Map Trenches Belgium sheets S.W. section 1 A. 1/20,000. D Coy was on the Right sub Sector. A Coy the centre, C Coy Left Right Flank sub & B Coy in Support. The line held was on the West bank of the RIVER YSER. No other newly-arrived Division had held the Eastern bank up to the 10th July. The 1st Division held this up to the 10th, but on 10/11th the Germans opened a very heavy barrage, attacked a portion of the 1st Div on East bank and after a gallant resistance the whole of Kings R. Battn the 1st Batt. K.R.R. and 1st Bat. Northants Regt. they if returns so far, when quite failing back over the Ribben bridges and 33 other ranks only escaping back over the river. Commanding Officers are now being brought into the Left Camp area Right & in relief of line being taken over & left behind. Report received...	

WAR DIARY or INTELLIGENCE SUMMARY

3/5th B (Erase heading not required.) Fus. RS

Place	Date	Hour	Summary of Events and Information	Remarks and references to Appendices
NIEUPORT BAINS	1917 July 16th		Badly knocked in from the bombardment (evening) of the 10th. July.	
DUNKERQUE "A"		17th	During the night of the 17th/18th dealt heavily shelled by the enemy.	
BELGIUM 1/100,000		20th	Battalion took up a wire burying work at O.O. 29.37 attached and marked Appendix IX	
		22nd	Battalion bore services by the 2/7 L.AN. Fus. the relief commenced at 11.10 pm, at this time the enemy opened up a very heavy bombardment on the left. Relaying the right, the bombardment continued until 1.0 am when it slackened, and the relief was continued at 2.0 am the bombardment was resumed with great intensity and continued until 3.30 am. The relief had eventually completed by 4.45 am. The Battn has been fortunate in having two casualties during the relief a Defence Scheme as O.O. N°142. Marked X	
		23rd	The Battn on its huts and tents at CAMP RINK gave day duties from 6.00 am to 6.00 am under the R.E's. Parties 00ST-DUNKERQUE BAINS Reference	X
	5		were sent each night to dig and bury the cable. During the early part of the september attached mr Nos 3 Rivet Section on night of July 31st [illegible]	
	9th		during the period the artillery line and both sides were intense. the enemy sheltered scattering from gas shells at night carriage the Battn.	

Army Form C. 2118.

WAR DIARY
or
INTELLIGENCE SUMMARY.
(Erase heading not required)

357th B^{try} H.R.E. Fus.^{rs} —

Place	Date	Hour	Summary of Events and Information	Remarks and references to Appendices
COXHYDE	July		Battalion moved from CAMP RINK this day into billets (unoccupied close)	
BAINS		30^{pm}	COXHYDE BAINS taking over from the 8th EAST LANCASHIRE REGT	
M^{id} R^y			who moved into CAMP RINK.	
DUNKERQUE		3¹⁵	Copy of letter received by Lt Col A S BATES DSO from General 5^e	
BELGIUM			Division COUTANCE V, Commanding DUNKERQUE on relinquishing	
1/100,000			Command of the Groupement ZUYDCOOTE Sept Sept 6 attached	
			as inset XII	
			Similar Communication attended to XIII	
			Buch orders: 38 Officers O.R. the ranks	
			Ration strength 36 10 36 20	
			40	
			Serving th Battery Ban au CONSEIL Permis 12/7/16 A. Brig Gen L. Dunn CB	
			Signed Commander of the Brigade Brig Gen O. C Brown D. O	
			to Brig Gen Sunlow	

Arthur Bates
Colonel

XIth Corps   2nd Division No.
                                                      G.S. 1215.

        All the Brigadiers and the Commanding Officers
that I have seen are most pleased with the arrangements
made by the 66th Division, Brigades and Battalions for
handing over the line.
        I should be glad if the G.O.C. 66th Division
might be informed as this Division has never taken over
a line under more comfortable circumstances.
                                (sgd) C.E. PEREIRA.
                                          Major-General.
26th June, 1917.   Commanding 2nd Division.

                        2.

Headquarters,   XIth Corps.
    Adv. First Army.   RHS.1194/14.

        I have much pleasure in forwarding this letter
for transmission to G.O.C. 66th Division.

                                (sgd) H.W. STUDD.
                                         B.G., G.S., for
XIth Corps,   Commanding XIth Corps.
27/6/17.

----

                        3.   First Army G.S. (O.A.)
XVth Corps   G.S. 647

        Will you please forward the attached letter to
G.O.C. 66th Division.

                                (sgd) W.H. ANDERSON,
                                        Major-General G.S.
28/6/17.   First Army.

----

                        4.   XVth Corps.
66th Division.   25/7 G.

        Forwarded.
                                (sgd) H. KNOX. B.G., G.S.,
30/6/17.   XVth Corps.

                        5.
197th Inf. Bde.   66th Divn.
                                                 339/I.G.

        Forwarded.   To be communicated to all ranks.

                                (sgd) A. R. BURROWES.
                                            Lieut.- Col.
                                            General Staff.
D.H.Q.   66th Division.
1/7/17.

                        6.
3/5th Bn. Lan. Fus.,   197th Inf. Bde.
                                                 BML 8/M/210.

        Forwarded. To be communicated to
all ranks.
                                (sgd) C.J. GASSON. Captain,
                                           Brigade Major.
B.H.Q.   197th Infantry Brigade.
2.7.17.

SECRET

OPERATION ORDER No. 2.
by
LIEUT. COLONEL. A.S.BATES D.S.O. 3/5th Lan. Fus.,
Commanding ZUYDCOOTE SUB-SECTOR.

Copy No. 7

Appendix No. 1

References – French Map (referred to as F.M.) and FRANCE & BELGIUM Sheet 19, 2nd Edition, 1/40,000, referred to as (Sheet 19) and Sun-print Map A.

DIVISIONAL SCHEME 358/G dated 6/7/17.
1. Copy No. 4/3 is attached.
Ref. para.(3) Appendices "A" & "B" already issued only to Battalions, give details of French garrisons referred to in this paragraph.

Battalions are distributed as follows:-

Battalion	Quartered in	Quartier.
(a) 2/5th E.LANCS.	BRAY DUNES	Bray Dunes.
(b) 2/10th MANCHESTER REGIMENT.	ZUYDCOOTE	Sanatorium.
(c) 3/5th LAN. FUS.,	(Sheet 19 C.20 & 21.)	Malo Terminus.

DEFENCES
2. (a) The QUARTIER BRAY DUNES at present has no constructed centres of resistance but 4, numbered 9 - 12 inclusive are being constructed.
(b) The QUARTIER du SANATORIUM has 4 well defined centres of resistance 5 - 8 inclusive.
(c) The QUARTIER MALO TERMINUS has 2 well defined centres of resistance 3 - 4 and in addition, "points d'appui" lettered "d" - "g" inclusive.

SYSTEM OF DEFENCE.
3. Os.C. Battalions will report their disposition to O.C. Sub-sector in accordance with para.4 of Divisional Scheme 358.G.
Posts will be held at all costs; should the enemy effect a landing, immediate counterattacks will be made by the nearest available troops to drive him back into the sea. Os.C. Centres of Resistance and points d'appui will make themselves acquainted with the gaps in the wire which could be used for counter strokes. In all cases the fullest information must be sent to Sub-sector Battalion Headquarters. Troops in Reserve must know the shortest way to their own Battalion's posts and also to the posts, whether British or Allied, on the immediate flanks of their own Battalion.

ALARM:-
4. The Alarm will be passed as follows:-
(a) By telephone from FRENCH H.Q. CHAPEAU ROUGE.
(b) By telephone from Sub-sector H.Q.
(c) By cyclist from Sub-sector H.Q.

REPORTS.
5. In case of a real, or practice alarm, reports on the situation will be forwarded direct to O.C. Subsector H.Q. Battle Headquarters are in the FORT DES DUNES, otherwise the Headquarters of the Sub-sector Commander are at the Estaminet CHAS. PICHON, Rue de FORT DES DUNES, LEFFRINCKHOUCKE (Sheet 19) G.21.c.15.80.

S.A.A. GRENADES.
6. Battalions will arrange for a supply of S.A.A. and detonated grenades to be kept in each centre of resistance to be occupied in case of alarm, and for the necessary guards and store-keepers to be placed over the ammunition.

RATIONS.
7. All available rations will be issued and carried.

-2-

WATER. 8. All water bottles will be filled and arrangements made for a reserve supply to be available should the garrison be in position for more than 12 hours.

LIASON. 9. Centres of Resistance Nos.3 and 12 will each have an interpreter attached for liason with the Allied posts on West & East respectively.

COMMUNICATION. 10. The Signalling Officer, 3/5th Lancashire Fusiliers will superintend this.

Every endeavour will be made to establish visual signalling between the different posts and Battle Headquarters of Battalions; also between the former and the barrage batteries marked with a green cross on F.M.

Battalions in whose QUARTIER the Barrage batteries are situated will report whether they can, in event of alarm, man the receiving stations at such batteries by signallers with a knowledge of French.

MEDICAL. 11. M.O's will make the necessary arrangements for establishment of R.A.P's and will report actions taken to the Sub-sector Commander when arrangements will be made with the A.D.M.S. for evacuations.

RELIEF. 12. In event of relief, these orders together with maps and documents referred to, are to be handed over to the relieving Battalion.

13. ACKNOWLEDGE.

Lieut.-Col.
8/7/17. Commanding ZUYDCOOTE Subsector.

Distribution

Copy No. 1. Colonel MILLOT.
2. 3/5th Lan. Fus.,
3. 2/5th E.Lancs. R.
4. 2/10th Manchester Rgt.
5. Signalling Officer (3/5th)
6-8. War Diary.
9. 66th Division (for information)
10. Spare
11. Spare

SECRET. COAST DEFENCE SCHEME ZUYDCOOTE SUB-SECTOR.   Copy No.4/3

66th.Div. 358 G.

Reference Sheet 19, 1/40,000. Map "A"(sunprint)
and XV Corps 54 G. of 29/6/17.

1. **SUB-SECTOR.** The Subsector includes the Coast defences from the Belgian Frontier at V.23.d.3/4 to C.14.c.0/4 both inclusive.

2. **COMMAND.** The senior British Battalion Commander will command the Subsector, his battle Headquarters are in the FORT DES DUNES, and he is, for the defence purposes, directly under the orders of the French Colonel commanding the EASTERN SECTOR, whose Headquarters are at CHAPEAU ROUGE at the intersection of the ROSENDAEL-TETEGHEM road and the DUNKIRQUE-FURNES Canal (C.85.c.6/0)

3. **TROOPS AND DISTRIBUTION.** In addition to the French garrison comprising M.G detachments and Searchlight detachments and coast watching troops, which are under the command of O.C.sub-sector, three British Battalions are detailed for this duty as follows.-
   One Battalion quartered in BRAY DUNES.
   One Battalion   "   " ZUYDCOOTE.
   One Battalion   "   " Map squares C.20 & 21.

4. **SYSTEM OF DEFENCE.** The O.C.Sub-sector is alone responsible that the troops and defences with which he is concerned are utilized to the best advantage; he will be guided by the following principles-
   (a) His troops will be held in readiness at two hours notice by day, and in immediate readiness by night or in foggy weather.
   (b) In case of alarm he will forthwith reinforce the permanent French detachments with a portion of his force.
   (c) To hold the bulk of his force in readiness for immediate counter-attack should the enemy effect a landing.

5. **COMMUNICATIONS.** Communications including visual alarm signals are directly under the A.D.A.S., XV Corps, any necessary work being carried out by the Signals of the Division furnishing the British troops, The O.C.sub-sector being responsible that his communications are adequate.

6. **ADMINISTRATIVE ARRANGEMENTS.** Although a scheme of this nature calls for no special administrative arrangements, the O.C.Sub-sector will personally satisfy himself that Battalion arrangements under the following headings are co-ordinated.
   (a) Interpreters to ensure smooth and rapid communication with the French troops.
   (b) Ammunition supply, including grenades.
   (c) Rations water and fuel.
   (d) Medical arrangements, especially from R.A.Ps rearwards.

7. **REPORTS.** In case of a real or practise alarm, reports on the situation will be forwarded direct to Divisional HQ.

(signed) A.R.BURROWES, Lt.Col,
General Staff,
66th.Division.

D.H.Q., 6/7/17

DISTRIBUTION.
Copy No.1/2 War Diary. No.3 FILE. No.4/7 O.C.ZUYDCOOTE sub-sector
  " No.8 XV Corps "G" No.9/10 Spare.
DISTRIBUTION by O.C.Sub-sector
Copy No.5 3/5th.LAN.FUS. No.6 2/10th.MANCHESTER R. No.7 2/5th.E.LANCS.
  " No.4/1 Colonel MILLOT. No.4/2,4/3 & 4/4 War Diary

OPERATION ORDER No.2
by
LIEUT. COL. A.S. BATES D.S.O.
Commanding 3/5th Bn. Lancashire Fusiliers.

No III   Copy No 12

wD2

Reference BELGIUM & FRANCE, Sheet 19, Second Edition, 1/40,000 and diagram attached to Operation Order No.1. (except as regards strength of garrisons.)

This order cancels Operation Order No.1 dated 30.6.17.

BATTALION FRONT. 1. The Battalion is responsible for the Coast Defence from C.14.c.0.4. to midway between point d'appui "g" and centre of resistance No.5 - about point C.11.c.3.9. Two well defined centres of resistance Nos.3 and 4 exist, and points d'appui "d", "e" (in 2 portions) "f" and "g" with certain other smaller portions of trench on the front.

DISPOSITIONS

2.
Centres of res-istance	Points d'appui	Garrison	Coy	In close support under O.C. Company.
No.3		2 platoons	"A"	2 platoons less 1 L.G.Section
	"d"	1 L.G.Section		
	"e"	2 L.G.Sections (1 in each position).	"D"	1 platoon. 2 platoons each less L.G. Section 1 platoon less rifle bombers & rifle sections.
	"f"	1 platoon less bombing & L.G. Sections.		
No.4		1 platoon plus 1 L.G.Section.	"B"	2 platoons
	"g"	1 platoon less 1 L.G.Section.		

In Reserve:- "C" Company at C.15.d.7.4.

The Battalion will be ready to take up above positions at 2 hours notice by day, and at immediate notice by night or in foggy weather.

ACTION. 3. Posts will be held at all costs. Should the enemy effect a landing, immediate counter attacks will be made by the nearest available troops to drive him back into the sea. Os.C. centres of resistance, points' d'appui, and supports will make themselves acquainted with the gaps in the wire which could be used for counter strokes.

In all cases, the fullest information must be sent to Sub-sector Battle Headquarters.

S.A.A. GRENADES. 4.   See Appendix "C"
"B" Coy will detail a bombing section from a Platoon in support to report immediately at Battalion Headquarters for the purpose of detonating bombs. The limber loaded with S.A.A. & 1 pack mule for "g" will report to Battalion Headquarters to load the boxes of detonated grenades. O.C. "B" Coy will arrange for a guide for the pack mule.
The above section will rejoin its platoon on completion of the work.

RATIONS 5. All available rations will be issued and carried.

- 2 -

WATER. 6. All water bottles will be filled. The watercarts will take up the nearest possible position to the 2 centres of resistance and petrol tins will be distributed as follows. Carrying will be done by troops in support.

Centre of Resistance	Pts d'appui	Tins of water.
3		11
	"d"	3
	"e"	4
	"f"	3
4		12
	"g"	6

LIASON. 7. M. ODDES will accompany O.C. "A" Coy for liason with the next Allied post on the West. M. JAMBON will accompany the C.O. to the FORT DES DUNES.

COMMUNICATION. 8. The signalling Officer will distribute the signallers so as best to assist in keeping telephonic communication open. He will also station signallers at BASTION 31 DUNKERQUE and the Barrage Battery at ZUYDCOOTE Battery.

Runners from	are to know the best routes to
Coast garrisons	Posts on either flank & Battle Headquarters.
Supports	Their own Coy posts & posts on each flank, also Battle H.Q.
Battle Headquarters	Other Battalion Battle Hdqrs and all Battalion posts.

BATTLE H.Q. 9. are at FORT DES DUNES. The following will accompany the C.O.; 2nd in Command, Adjutant and other H.Q. Officers less Transport Officer and Q.M. All Headquarters runners, after accomplishing initial duty of passing the Alarm - M. JAMBON.

MEDICAL ARRANGEMENTS. 10. R.A.P's will be established as follows:-
(a) Under canvas on the FORT DES DUNES - BATTERIE DE ZUYDCOOTE Road, North of the railway.
(b) In the corner house at C.20.b.2.4.

REPORTS 11. In case of real or practice alarm reports on the situation will be sent to Battalion Headquarters.

RELIEF. 12. In event of the Battalion being relieved, these orders will be returned to Battalion H.Q.

13. ACKNOWLEDGE.

Lieut. & Adjt,
9/7/17. 3/5th Battn. Lancs. Fuslrs.,

DISTRIBUTION
Copy No. 1 C.O.   Copy No.2 Colonel MILLOT
3. "A"   4. "B"
5. "C"   6. "D"
7. 2nd in Comnd   8. Adjutant
9. M.O.   10. Interpreters
11. H.Q. Officers   12. Transport Officer
13-15. War Diary   16-18. Spare.

APPENDIX "A"

Extract from, **as far as concerns the 3/5th LAN. FUS.**,

French troops stationed in the ZUYDCOOTE Sub-sector.

QUARTIER	Units	Normal Stations.	Alarm Stations	Reserve
MALO TERMINUS.	1/2 Cie Mitr. 103rd R.I.T. ½ Cie du Genie	FORT DES DUNES	West of FORT DES DUNES	du Gouverneur du Secteur.

R.I.T. - - Regiment d'Infanterie Territoriale

APPENDIX "B"

Extract from, **as far as concerns the 3/5th LAN. FUS.**

French troops on watch each night in the Sector.

QUARTIER	POSITION	½ PLATOONS	Sections of Mitrailleuses	Remarks.
MALO TERMINUS	N.W. Battery de ZUYDCOOTE		/18th A.P.F.	(A.P.F. --
	Point d'appui "C"	/18th A.P.F.	/18th A.P.F.	(Auxiliaire (de Place (Porte

9/7/17.

Lieut.
Adjutant, 3/5th Bn. Lan. Fus.

DISTRIBUTION

Copy No. 1. C.O.
2. "A"
3. "B"
4. "C"
5. "D"
6/8. War Diary

APPENDIX "C"

S.A.A. & GRENADE RESERVE

1. The following boxes of S.A.A. and detonated grenades have been distributed.

Centre of Resistance	By Coys	Boxes S.A.A.	Boxes Grenades	Remarks
3	A	22	29	Of these 4 boxes SAA & 5 boxes grenades will be fetched by garrison of point d'appui "d" on alarm
4	B	18	24	

2. In event of alarm the following boxes S.A.A. and detonated grenades will be taken by Companies as under:-

Point d'appui	Method	Boxes S.A.A	Boxes Grenades	Coy	Remarks
"e"	)	8	5	"D"	This limber will be taken as near to the posts as possible & the boxes carried by the garrison to their respective posts. The limber & distribution will be superintended by Lieut. MORLEY who will report completion to the C.O.
	) 1 limber)				
"f"	)	8	6	"D"	
"g"	4 pack mules.	6	6	"B"	

3. Remaining 2 pack mules to take 4 boxes SAA to C Coy in Reserve and to return to the transport. The 4 pack mules used by B Coy will return to the transport and all 6 will continue to take Boxes from there to C Coy until 26 Boxes are dumped there for reserve. Lieut Thompson will superintend this report completion to the CO

SECRET

XV Corps 54/10 G.
66th Divn 358/10.

Subject:- Practice Alarm.

To:- O.C.
ZUYDCOOTE Sub-sector.

As instructed, I have to report as follows:-

1. A practice alarm was held to-day, the message being received from the CHAPEAU ROUGE at 6.10 a.m.

DISPOSITIONS 2. The dispositions of the Battalion were:-

Centre of resistance	Points d'appui	Garrison	Coy	In close support
3		2 platoons	"A"	Balance of Company
	"d"	1 L.G.Section		
	"e"	2 L.G.Sections (1 in each post)	"D"	Balance of Company
	"f"	1 platoon less bombing & L.G. sections.		
4		1 platoon plus 1 L.G.Section	"B"	Balance of Company
	"g"	1 platoon less 1 L.G.Section		

In Reserve at C.15.d.7.4. - - "C" Company.

3. The following schedule gives details of time of despatch to, and receipt of messages by the different Companies, and the hours at which they were in position.

Coy.	Message Sent by cyclist a.m.	Received a.m.	Coy in position a.m.	Time between receipt of message and being in position
"A"	6.11	6.20	7.27	1 hour. 07'
"B"	6.11	6.16	7.30	1 hour. 14'
"C"	6.11	6.23	7.35	1 hour. 12'
"D"	6.11	6.18	7.10	0. 52'

4. The Billets of the Battalion are very scattered and if the Alarm was given in the dark, I do not think the times shewn in the last column of the above schedule could be adhered to.

COMMUNICATION 5. Telephone communication between Centres of resistance 3 and 4 and Battalion H.Q. at the FORT DES DUNES worked well - also visual signalling between these points and the Barrage Batteries at Bastion 31 and the Battery de ZUYDCOOTE. Battalion Signallers were sent to each of these Batteries and touch was made with the former at 7.20 a.m.

AMMUNITION 6. S.A.A. and grenades (detonated) had been previously dumped

-2-

No. IV

AMMUNITION 6.(continued)

dumped/
in the centres of resistance. A reserve dump of S.A.A. was made with the Reserve Company.

WATER 7. Water carts filled, with empty petrol tins, were taken as close as practicable to centres of resistance 3 and 4, and the tins filled and distributed by the Support troops.

LIASON. 8. Touch was kept with the French post to the West of centre of resistance 3. An interpreter being attached to centre of resistance 3 for this purpose.

MEDICAL. 9.(a) The 2/1st E.Lancs. Field Ambulance formed a R.A.P. at an empty corner house on the East side of the road at G.20.b.2.4. The Field Ambulance was connected with Battalion Headquarters by telephone for purposes of giving the alarm and of being informed when ambulances were required. Captain PORTER SMITH, R.A.M.C.(T) was in charge and was in position before the troops, which his R.A.P. served, were at their posts.

(b) The Battalion M.O. formed a R.A.P. in 3 tents (struck from the Transport Lines) just off the road to the Battery de ZUYDCOOTE, North of the Railway. A 50 gallon tank was filled at the Battery and then left at this R.A.P.

CONCLUSION 10. If it is seriously believed that the enemy can land a force of any size, other than a few men, without detection by the French troops watching the coast, I think the Battalion should be situated under canvas closer to their battle positions.

Lieut.- Col.

10/7/17.   Commdg 2/5th Battn. Lancashire Fusilrs.

DISTRIBUTION

Copy No. 1.   O.C. ZUYDCOOTE Subsector
         2.   O.C. ZUYDCOOTE Subsector
         3.   War Diary.
         4.   War Diary.
         5.   Spare
         6.   Spare

Subject:- Practice Alarm.

XV Corps 54/G
66th Div.358/1G

From:- O.C.
ZUYDCOOTE Sub-sector.

To :- Le Commandant,
Eastern Sector,
DUNKIRK Coast Defences,
CHAPEAU ROUGE.

I have the honour to report as follows:-

ALARM.
1. The message giving the practice Alarm was received at 6.10 a.m. 10th July.

ACTION.
2. The following schedule shews actions taken together with hours of despatch. All messages, both for real and practice alarm, had been previously written ready for despatch.

PRIORITY TELEPHONE		UNIT & QUARTIER	Confirm- -ation by Cyclist & time of receipt	Unit reported wholly in position
Stated to get through	Message sent			
6.12 a.m.	6.30 a.m.	2/5th EAST LANCS. BRAY DUNES.	(x) 6.50 a.m. 7.35 a.m.	9.0 a.m.
6.12 a.m.	6.30 a.m	2/10th MANCHESTER.R SANATORIUM.	(x) 6.50 a.m. 7.18 a.m.	7.30 a.m
6.12 a.m.	6.23 a.m.	2/1st EAST LANCS. FIELD. AMB.	--	7.15 a.m
Cyclist Orderlies and runners	6.11 a.m	3/5th LAN. FUS. MALO TERMINUS	--	7.35 a.m

(x) The reason of the lateness of these confirmatory messages was that all cycles were in use in my own Battalion Sector.
In addition the BATTERIE de ZUYDCOOTE was telephoned to, also the FORT DES DUNES.
Therefore 2 hours 3 minutes elapsed between receipt of message and the troops being in position. This was under favourable conditions.

3. I reached the FORT DES DUNES, Subsector Battle Headquarters at 6.30 a.m. and took over. It was reported to me that 28 French soldiers remained in the Fort under my orders.

4. Knowing that the 2/6th Bn MANCHESTER Regt was under canvas between the FORT and the Battery de ZUYDCOOTE, I asked its C.O. if I could count on his support in the event of the enemy landing and my being in difficulties. He replied "Yes".

NARRATIVE. 5. At 6.30, I opened the envelope given me and reported its contents, viz:-

" A violent cannonade is heard in a N.E. direction" to CHAPEAU ROUGE.

At 8.32, I received the following message despatched 8.15 from 2/10th MANCHESTERS :-

"15 barges have been sighted sailing towards coast "between ZUYDCOOTE SANATORIUM and BRAYDUNES"

This message was repeated to CHAPEAU ROUGE at 8.35 and to 2/5th EAST LANCS. at 8.37 in case the latter had not received this news. The same message was also sent at 8.40 to the Battery de ZUYDCOOTE.

At 9.03 touch was gained with the French post to the West of Centre of Resistance No.3 by the garrison of the latter. At 9.15, I received from CHAPEAU ROUGE a message with the information that 1 Platoon of French troops had been sent to LEFFRINCKOUCKE Bridge and a ½ Company of Douaniers to the Bridge at FIRMINY Waterworks

At 9.34 I received a telephone message from 2/5th EAST LANCS. sent off at 8.15 and delayed by the exchange to the effect that it was in position.

At 9.46 a.m. I received message from 2/5th EAST LANCS. timed 9 a.m. confirming message about the 15 barges from centre of resistance No.9.

At 9.57 received message from 2/10th MANCHESTERS to the effect that several hostile Battalions were landing on the beach between Centre of Resistance No.6 and BRAY DUNES, that the French 75,s were in action. This message I passed on at 9.59 to CHAPEAU ROUGE.

At 10.20 received message from 2/10th MANCHESTERS that enemy were attacking all his 4 posts and BRAY DUNES and that the coast defence troops were holding their own. This was passed to CHAPEAU ROUGE at 10.21.

At 10.24, I ordered O.C. 3/5th LAN. FUS., to move 2 platoons from his reserve Coy to a position behind point d'appui "g" in case the SANATORIUM QUARTIER should need assistance. This was reported to CHAPEAU ROUGE at 10.27 and to the O.C. SANATORIUM QUARTIER at 10.30 a.m. and he was told he could call on them if required. These 2 platoons were in the new position at 11 a.m.

At 10.28 received message from O.C. 2/5th EAST LANCS. confirming the news of the landing of the enemy and adding that he had reinforced No.9 Centre of Resistance with 2 platoons.

At 10.53 I was handed translation of message sent from CHAPEAU ROUGE at 10.25 giving the movements of troops ordered by the Sector Commander

At 10.55 a.m. received following from GENERAL GOUVERNEUR:-

"Pas ordres du General Gouverneur fin de l'alert "à 10.30 le 10 Juillet 17 P.O. le chef d'Etat M. aaa "Please pass on."

This had been spoken to me by Lieut.-Col NORTON, A.S.O. 2/10th MANCHESTERS at 10.45 a.m.

I accordingly sent out a message declaring the Test Alarm to be at an end.

COMMUNICATIONS. 6.

Office of origin	Time despatched	Time received.	Time in transmission.
SANATORIUM	7.30	7.42	12'
	8.15	8.32	17'
	9.45	9.57	12'
	10.12	10.20	8'
BRAY DUNES	8.15	9.34	1 hr 19'
	9.00	9.46	46'
	10.00	10.28	28'
	11.05	11.30	25'

Above table shews that while the communications with the SANATORIUM QUARTIER was more or less satisfactory those with BRAY DUNES are certainly capable of improvement.

REPORTS. 7. I attach herewith reports on the exercise from the Officers Commanding
(a) 3/5th LANCASHIRE FUSILIERS – MALO TERMINUS.
(b) 2/5th EAST LANCS. Regt – BRAY DUNES.
(c) 2/10th MANCHESTER Regt – SANATORIUM.
(d) 2/1st E.LANCS.FIELD AMBULANCE.

Reference (b) para.1. It would surely have been better had the Battalions paraded without breakfast and taken their rations with them. I know one Unit cooked their breakfasts in their posts.

Reference (c) Recommendations, page 2, paragraph marked in blue. The French map sent to O.C. QUARTIERS clearly marked the barrage batteries covering the different sections of the coast. My 105 dated 4/7/17 and para.10 Operation Order No.2 dated 6/7/17 instructed Units to get into touch with the Barrage Batteries marked with a green cross on their maps
I am probably to blame for not making it quite clear that the Corps instructions 358 G dated 6/7/17, para.3 (copies of which Units received) delegated command to the Os.C. QUARTIER.

DEFENCES. 8. To make these better would not take much work, especially for the flanking L.G. positions which require cover from the sea.

CONCLUSION. 9. (i) I regret that in handing over Command of the Subsector tomorrow I shall probably not be able, owing to the recent reliefs in the troops, to hand over the scheme complete in detail.
(ii) I have been hampered by lack of any assistance in the clerical or staff work so far as paper work is concerned, beyond that found by the Orderly Room Staff of my Battalion which has the normal work of the Battalion to attend to.
(iii) This must be my excuse for the delay in rendering this report and for its length and drafting which is disjointed.

11.7.17.

Lieut.- Col.
3/5th Bn. Lanc. Fus.,
Commanding ZUYDCOOTE Sub – sector.

S E C R E T.

XV Corps 54/10 G.
66th.Div. 358/1G.

N° VI

Le Cdt. le Secteur EST
   de la Place de DUNKERQUE.
     CHAPEAU ROUGE.

Subject. Alarm on night July 10/11th. 1917.

ALARM.
1. (a) The following message was received from 66th.Div.
at 10.45 p.m.
"G.S.18. Enemy has attacked the Corps front AAA
"Troops on coast defences will be particularly
"alert forthwith AAA."
(b) The above was followed by the following received at
10.58 p.m.
"In continuation of my G.S.18 take precautionary
"measures AAA Acknowledge AAA."

ACTION.
2. Both above messages were, at once, repeated to you and to the Os.C.Quartiers. I asked you to warn all the French troops in the Sub-sector. There seemed some doubt at your H.Qrs. as to whether the alarm was a genuine one or not. This probably arose owing to there having been a Test Alarm earlier in the day.
Message (b) above was handed to my signal office at 11.1 p.m. and was received by telephone as under,
    2/10 MANCHESTERS at 11.25 p.m.
    2/5 EAST LANCS. at 11.35 p.m.
At 11.10 p.m. the 3/5th.LAN.FUS. instructed 1 platoon to garrison Centre of resistance No.3 and 1 platoon to garrison Centre of resistance No.4. The Battalion dressed and was ready to move at a moments notice. Telephonists, instruments and lamps were sent to Bastion 31, The Battery de ZUYDCOOTE and the above 2 Centres of resistance. This information was passed on to your H.Qrs. and to the other 2 Battalions.
At 11.45 p.m. the 2/6th.MANCHESTERS, under canvas North of the FORT DES DUNES was warned of events and action taken in case of attack.
At 12.50 a.m. I received a message from the 2/10th MANCHESTERS that they had ordered Centres of resistance Nos.5 & 8 to be manned by a platoon each, and Centres of resistance Nos.6 & 7 by a Lewis gun section each. Telephones and operators were also sent to each Centre. This information was passed to your H.Qrs. at 12.55 a.m.
Centre of resistance No.3 was occupied at 12.45 a.m. & Centre of resistance No.4 at 12.50 a.m. by the platoons of the 3/5th.LAN.FUS mentioned above. Their orders had been received by both Company Commanders concerned at 11.25 p.m.. The platoons took, therefore, 1hr.25' to get into position.
No report has been received by me as to the orders given or action taken by the 2/5th.EAST LANCS.
During the night reports on the situation were received from the 3/5th.LAN.FUS. posts hourly. No others were received
At 3.40 a.m. I telephoned to your H.Qrs. and confirmed my view that, by daylight, the coast guard troops of the French were sufficient and that no British garrisons were required. I ordered (3.43 a.m.) the 3/5th. to vacate their posts at 4.30 a.m. and telephoned to the other Battalions that "Posts need not be garrisoned by day". I also telephoned to 66th.Div. to this effect.

11/7/17

Lieut.Colonel,
Commanding 3/5th.LAN.FUS.
and ZUYDCOOTE Sub-sector.

Situation on Corps front-- Night of 10th/11th July 1917.

Summary of messages received up to noon 11/7/17.

10/7/17.

8.45 p.m. 3 Battalions of the 199th Bde. and 3 Battalions of the 198th Bde to be held at 1 hour's notice to move. Enemy attacked at 7.45 p.m. and took front trenches of 1st.Div. 32nd.Division situation not clear.

10.00 p.m. 197th.Bde.H.Qrs ordered to move at once to 32nd.Div. and take over command of the 3 Battalions 197th.Bde. at OOST DUNKERQUE and AVECAPELLE. O.C.ZUYDCOOTE Sub-sector ordered to have all Battalions on the alert and to take precautionary measures.

11/7/17.

12. midnight. 32nd.Div. report enemy in NOSE SUPPORT, M.22.b. Bridges practically destroyed.

12.10 a.m. Corps orders M.G.companies and L.T.M.batteries to be ready to move with the Battalions of the 198th.Bde.(two lorries earmarked by S.M.T.O for transport of L.T.M.Bs)

12.15 a.m. G.319 from XV Corps ordering 32nd.Div. to do utmost to regain original front, and for 1st.Div. to hold the left bank of the YSER.

2.10 a.m. 32nd.Div. now holding NEW TRENCH, NASAL SUPPORT to M.28. b.7.8., NASAL LANE as front line. Situation NASAL WALK not known. 1st.Div. holds S.W. bank of the YSER.

2.30 a.m. Enemy bombed MALO & DUNKIRK from aeroplanes.

2.50 a.m. Orders from Corps that Battalion of 197th.Bde. at AVE-CAPPELLE is to move by lorry to KUMNA CAMP and 197th.M.G. Company by march route to CAMP JEANNOT as soon as possible. 197th.Bde.Units to be prepared to move in battle order at one hour's notice.

7.11 a.m. 32nd.Div.report that they have reoccupied the whole of their original front line. This requires confirmation.

7.30 a.m. 1st.Div. report about 4 Officers & 33 O.Rs. from troops E. of river swam river & rejoined. Considerable hostile shelling up to 2.30 a.m.

11.17 a.m. 32nd.Div. report that their left Bde. reported at 4.55 a.m. they were holding original line with defensive flank thrown back facing GELEIDE BROOK. Garrison of NEW TRENCH in touch with 1st.Division.

11.31. a.m. 32nd.Division report enemy attacking LOMBARTZYDE sector at 10.25 a.m.

11.57 a.m. 32nd.Div. report situation as regards bridges as follows. Bridges East of Five bridges serviceable, Five bridges damaged but will be serviceable in an hour. VAUXHALL & PUTNEY bridge serviceable for infantry. Enemy now shelling front system in LOMBARTZYDE sector. Small bodies of enemy seen coming down from WESTENDE.

P.T.O.

12.40 p.m. 59nd. Squadron R.F.C. report shrapnel barrage opened
on trench line from M.21.b.8.1 to M.22.a.9.8.
Barrage eased at 2.a.m., but this line is still being
shelled consistently. This is probably the front line
held by our infantry. The ground has been very heavily
bombarded and is torn up more than any other part.

Copies to C.R.A.
        197th Inf.Bde.
        198th .. ..
        199th .. ..

66th.D.H.Q.,
  11/7/17
                                                       Captain,
                                                General Staff,
                                                66th.Division.

197th Brigade.

66th Division.

3/5th BATTALION LANCASHIRE FUSILIERS AUGUST 1917.

CONFIDENTIAL

WAR DIARY

OF

3/5th Bn. LANCASHIRE FUSILIERS

From:- 1/8/1917   To:- 31/8/1917.

(VOLUME:- 7.)

----------o---------

Army Form C. 2118.

WAR DIARY
or
INTELLIGENCE SUMMARY.

35th Bn Lancashire Fus.

Place	Date	Hour	Summary of Events and Information	Remarks and references to Appendices
COXYDE BAINS (DUNKERQUE)	1917		MINDEN DAY. Rose as Usual for the Day. Special Order of the Day issued by C.O. See Appendix 1. Parties to mourner parade will Take part in the great offensive which was to have to commence	708.1
BELGIUM (100,000)			from YPRES to the Sea. Performance orders issued as follows:	
			1. Ammunition Orders (Bralin. No.1 marked Appendix 2	No.2
			2. Ammunition Orders, No. 2	No.3
			3. Operation Orders No.1	No.4
			4. do do No. 2	No.5
			5. do do No. 3 & 4	No.6
			6. Survey to above orders Appx 5,6,7 &	No.7
			Very heavy firing during the night. Ground unsuitable. Aeroplanes in Observation by the Germans for several days late. Owing to this enemy extensively covered fighting line aged by German Supplies in billets COXYDE BAINS to death.	
Aug 12th			last night. Reference. Electric Candelumes & Motorcycle Kitchen M.T. of 2nd Rank. Helper received by 197th INF BDE from MAJOR SHARP Comdg 143rd	

WAR DIARY
or
INTELLIGENCE SUMMARY.

3/5TH BATTALION R.F. FUSILIERS

Army Form C. 2118.

Place	Date	Hour	Summary of Events and Information	Remarks and references to Appendices
COXYDE BAINS	1917 Aug. 12th		Field Company Royal Engineers examined the Battalion from all Ranks in two matches.	
(DUNKERQUE (A)) BELGIUM 1/100,000		20th	The Batt when relieved the 2/6th Manchester Regt in the front line reserve taking over the Left Sub sector in NEWPORT BAINS on the night of the 20/21st	
		10pm	Artillery on both sides very active. Enemy shell supply 3/5/7.2 seemed more of a nuisance or 100 shells into NIEUPORT. We were ourselves very heavily sheller in the out- post lines, as well as on our billets few casualties from shell fire during the day	
		28th	Oatlaken relieved during the night of the 28/29th by the 2nd Battn Pts Queeen's & 11th MIDDLESEX Con.R Regt 0057-DUNKERQUE BAINS. LIEUT GELL rejoined M950 Gunnery who had been attached to the Batt. during the time in the	

Army Form C. 2118.

WAR DIARY
or
INTELLIGENCE SUMMARY.
(Erase heading not required.)

3/5th B. S.H. R.E. FUSRS.

Place	Date	Hour	Summary of Events and Information	Remarks and references to Appendices
OOST-DUNKERQUE BAINS	Aug 29 30 31st		French's Memorandum and his resort on no liaison to be 2nd in command was held behind with the following Batts. Casualty list for month attached marked 8. Battalion strength 38 officers and 874 other ranks. Ration strength 28 and 943.	No. 8
DUNKERQUE 1 A				
BELGIUM 1/100,000			After all the preparations which had surrounded him wants to cover the YSER by the Division it has been a month of disappointment and handed that at any rate for the present all chances of an offensive on the front of the immediate Division have been abandoned. Nothing officially on the subject has been divulged nor any reason given, but we are left to draw for ourselves a conclusion. The G.O.C. tells the C.O. that the programme for the next month was a fortnight in coast defence and a fortnight training.	

Arthur Blake
F.O.G.
Commanding 3/5th Bat. R. Fus.

SPECIAL ORDER OF THE DAY
BY LIEUT.COL.A.S.BATES, D.S.O.
COMMANDING 3/5th.LAN.FUS.

On the eve of what will, probably, be the greatest Offensive on the Western Front, the Commanding Officer wishes to congratulate all ranks on having the privilege of fighting as Lancashire Fusiliers.

Made up, as the Battalion is, of pre-war Territorials, men who enlisted on the outbreak of war and those whom our Country called to it's service, it has most glorious traditions to uphold stretching from DETTINGEN and MINDEN in the past, through the PENINSULAR, CRIMEA and MUTINY to SOUTH AFRICA 1899-1902 and those in the present war.

It has the old historical traditions of the XXth. to follow, in addition those of the regular Battalions of the LANCASHIRE FUSILIERS and, lastly, those of it's 1st and 2nd. line Territorial Units to emulate.

It is, probably, impossible, to surpass any of these, but there is no reason why, in years to come, this Battalion should have any cause to look back upon the battle of the DUNES with any other feelings than pride.

The only necessity is that all ranks must always remember that the Battalion will be judged by it's own action and that the latter is in their own individual hands.

The Commanding Officer is content to leave the Honour of the Battalion in the hands of the Officers, N.C.Os and men convinced as he is that they will not allow it to be sullied: and sure that added lustre will be given to the Regimental Honours in the days in the immediate future.

This Order will be communicated to all ranks.

Lieut. & Adjutant,
3/5th.LAN.FUS.

MINDEN DAY. 1917

SECRET AND CONFIDENTIAL   Copy No. 11

ADMINISTRATIVE OPERATION ORDER No.1.
by Lt. Col. A.S. BATES D.S.O. Comdg. 3/5th Lan.Fus.

1. These orders will be referred to as A.O.O. No.1.
2. These orders are to be returned to the Orderly Room prior to any offensive action being taken by the Battn.

OFFICERS & O.R. LEFT BEHIND.
3. The following Officers and other ranks will remain behind when the Battalion takes part in the forthcoming operations.
Major W. WIKE. Captains S.J. GOWLAND and H. HASTINGS.
Lieuts. N.D. THOMSON, F.R. CROUCH & R.S. MORLEY.
Sec.Lts A.F. SENIOR, C.F. TWEEDY, S.E. REID, J.W. PICKETT W. HALL and F.W. BELL, if the latter's duties as subarea salvage Officer necessitate it.
No. 202086 R.S.M. INGHAM, No. 201338 C.S.M. DOODSON. No. 204416 C.S.M. PENDLEBURY. No. 201261 Pioneer Sgt PRATT. No. 202031 Sgt BARON. No. 201345 L/Cpl TAYLOR and No. 202539 Pte CHEW.   33% of the signallers to be nominated by the Signalling Officer and 33% of the runners to be nominated by the Adjutant.
1 Sgt, 1 Cpl and 1 L/Cpl per Coy to be nominated by Os.C. Coys.
1 Rifle bomber, 1 Scout & Sniper and 2 Lewis gunners per platoon to be nominated by Platoon Commanders.

COMMAND
4. Lieut. STEVENS will command "A" Coy.
Captain BENTLEY will command "B" Coy.

ACTING R.S.M.
5. No. 201395 Sgt HARPER will act as R.S.M. during the forthcoming operations.

INFORMATION & IDENTITY.
6. No Officer, N.C.O. or man will carry on his person any maps, letters, documents or orders which, if they fell into the enemy's hands would be of value to him.

PRISONERS.
7. Any troops capturing prisoners are responsible for passing them back under escort. Further instructions as to collecting posts will, probably, be issued. No Commander must weaken his unit to the danger of his line by sending back prisoners. Officers prisoners will be kept separate from O.R. and must not be allowed to converse with them. Nothing is to be taken from prisoners except their arms and any papers which may be of value to "Intelligence". These latter will be sent to Battalion H.Qrs as soon as possible.

LOOTING.
8. Looting is strictly forbidden and the severest disciplinary action will be taken against any one caught in the act or found in possession of loot.

WATER.
9. Arrangements will be made to send up water at the earliest possible moment. While no water should be drunk from enemy sources until they have been passed as fit, all ranks are reminded that water in enemy waterbottles will be good and that waterbottles can be collected from our own casualties. The water carried on the men should be very sparingly used, especially early in the day.

ORDERLY ROOM
10. Lieut. R.S. MORLEY will be in charge of this at the Transport Lines and will be assisted by No. 202016 Sgt CALVERT and No. 203084 L/Cpl GOWLAND.
No. 203076 Pte KING will accompany the Adjutant.

SIGNALLERS & PIGEON MEN
11. Signallers and Pigeon men will be under the command of the Signalling Officer.

Distribution 1. C.O. 2. Major Wike 3 Adjt & File
4. "A" Coy. 5 "B" Coy 6. "C" Coy 7. "D" Coy
8. H.Qrs Coy. 9. M.O. 10/11 War Diary 12 Spare.

Lt & Adjt.
3/5th Lan.Fus.

30/7/17.

SECRET AND CONFIDENTIAL.   Copy No. 11 wd.

ADMINISTRATIVE OPERATION ORDER No. 2.
By LT.COL.A.S.BATES, D.S.O. Comdg. 3/5th.LAN.FUS.

1. These orders will be referred to as A.O.O.No.2.
2. These orders are to be returned to the Orderly room prior to any offensive being undertaken by the Battn.

UP & DOWN TRENCHES. 3. The strictest attention must be paid by all ranks, including casualties, to any notice boards stating the direction of traffic in any trench in the battle area.

SALVAGE. 4. All parties should carry back salvage when returning from the front area. It should be regarded as a point of honour that no individual returns empty handed.

NOTICE BOARDS. 5. The Adjutant will have the following boards prepared. They will be taken up by Battalion runners and fixed under the supervision of the A/R-S-M. The latter will be responsible that the boards are carried forward if Battalion H.Qrs. moves.
  (a) 5 boards, 2 with arrow to the right, 2 with arrow to the left and 1 without an arrow. "BATTN.HQRS. UNBEND"
  (b) 5 boards, as above, "REGTL.AID POST"

PRISONERS. 6. With further reference to A.O.O.No.1 para.7 the following extracts from XV Corps No.A.C/7524/6 are published for information.
  (a) Prisoners, except Officers, will not be searched on first being captured but will at once be deprived of all arms.
  (b) Officer prisoners will be searched immediately on capture and all papers, documents etc. will be taken from them and tied into separate bundles under the Officer's name. These will be handed over to the escort.
  (c) Under no circumstances will the pay book or identity disc be taken from either Officers or men.
  (d) At all times Officers, N.C.Os and men, who are prisoners, will be kept separate.
  (e) No Officers, N.C.Os or men, escorts, interpreters or civilians are to be permitted to converse, or in any way, communicate with prisoners. This does not apply to Staff Officers.

ESCORTS. 7. As a rule an escort of 1 man per 10 prisoners is sufficient, the latter being made to walk with their hands up. Officer prisoners will be specially escorted.

SANDBAGS. 8. The Adjutant will issue instructions to all runners who go back to Bde.H.Qrs to endeavour to return with at least 20 sandbags each. If this is practicable runners will carry them to Companies when taking messages.

MESSAGES. 9. All messages are to be written with black pencils and not indelible ones. If the duplicate copies are more legible than originals the former will be sent. All Officers will prefix the number of their messages by their full initials. Time and place will, always, be given.

LEWIS GUNS. 10. If opportunity offers it is suggested that empty L.G. drums will be more easily filled at Battalion H.Qrs. than in the line. Not more than 8 drums will be away from the gun at any time. Empty drums above this number must be filled at the gun.

OFFICERS. 11. Each Company will have 4 Officers. Os.C.Coys will be prepared to leave 1 at Battalion H.Qrs to be sent up subsequently if the situation demands.

CODE NAMES. 12. All ranks must know the code name for this Battalion "UNBEND" and for the 2/6th.LAN.FUS. "UNBORN"

Distribution.
As for A.O.O.No.1.

1/8/17   Lt. & Adj.
                                                          3/5th.LAN.FUS.

SECRET.   Copy No. 12

                                                                      4

OPERATION ORDER No.1 by LT.COL.A.H.BATES, D.S.O.
              COMMANDING 2/5th.LAN.FUS.

Reference Secret Trench maps 1/10,000 & sheets 11 S.E. & 12 S.W.1/20,000.

                   1. These orders will be returned to the Orderly room prior to any offensive action being taken by the Battalion.

INFORMATION. 2. The enemy holds the Eastern bank of the YSER from the sea to the GELEIDE BROOK and thence from M.29 b.10.90 South of LOMBARTZYDE to the NIEUWLAND POLDER about ROSE trench.

INTENTION. 3.(a) At a date, to be fixed later, the 32nd.Div, on our right will capture the enemy position about LOMBARTZYDE from the GELEIDE BROOK along LOVERS & HAMBURG WALKS -- RAVEN trench and will establish posts N.E. of the GEL-EIDE BROOK.
(b) The 66th.Div, the 198th.Bde being in the line, will assist this attack by a demonstration as follows;
  (1) 18 pr. and T.M. programme on the area bounded by the sea, the PAVEE roads and a line drawn N & S through M.5.d.2.2.
  (2) Smoke barrage by the R.A., if the weather permits.
  (3) R.E. activity with dummy rafts etc. covered by a smoke screen on the left bank of the river, densest at it's mouth.
  (4) M.G.programme.
  (5) L.G. fire from the Infantry in the line.
  (6) Smoke candles lit from the mouth of the river to BOSCHE trench by the Infantry in the line.
(c) Forty eight hours after the success of the operation detailed in sub-para.(a) above the 66th.Div. will force a crossing over the river YSER near it's mouth and will establish a bridge head E of the river. This task is allotted as follows;
  (1) Bridging the YSER at NIEUPORT BAINS.
The 198th.Bde will undertake
  (2) Establishing a covering party on the DUNES about BACK WALK.
  (3) Passing sufficient troops across the YSER to force their way along the DUNES to the vicinity of BLUE trench and to join hands with a force on our right operating from the line of the GELEIDE BROOK.
The 197th.Bde will assemble in NIEUPORT BAINS as the river is forced and will be prepared for
  (4) A subsequent operation of advancing from BLUE trench to line LOMBARTZYDE BAINS -- PUNCH trench.
The 199th.Bde.will take over the defence of the coast and line.

TROOPS
ALLOTTED. 4. In addition to the Infantry.
(a) Artillery, coordinated by the Corps.
(b) R.E. 1 section "F" Coy and 1 Coy. Pioneers in addition to the bridging parties.

ZERO HOUR. 5. Will be notified later. At this hour the actual work of bridging and passing covering parties over will commence.

FIRST
OBJECTIVE. 6. Will be the line of BLUE trench or it's vicinity.

METHOD OF
ATTACK. 7. A standing barrage to cover the crossing will be established along BACK WALK from Zero to Zero plus 4 hrs. when it will move to the "Blue" line, and finally to the "Brown" line in front of the covering party as detailed. (These coloured lines are not specified) The covering party will occupy a position on the high ground N.E. of BACK trench until such time as the attacking troops, formed in the dead ground between the YSER & the DUNES are ready to advance.

The standing barrage will then become a creeping one moving at the rate of 50 yards in every 3 minutes, until it again becomes a standing barrage.
The attack will be delivered on a two Battalion front (a third Battalion being in reserve) which will include the high ground between BACK and DARE trench.
A defensive flank will be formed on the right from which patrols will be pushed in the direction of the GELHIDE BROOK in the event of possible cooperation by the troops on our right.

COMMUNICATIONS. 8. It is of special importance that the most forward Infantry should, at all times, be ready to light flares when they are called for by a contact aeroplane.

CARRYING PARTIES. 9. The 2/5th.LAN.FUS. will be prepared to act as carrying parties when the second objective (see para.3(c.4)) has been captured.

POSITIONS OF ASSEMBLY 10. At Zero the 197th.Bde will, probably, be just West of the OOST DUNKERQUE--OOST DUNKERQUE BAINS road.

ROUTES. 11. From Zero onwards;
BATH AVENUE an UP road.
BLIGHTY AVENUE a DOWN road.
BATH LANE reserved for troops in actual occupation and for evacuation of wounded.

Arthur
Lieut.Colonel,
Commanding 2/5th.LAN.FUS.

Distribution.
No.1. C.O.
2. Major WISE.
3. "A" Coy.
4. "B" Coy.
5. "C" Coy.
6. "D" Coy.
7. H.Qrs. Coy.
8. Adj. and file.
9. Signalling Officer.
10. Intelligence Officer.
11. Medical Officer.
12. War diary.
13. War diary.
14. Spare.

August 1st. 1917.

SECRET.   Copy No. 12 WD 5

OPERATION ORDER No. 2 by   Lt.COL.A.S.BATES, D.S.O.
COMMANDING   2/5th.LAN.FUS.

Reference Secret Trench maps 1/10,000 & sheets 11 S.E. & 12.S.W. 1/20,000

    1. These orders will be referred to as O.O.No.2.
    2. These orders will be returned to the Orderly room prior to any offensive action by the Battalion.

A.O.O.No.1   3. Reference para.3 line 6 after "C.F.TWEEDY" add "C.H.TYE"

A.O.O.No.2   4. Reference para.9. In all cases the copy and not the original of the message will be sent. They will be legibly written, dated as well as timed and signed. All Officers are entitled to read messages during active operations, but orderlies must not be delayed.

INTENTION.   5. Reference OO.No.1 para.3.c.(2) & (3) the 2/5th E.LANCS. & 2/9th MANCH.R. will carry out this. The 2/10th MANCH.R. will be in reserve. The 2/4th E.LANCS. will assist the R.E. with bridges, see O.O.No.1 para.3.c.(1).

FRONTAGES.   6.(a) Right Battalion from S.E. edge of DUNES (about M.15.d.2.8) and in the "yellow" line from junction of C.T. and BARE tr. at M.15.b.45.35. to BLUE AVENUE inclusive.
   (b) Left Battalion from BLUE LANE AVENUE exclusive to the Sea. (BLUE AV. is the C.T. running South of the PAVE Rd up to BLUE trench)
   (c) When the objective "yellow" line has been captured the Left Battalion will push detachments forward before consolidation in the "yellow" line begins, without a check, and occupy and consolidate BLACK DUNE (M.15.a.8.8) and the PIMPLE (M.9.c.4.9)
   (d) The Reserve Battalion will cross after the assaulting Bns. and take up it's position along & West of the "blue" line.

STRONG POINTS. 7. Will be constructed at about M.15.a.8.0, M.15.a.3.4 and M.14.b.8.9.

ARTILLERY.   8. Reference O.O.No.1 para.7 the creeping barrage, when it passes the "yellow" line will move in lifts of 100 yards every 3 minutes.

ARRANGEMENTS FOR ASSEMBLY   9.(a) At ZERO it is probable that the dispositions will be
   2/5th & 2/7th L.F. in CAMP LEFEVRE.
   2/6th & 2/8th L.F. in CAMP BADOR.
   All C.Os will be at CAMP JUNIAC by ZERO Hour.
   (b) After ZERO the 197th Bde will be prepared to move up and support the 198th.Bde.
The 2/5th.LAN.FUS. "D" Coy leading followed by "B","A" and "C" Companies, will move into the area vacated by the 2/9th MANCH.R. in the trenches between the STATION & the SEA, cellars in NIEUPORT BAINS as far back as M.13.d.5.0 (cross roads). Prior to getting into this position it may be necessary for the Battalion to occupy the position vacated by the 2/10th.MANCH.R. (the left rear Battn. 198th.Bde.) in the remainder of NIEUPORT BAINS cellars and Reserve Trench.

ROUTES and TRAFFIC.   10.(a) Reference O.O.No.1 para.11, authorised runners may use any route either UP or DOWN and will be given PRIORITY to all traffic.
   (b) Traffic at bridges & rafts will be regulated by the R.E. Walking wounded & prisoners may, at the discretion of the O.i/c Traffic, return in boats etc. from the East bank.

PRISONERS.   11. Reference A.O.O.No.2 para.6 All prisoners will be returned to Bde.Collecting post in shelter under the foot bridge running from M.14.a.40.25. They will be taken over from fighting escorts at OOST DUNKERQUE BAINS straggler post R.27.c.9.7.

CARRYING PARTIES.   12. Os.C.Coys will each detail 1 N.C.O & 14 men to remain at or near Battn.H.Qrs under the Intelligence Officer.

2.

DRESS AND EQUIPMENT.	13.(a) As laid down in S.S.135 section XXXI except para.1. Officers will wear Officers' jackets. para.2. sub-para.VI Cap comforter, Cardigan jacket & spare oil tin will NOT be carried. No great coats will be carried. (b) Reference S.S.135 section XXXI para.4 sub-para.(I) S.A.A. detailed there will NOT be taken. .. (II) 128 wire breakers attached to rifles will be carried (i.e.32 per Coy.) 48 wire cutters will be carried (i.e.12 per Company) .. (III) 75% of the Battalion will carry shovels. Nos.1 & 2 of L.G.teams & Bomb throwers will NOT carry them. .. (IV) 8 rifle grenade S.O.S signals will be carried per Company. .. (V) Artillery flags will be issued later. .. (VI) "P" grenades will not be carried. .. (VII) Bomb throwers will carry 5 bombs. Bomb carriers will carry 12 bombs in slung bomb buckets with sandbag covers. Rifle bombers will carry 12 rifle grenades (Nos.20,23 or 24) in belt bags with holes in the bottoms. Cartridges will be carried in small bags (these latter will be supplied by the Bombing Officer). Delete sub-para.(VII) re spare rods.
VERY PISTOLS.	14. Two per Company will be carried.
SIGNALS.	15.(a) S.O.S. A rifle grenade, variation "C", bursting into 4 green lights, to be repeated until acted upon by the Artillery. (b) Lengthen range signal for Artillery, a Very light changing from white to red. These will be issued at the rate of 20 per Coy with 20 in reserve at Battn.H.Qrs.
MOPPERS UP.	16. Reference "Instructions No.1" para.10 the Battalion will find it's own "Moppers up". All attacking waves will be organised as laid down to include "Moppers up".
COMMUNICATIONS.	17.(a) 16 pigeons, at least, will be allotted to the Battn. They will be distributed by the Signalling Officer. (b) A Brigade relay post will be established at M.14.a.2.2 (the French 75 mm gun emplacement) When the Battalion is across the river all runners forward and backward will report there, when messages will be despatched under arrangements of the Bde. Signalling Officer. (c) Reference O.O.No.1 para.8 the Appendix "B" to S.S.135 will be brought to the notice of all ranks.
SYNCHRONISATION OF WATCHES.	18. The Signalling Officer will arrange for at least two watches to be synchronised at Bde.H.Qrs at ZERO minus 1 hour and at ZERO plus 3 hours. Os.C.Coys. will send watches to Battalion H.Qrs. half an hour after these hours.
BATTLE STRAGGLERS POST.	19. The Battalion Provost Sergt and 5 police will be posted at R.27.b.5/07.1 OOST DUNKERQUE BAINS. Special orders will be issued to the Provost Sergeant.
BRIDGES.	20. MORTLAKE. Pontoon ready at ZERO plus 9 hours. RICHMOND. .. .. 11 hours. Capacity of each of the above 1,000 men per hour. MORTLAKE BARREL ready at ZERO plus 40 hours. RICHMOND BARREL .. .. 48 hours. Capacity of each of above 4,000 men per hour.
ENEMY RUSES.	21. Attention is drawn to memorandum distributed with copies 1,3 to 6, 9 & 11 of these orders on the subject of enemy ruses. All ranks must be warned. They are less likely to be found if the enemy offers resistance than if he retires with small, or no, opposition.

3.

WHITE FLAGS.	22.	The display or hoisting of a white flag by the enemy is not a sign of surrender, but merely implies that he has a communication to make. If a white flag be displayed during an action firing WILL NOT be discontinued on any account. The fact that a white flag has been displayed will be at once reported to Battn. H.Qrs. This is to be made known to all ranks.
MEDICAL ARRANGEMENTS.	23.	Dressing stations. NIEUPORT BAINS M.13.d.4.3. LAITERIE ROYALE R.33.d.9.1. An A.D.S. will be opened when the situation permits by the beach at M.14.b.3.6. R.A.M.C. guides will wear a special badge on left arm.
DETAILS.	24.	Will be in CAMP JUNIAC (YORKSHIRE) under the command of the senior Officer. Lt. JONES, 2/7th.L.F. will act as Bde Transport Officer.

DISTRIBUTION.

No.1. C.O.
    2. Major WIKE.
    3. "A" Coy.
    4. "B" Coy.
    5. "C" Coy.
    6. "D" Coy.
    7. H.Qrs. Coy.
    8. Adj. & file.
    9. Signalling Officer.
10. Intelligence Officer.
11. M.O.
12. War diary.
13. War diary.
14. Spare.
15. 197th. Inf. Bde. (for information)

Arthur Wate
Lieut.Colonel,
Commanding 2/5th.LAN.FUS.

3/8/17.

SECRET.   Copy No. 13

OPERATION ORDER No. 2 by   LT.COL.A.G.BATES, D.S.O.
        COMMANDING   2/5th.LAN.FUS.

Reference Maps as before.

              1. This order will be referred to as O.O.No.2. It will be
              handed in to the Orderly room prior to any offensive
              action being taken by the Battalion.

O.O.No.1   2. In para.(b) for "R" read "Field".
              In para.11 delete at end from "and" to "wounded".

HEADQUARTERS. 3. On leaving CAMP LEFEVRE will be composed as follows:

         Officers   Other ranks.

         C.O.   A/R-S-M. .... 1.
         Adjutant.   Signallers........... 1.
         Signalling Officer.   M.O's staff.......... 4.
         A.T Intelligence ..   H.Q. batmen.......... 5.
         Medical Officer.   Runners.............. 14.
                                    Water duty........... 5.x
                                    Sanitary duty........ 2.
                                    Gas duty............. 1.
                                    Clerk................ 1.
                                    Pigeon man........... 1.
                                    H.Q.cook............. 1.
                                    Carrying party....... 31.
                                                     107.

          x These may be sent back, if the M.O. so
            directs, when the Battn Crosses the river.

COMPANY   4. Are as follows, any reductions to be reported at once.
STRENGTHS.   "A" Coy 119 Other ranks
              "B" Coy 108   ..   ..
              "C" Coy 110   ..   ..
              "D" Coy 104   ..   ..
                    441

BATTALION   5. The Battalion should go into action with 21 Officers
STRENGTH.   (incl. M.O.) and 544 other ranks.
TO BE CARRIED 6. Appendix "A" is issued herewith which shews what Amn.,
              stores etc have to be carried and the method of distri-
              bution. Officers detailed in the last column will ensure
              that each N.C.O. and man knows exactly what he has to be
              in possession of when the Battn. leaves CAMP LEFEVRE.
              Os.C.Coys. will each return 3 Very pistols to the Orderly
              room at once.

OFFICERS.   7. Reference A.O.O.No.1 para.11 the Officers per Coy. to be
              left at Battalion H.Qrs. will report there on their Coys.
              receiving orders to cross the river. Os.C.Coys. will
              send in names of the Officers selected on arrival at
              CAMP LEFEVRE.

DISTRIBUTION.

As for O.O.No.1.

4/8/17
                                                      Lieut.Colonel,
                                         Commanding 2/5th.LAN.FUS.

SECRET

Copy No. 13

OPERATION ORDER No.4.
by
LIEUT. COL. A.S. BATES D.S.O.
Commanding 3/5th Battn. LAN. FUS.,

1. This order will be referred to as O.O. No.4 and will be returned to the Orderly Room prior to any offensive action being taken by the Battalion.

MESSAGES.
A.O.O.No.2 para.9
O.O. No.2 para.4

2. Messages will be written in triplicate, and, if sent by runner, the second copy is to be sent 100 yards behind the first. On the east of the river runners will work in pairs.

DETAILS.
O.O.No.2 para.24

3. At 4 p.m. on "Y" day the Transport, Q-M stores and details (- if the latter have not already gone to the Corps Camp) will be ready to move in to Camp JUNIAC The kits of Officers going into action, orderly room boxes, mess boxes, etc., will be loaded by 3 p.m. Brigade orders detailing accommodation in Camp JUNIAC have been given to the Transport Officer and Q.M.

O.O.No.2 para.19.

4. Detailed orders for the Battle Stragglers Post have been issued to the Provost Sergeant.

APPENDIX "A"

5. (a) Ref. footnote (j) the artillery lengthening signals are $1\frac{1}{2}$" This footnote can be deleted.
   (b) V.P.$1\frac{1}{2}$" Each Coy will carry 1 V.P.$1\frac{1}{2}$" If a second can be procured per Coy it will be issued.
   (c) 12 rifle grenades (not 8) will be carried by each rifle bomber in accordance with O.O.No.2 para.13(b)

Appendix "A" is to be added to and amended accordingly.

Lieut.- Colonel.
Commanding 3/5th LAN. FUS.

Distribution.

Copies 1 to 16 as for O.O.No.2
Copy No.17 to Transport Officer & Q.M.

5/8/17.

SECRET INDEX TO ORDERS ETC. Copy No. 12 W.D.

	INS. No.1	ADMINISTRATIVE OPERATION ORDER No.1	No.2	OPERATION ORDER No. 1.	No. 2.	No. 3.	No. 4.	APPDX. "A"
Acting R-S-M.	1		6					
Barrage	2				7	6		
Battalion strengths							5	
Battle stragglers posts						19		4
Bridges						20		
Carrying parties					9	19		
Casualties	3							
Code names				12				
Command of Companies			4					
Communications					8	17		
Company strengths							4	
Consolidation	6							
Counter-attack	7							
Details						24		3
Dress & equipment						13			X
Enemy ruses						21		
ESCORTS				6&7				
First objective					6			
Frontages					6			
Grenades	8					12		6	X
Headquarters							3	
Hints during attack	13							
Information	11		6		2			
Intention					3	5		
Lewis guns	5			10					X
Looting			8					
Medical arrangements						23		
Messages					3	4		2
Method of attack					7			
Misbehaviour	4							
Moppers up	10					16		
Notice boards					5				X
Officers & O.R left out			3				3	
Officers					11		7	
Orderly room			10					
Pigeon men			11					
Positions of assembly					10	9		
Prisoners			7	6		11		
Routes					3	11	10	
Salvage				4				
Sandbags				8					X
Signals						15			X
Signallers			11					
S.A.A	12							
Strong points					7			
Synchronisation						18		
To be carried							6		X
Tools	9								X
Troops allotted					4		2	
Up & Down trenches				3	11	10		
Very pistols						14		5	X
Water			9					
White flags						22		
Wire cutters & breakers	12				5	13			X
Zero hour					5			

Distribution as for O.O.No.3.

5/8/17

Lieut. Colonel,
Commanding 3/5th. LAN. FUS.

APPENDIX "A"

DISTRIBUTION OF AMMUNITION, STORE, &c TO BE CARRIED

	L.G. Drums per team (a)	L.G. Drums spare (a)	Shovels	Bombs	Rifle grenades	S.O.S. Grenades	Artillery lengthening signals (f)	Flares	Wire cutters	Wire breakers	Sandbags	Notice boards	Very Pistols, 1"	Very Pistols 1½" (h)	V.P.A. 1" white	V.P.A. 1½" white (h)	Artillery flags (h)	Pigeons (k)	Stretchers	Signalling stores	Officer responsible for correct loads being taken
Lewis Gunners	24														12 (e)						Os..C. Coys
H.Q. excluding carrying party			60	2 per all O.R. 5 per thrower 12 per carrier.	8 per rifle bomber in Coys.			2 per all O.R. in the Coys and carrying party.			3 per all O.R.	10 (b)	12 (d)		60 (d)		8 (a)		3 (b)	2 loads (b)	Signalling officer.
"A" Company			95			8	20		12	32			1 (c)		12 (c)		2 (k)		1 (f)		O.C. "A" Coy
"B" Company			85			8	20		12	32			1 (c)		12 (c)		2 (k)		1 (f)		O.C. "B" Coy
"C" Company			89			8	20		12	32			1 (c)		12 (c)		2 (k)		1 (f)		O.C. "C" Coy
"D" Company			83			8	20		12	32			1 (c)		12 (c)		2 (k)		1 (f)		O.C. "D" Coy
Carrying Party		192					20			12/32									4 (g)		Intelligence Officer.
TOTALS	24	192	412	—	—	32	100	1002	48	128	163210	16	300				16		16	11	

(a) 128 drums will remain in reserve with Details
(b) carried by Sanitary men, gasman & Runners
(c) .. Coy Hdqrs
(d) .. as for (b) made up into 4 sandbags of 3 V.P. and 15 V.P.A.
(e) per te an
(f) To be dumped at Bn.H.Q. at NIEUPORT BAINS.
(g) Up to NIEUPORT BAINS will require 2 men each. Forward of that 1 man for stretcher when the 3 details carried by HQ will be taken by carrying party) details will be published when known. (party)
(h) size at present unknown.
(j) (iv) in brackets
(k) in brackets

3/5th Battn. LANCASHIRE FUSILIERS

CASUALTIES FOR MONTH OF AUGUST, 1917.

Date.	KILLED Officers	Other Ranks.	WOUNDED Officers	Other Ranks.
4/8/17				203053 L/C MITCHELL.A.
				202484 Pte SIMPSON.W.
				204360 " HALES.H.
				203577 " NORMAN.H.E.
6/8/17				201320 " PERCIVAL.J.
				204430 " TRAVIS.J.
				201159 " DIGGLE.R.
				3/17070 " ROBINSON.H.
20/8/17				202688 " LAMB.T.
				203657 " BARNES.W.E.
22/8/17		203263 Pte SIMPSON.W.		202025 L/C EASTWOOD.W.
24/8/17				202370 Pte MAY.J.
25/8/17				203122 " HOUGHTON.T.
				203164 " BLACKBURN.H.
				203180 " WOODBURN.D.
26/8/17				201306 Sgt POOLER.J.
				202027 Cpl INGHAM.J.
28/8/17				204352 L/Sgt LOUDEN.L.W.
31/8/17				202529 Pte MOORE.J.J.

197th Brigade
66th Division.

3/5th BATTALION LANCASHIRE FUSILIERS SEPTEMBER 1917.

ORIGINAL

CONFIDENTIAL.

WAR DIARY

OF

3/5th BATTALION

LANCASHIRE FUSILIERS.
---o---

From:- 1/9/1917   To:- 30/9/1917.

VOLUME 8.

Army Form C. 2118.

WAR DIARY
3/5th BATTN of LANCASHIRE FUSRS
INTELLIGENCE SUMMARY
(Erase heading not required.)

Instructions regarding War Diaries and Intelligence Summaries are contained in F. S. Regs., Part II. and the Staff Manual respectively. Title pages will be prepared in manuscript.

Place	Date	Hour	Summary of Events and Information	Remarks and references to Appendices
LA PANNE	1917 Sept 3rd	3 p	On the 3rd the Battn. left MIDDLESEX CAMP (OOST-DUNKERQUE BAINS)	
DUNKERQUE			and went into billets at LA PANNE, relieving the 2/7th MANCHESTER REGT.	
1A			The Reg took over the left section of the Belgian Coast defence	
BELGIUM			having 2 1/2 Companies in Front Line 2 1/2 Companies in Support	
1/10,000			and 1 Company in Reserve.	
			Preliminary Coast Defence Scheme attached and marked A	"A"
		4th	In the evening of the 4th 5th twenty aeroplanes dropped	
			bombs on LA PANNE, our casualties were 1 killed + 12 wounded,	
			6 of these being very slight.	
		6	Training has carried on when available, & in general defence	
			Sea bathing has much enjoyed, the weather being very good	
		18th	Preliminary Civil Defence Scheme Amendment attached marked B	No. B
			" Coast Defence Orders " " C	No. C

Army Form C. 2118.

WAR DIARY
3/5th BATTN of LANCASHIRE FUSRS –
INTELLIGENCE SUMMARY.
(Erase heading not required.)

Instructions regarding War Diaries and Intelligence Summaries are contained in F.S. Regs., Part II. and the Staff Manual respectively. Title pages will be prepared in manuscript.

W.W.

Place	Date	Hour	Summary of Events and Information	Remarks and references to Appendices
LA PANNE DUNKERQUE BELGIUM 1/40 000	1917 Sept. 1st	18th	The Battn. manoeuvered by the 2/10th MANCHESTER REGT and went into Camp at ST IDESBALD, taking over from the 2/6th MANCHESTER REGT. During the 6 days Battn. was there no Coast defence &c. following work was done – 4 Double Lewis Gun Emplacements been constructed. 5 (issued) Sentry and Obs Shelters. 1 Snipe Shelter erected. 8 Bench Dug-outs cleaned. 2 Officers Dug outs erected. 3 Officers Dug outs cleaned. 1 Drill Ays T. 3 Tub & Clean Shelters 3 Officers Shelters attached and worked D Repair for Defence and Works – The Battn. left LA PANNE. 3 Coys & Batt: Hqts. B Coy having been attached to the AUSTRALIAN TUNNELLING Coy and went into Camp at ST IDESBALDE for training. Map of Training area attached with marked. On this date the 66th Division manoeuvered in the NIEUPORT - NIEUPORT BAINS Sector by the 42nd Division. No 190 1st Line Made Division. the Battalion going into Camp at MALO TERMINUS near DUNKIRK and taking over the same QUARTERS	W.D. T.E. T.E.

T2134. Wt. W708-776. 500000. 4/15. Sir J. C. & S.

WAR DIARY

Army Form C. 2118.

3/5th Battalion Lancashire Fus.

INTELLIGENCE SUMMARY

(Erase heading not required.)

Place	Date	Hour	Summary of Events and Information	Remarks and references to Appendices
ZUYDCOOTE	1917		In the training held in JUNE/JULY previous held by 1.	
DUNKERQUE	Sep 24th	2.45	On the 27th the Division arrived/moved for Battle Areas	
		6	relieved by the 11th QUEENS ROYAL WEST SURREYS (R.F.C.)	
BELGIUM	29th		OTTER M.C. commdg. — 41st Division. The Bath rested	
1.10.00.b			1/6 ARQUES near ST OMER on night char-a-banc and	
			went into billets there on the same evening in the village of CAMPAGNE	
			Coast Defence Orders No.1 attached and marked "F"	No. F
			Addition to do do G	No. G
			do do H	No. H
			Barrage detail — APPENDIX B I	No. I
			Casualty List for month of September " "	No. L
	30th		Battalion strength 30 Officers and 852 other ranks.	
			The Division which had been part of the XI Corps on leaving the IInd Army Area	
			now came into the IInd Army and became part of the IInd ANZAC Corps which	
			consisted of 3rd Australian Divn, NZ Division, 41st Division + 66th Division.	
			2/Lt DC HALSALL joined the Battn on the 29th from	
			the 3rd Battn. Lan. Fus. (RESERVE)	

Arthur Dale Lt Col.
Commanding 3/5th Battn Lan Fus.

SECRET.   Copy No. 15

PRELIMINARY COAST DEFENCE SCHEME
3/5th Bn. LAN. FUS.

Reference Sheet 11 S.E. 1/20,000.   A

FRONTAGE.   1. The left Section, occupied by the Battalion stretches from INFANTRY TRENCH on the East at W.9.d.9.9. (exclusive) to the Franco-Belgian Frontier at V.23.d.3.5. a length of about 4,900 yards.

DEFENCES.   2.(a) Consist of
       (i) Continuous belt of wire.
       (ii) Trenches ar irregular intervals.
       (iii) Open L.G. Emplacements for 4 pairs of guns.
       (iv) Dug-outs for reserve troops in rear of the front line of SAND DUNES.
       (v) Observation post in HOTEL TERLINCK.
(b) Posts under (ii) and (iii) are permanently garrisoned as follows (details have been handed to Os.C. Coys)
     N. O. P. Q & R by "D" Coy
     S. T. U. & V by "B" Coy
These are all day and night posts except N which is day only.
(c) Patrols of 1 NCO & 2 men go from each post to visit flank posts at irregular intervals during the night and in foggy weather moving along the beach. Post N will maintain touch with the 2/7th Lan. Fus., and Post V will maintain touch with the French Gendarme post across the Frontier. Patrols will record the hours they visit other posts and the latter will record the hours at which they are visited.
(d) An Officer of each front line Company will visit all his Company's posts once by day and once by night (after midnight.)

DISTRIBUTION OF TROOPS.   3. Front Line   2 platoons each of "B" & "D" as in para 2(b) & in huts near their posts.
Support.   The remaining 2 platoons of "B" & "D" in immediate support near the front.
Reserve.   "A" & "C" Coys in billets in LA PANNE.
Battn. H.Q.   VILLA DES ANCRES W.15.a.0.8.

ACTION IN CASE OF ATTACK.   4.(a) Posts will repel the enemy by Rifle and L.G. fire.
(b) The 2 supporting platoons will move up at once to positions of readiness in rear of "O" & "U" Posts respectively ready to counter attack at once or reinforce as required.
(c) Right Reserve Coy "C" will assemble near Crossroads W.15.a.30.45
Left Reserve Coy "A" will assemble near road at W.14.c.78.70.
Both will send runners to Battalion Headquarters & await orders for counter attack or reinforcing.
(d) Transport will harness up all S.A.A. & Bomb limbers.
(e) HdQr Company, less Signallers & Runners will report to R.S.M. at Transport Lines and load up limbers & act as carrying parties to front line & reserves.

LOOKOUTS & ALARM SIGNALS.   5.(a) The French Naval Authorities & H.M's ships which lie off LA PANNE at night are responsible for the lookout over the Sea.
(b) Battalion sentries & O.P's are responsible for lookout on the beach.
(c) The alarm of an impending hostile landing is given as follows :-
    (1) by telephone.
    (2) By the Naval lookout posts burning a whitw & green flare.
    (3) By the ships at sea sending up green & white rockets or a green Very light.

-2-

LOOKOUT & ALARM SIGNALS (cont.)

5. Ref. (1) the signaller at the post giving the alarm will call up H.Q. Coast Defences & BUZZ "Raid near...........post". The message will be confirmed by runner.
(d) In case of a raid the Bugler at "R" Post will sound the "ALARM".

COMMUNICATIONS.

6. Bn. HdQrs is connected through "R" post to Belgian Exchange and through the latter to "Q" & "S" posts. "R" & "S" posts are in communication with each other through Belgian Exchange. All above by ringing telephone.
"S" & "V" posts are in communication with each other by D III telephones. A line is being laid through 66th Divn. to Brigade Hdqrs at COXYDE BAINS.

A.A. DEFENCE.

7. One Lewis gun of each pair will be told off for A.A. work & will be ready for action at 1 minutes notice during hours of L.G. training and at a moments notice at other times. One gun from "T" post will be mounted on the dunes exclusively for A.A. work.

STANDING ORDERS

8. (a) Companies in the front line will be ready to move immediately by day & night. They will normally be employed by day on work on their posts.
(b) Reserve Coys will be ready to move at 2 hours notice by day & at 10 minutes notice by night.
(c) Front line Companies are responsible for all work on their posts - definite schemes will be drawn up by Os.C. L. these Coys and submitted to Bn. Hqrs.
(d) Positions of readiness in the dunes for supporting platoons, if not already marked will be marked by notice boards with lines of white posts shewing route from Coy Hdqrs.
(e) An extra 100 rounds per man of the garrison will be kept in the posts.
(f) L.G. teams will carry 25 drums per gun.
(g) Between 8 p.m. & 4 a.m. the beach in front of the belt of wire will be treated as NO MAN'S LAND. Anyone seen there will be challenged & if necessary fired on.
(h) L.G's will be tested by being fired daily in the early part of the evening.
(j) Orders for sentries & patrols attached - issued to Coy Commanders only.

Arthur Water
Lieut.- Colonel
Commanding 3/5th Bn. Lancashire Fusil

DISTRIBUTION

Copy No. 1. C.O.
2. Major Wike.
3. "A" Coy
4. "B" Coy
5. "C" Coy
6. "D" Coy
7. Adjutant
8. L.G.O.
9. Bombing Officer
10. Signalling Officer
11. Transport Officer.
12. Quartermaster.
13. Medical Officer.
14. War Diary.
15. War Diary.
16. File.
17. Spare.
18. 197th Inf. Bde for information.

2/9/1917.

Headquarters,
197th Infantry Brigade.

Herewith, as directed by Brigade Major.

SUMMARY OF WORK DONE DURING TOUR OF COAST DEFENCE

Double L.G. emplacement constructed.	Covered sentry shelters erected.	Signal Station erected	French dugout cleared.	UNDER R.E. SUPERVISION			
				Company Hdqrs cleared & repaired.	Officers' hut erected & repaired.	Mens' Hut cleared & repaired.	Mens' cookhouse erected.	Well dug.
No.2 Post	No.2 Post	No.2 Post	Four at No.8 Post	No.7 Post	No.8 Post	No.7 Post	No.8 Post	No.9 Post
No.3 Post	No.5 Post		Four at No.9 Post		No.9 Post	No.9 Post	No.9 Post	
No.6 Post	No.6 Post						No.7 Post	
No.8 Post	No.7 Post							
	No.9 Post							

In addition, trenches to be occupied in case of attack have been cleared daily.

16/9/17.

Lieut.-Colonel.
Commanding 3/5th Bn. LANCASHIRE FUSILIERS.,

SECRET   AMENDMENTS TO PRELIMINARY COAST DEFENCE   Copy No. 14
SCHEME   10/9/17.
3/5th Bn. Lan. Fus.,

DISTRIBUTION

On relief to-day posts will be held as follows:-
Nos. 1 - 7 By the right Coy "C" with 2 L.G.Sections from "A" Coy.
Nos. 8 - 9 By the left Coy "A" less 2 L.G.Sections.
Support to Nos. 1 - 7 found by 2 "C" Coy.
" " " 8 - 9 " " "A" Coy.
Reserves:- "B" & "D" Coy in billets in LA PANNE.

COMMUNICATIONS

"R", "U" & "V" posts are connected to Battalion Hdqrs and to one another by one line communication being by D.III telephone. "Q" post is directly connected to Battn. Hdqrs by ringing telephone. Battn Hdqrs is in direct communication with 66th Divn. Hdqrs and through their exchange with Hdqrs of 197th Bde. It is also directly connected to the Belgian Exchange through which in case of necessity, communication may be obtained with "Q", "R", "U" & "V" Posts.

There is also auxiliary visual communication between "V" & "Q", & "U" & "Q" posts, "Q" delivering to Battn. Hdqrs.

Captain,
Adjutant 3/5th Lan.Fus.

10/9/17.

DISTRIBUTION
As in Preliminary Coast Defence Scheme d/d 2/9/17.

SECRET   Copy No. 10

                        COAST DEFENCE ORDERS
                          LA PANNE SECTION.
                                 by
                      Lieut.-Col. A.S. BATES D.S.O.
                Commanding 3/5th Bn. LANCASHIRE FUSILIERS.

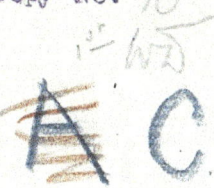

FRONTAGE.   1.   4,900 yards from W.9.d.9.9. on the East to the Franco
                      Belgian Frontier on the West at V.23.d.3.5.

DEFENCES.   2. (i)   A belt of wire, with gaps in places, buried in many
                         places within a foot of the top.
                  (ii)   Trenches at irregular intervals.
                  (iii) L.G. & M.G. emplacements.
                  (iv)   Dug-outs and huts for reserve troops.
                  (v)   O.P. at the TERLINK HOTEL.
                  (vi)   Two Belgian Searchlights (positions not yet defined.)

GARRISONS.   3. (a)   As per Appendix "A" & map attached, 1/10,000.
                         Each post patrols to the post on either flank at
                         irregular intervals through the night and in foggy
                         weather.
                   (b)   1 Platoon and 2 sections of Right Front Company in
                         support in billets in LA PANNE BAINS.
                   (c)   In reserve 2 Companies in LA PANNE BAINS.
                   (d)   Battalion Headquarters at the VILLA DES ANCRES.

POLICY OF
DEFENCE.   4. (1)   To hold the Sector with a front line of M.G. posts
                         which are to be permanently manned.
                   (2)   To hold a proportion of the Infantry (not exceeding
                         25%) ready for the reinforcement of the front line.
                         (Platoons & Coys. in Support)
                   (3)   To keep the remainder of the Infantry as a striking
                         force.
                   (4)   To counter-attack the enemy at once, & to drive him
                         into the sea should he effect a landing.
                         The role of the striking force will therefore be for
                         counter-attack rather than for reinforcing the front
                         line of defence.

ACTION IN CASE
OF ATTACK.   5. (i)   Posts will be manned and the enemy repulsed by
                         rifle & L.G. fire.
                  (ii)   One platoon and 2 sections of the Right front Coy in
                         billets & No.8 post will counter attack at once and
                         drive the enemy into the sea.
                  (iii) The Reserve Coys will assemble as follows:-
                             The Right at the crossroads W.15.a.30.45.
                             The Left at about W.14.c.78.70.
                         Both sending runners to Battalion Headquarters.
                  (iv)   Headquarter Company, less Signallers & Runners, will
                         report to the R.S.M. at the Transport Lines and load
                         up limbers & act as carrying parties.

LOOKOUTS AND
ALARM SIGNALS. 6.(a)   The French Naval Authorities & H.M's ships which lie
                         off LA PANNE at night are responsible for the lookout
                         over the Sea.
                   (b)   Battalion sentries & O.P's are responsible for
                         lookout on the beach.
                   (c)   The alarm of an impending hostile landing is given
                         as follows:-
                             (1) By telephone.
                             (2) By the Naval lookout posts burning a white
                                 and green flare.
                             (3) By the ships at sea sending up green &
                                 white rockets or 3 green Very Lights in
                                 succession.
                         Ref. (1) the signaller at the post giving the alarm
                         will call up Headquarters Coast Defences & BUZZ
                         "Raid near............Post". The message will be

-2-

         confirmed by runner.
    (d) In case of a raid the Bugler at No.4 Post will sound the "ALARM".

COMMUNICATIONS   7. See Appendix "B" for telephonic communications.

A.A.DEFENCES.   8. See Appendix "A"

[signature: Arthur Salter]

Lieut.-Colonel.
Commanding 3/5th Bn. LANCASHIRE FUSILIERS.

14/9/17.

DISTRIBUTION

Copy No. 1. 197th Inf. Bde.
       2. C.O.
       3. "A" Coy.
       4. "B" Coy
       5. "C" Coy
       6. "D" Coy
       7. H.Q Coy
       8. File
       9. War Diary
      10. War Diary
      11. Spare
      12. Spare.

APPENDIX "A"

LA PANNE SECTION COAST DEFENCE

No. of Post.	Map reference.	Garrison	A.A.L.G.Day position	Nature of shelter & situation.	Remarks.
			RIGHT COMPANY plus 2 L.G. Sections.		
1.	W.9.d.36.55	1 section		Elephant W.9.d.46.42	Finds a patrol to either flank. A fairly good trench exists. No day sentry
2.	W.9.d.10.32	2 L.G.sections W.9.d.23.44		Small dugouts W.9.d.17.36	The night posts for the L.G's are at W.9.d.23.44 firing to the right & W.9.d.27.48 firing to the left.
3. TERLINK	W.15.a.10.75	2 L.G.sections		Dugouts	
3. TERLINK O.P.	W.15.a.13.70	3 signallers & 3 men & NCO.		Billet in hotel.	Observation post day & night on top of TERLINK HOTEL in telephonic communication with Bn.H.Q.
4.	W.14.b.70.53	3 sections		Billets "AY HOPE"	Trenches exist
5.	W.14.a.80.01	1 section		Dug-outs	Only finds sentry post by day and night.
6.	W.14.c.03.57	1 section & 2 L.G.sections	W.13.d.93.45	Hut & dugouts	
			LEFT COMPANY		
7.	W.19.a.95.99	1 Platoon less L.G.Section.		Huts. W.19.a.95.99 W.19.a.65.55	Company Headquarters W.19.a.79.80.
8.	V.24.b.36.32	1 Platoon plus L.G.Section.	V.24.b.43.20 to be constructed	French dugouts between V.24.b.35.15 & V.24.a.63.21.	Double L.G. emplacement V.24.b.36.32 Trenches exist.
9.	V.23.d.85.67	2 Platoons		3 French dugouts between V.24.c.07.50 & V.24.c.56.75 A hut at V.23.d.60.58	Officers' Hut at V.23.d.93.51. A well is being constructed at about V.23.d.85.25 Trenches exist - only 1 L.G. emplacement.
	V.23.d.74.65	2 M.G's		V.24.c.23.76 French dugout	The other gun is in reserve

Appendix B

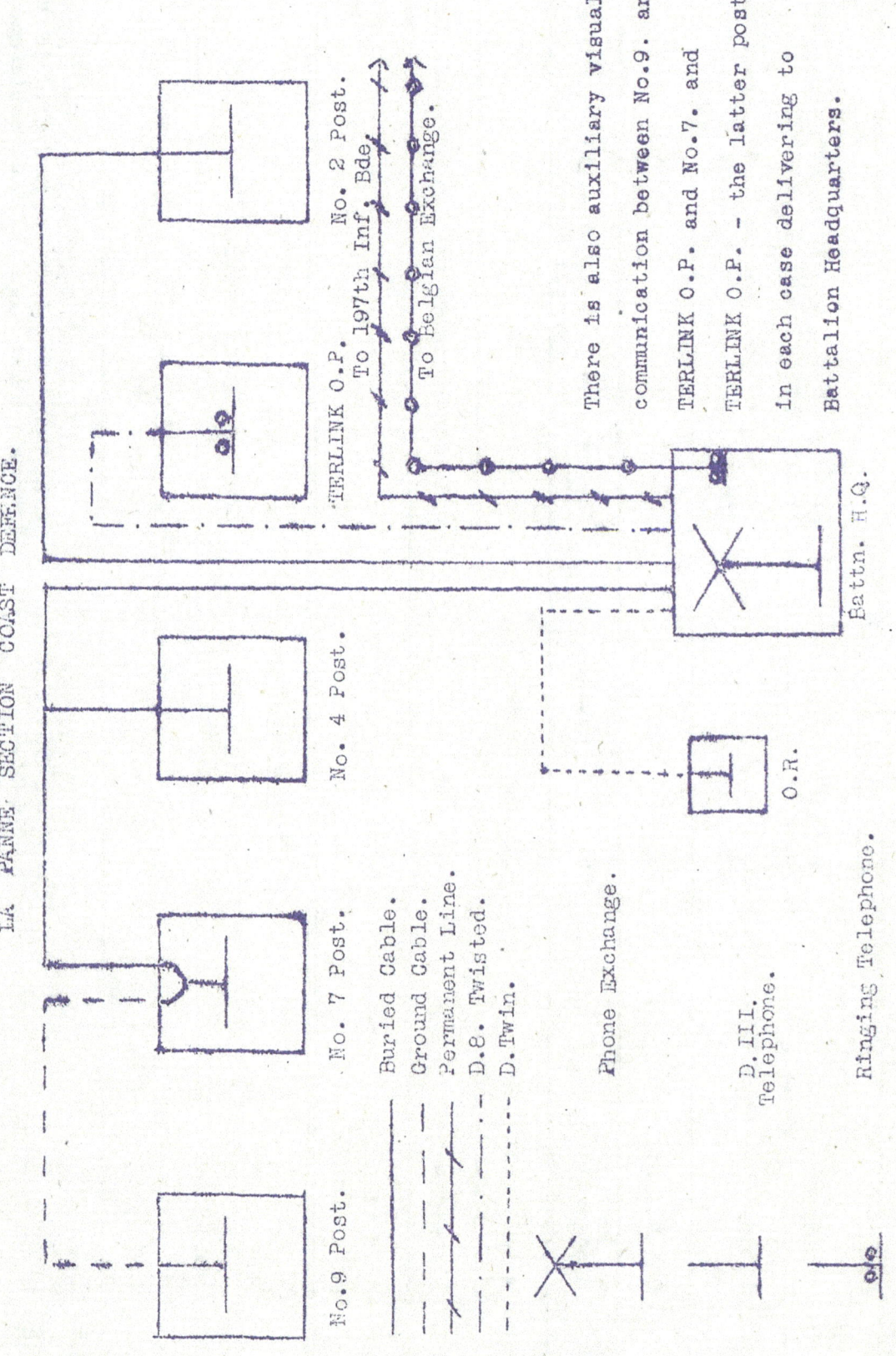

ORDERS FOR SENTRIES

1. They will keep a sharp look-out to sea and report to N.C.O. i/c all war vessels and all rocket lights, especially GREEN or GREEN and WHITE, seen at night.

2. The N.C.O. i/c will report to Officer i/c Post the times at which above are seen.

3. They will arrest all persons with cameras and conduct them to Officer i/c Post.

4. They will report landing of aircraft in their sector to the N.C.O. i/c.

5. Between the hours of 8.0 p.m. and 4.0 a.m. every person will be challenged twice and if possible, apprehended. If such person endeavours to evade apprehension after being challenged, he will be fired on.

6. Sentries must use their common sense in reading orders. Fire will not be opened by day unless circumstances demand it. Obvious British Officers and men should be stopped and warned of their danger.
British aeroplanes, horses, etc., must not be fired on.

-------o-------

ORDERS FOR PATROLS

1. They will see that no person is on the beach in their sector between the hours of 8.0 p.m. and 4.0 a.m.

2. Any person so found will be twice challenged and if possible, apprehended.

3. They will see that all lights on the sea front are shaded. The number of house and name of unit of occupier will be taken in case where this is not complied with.

4. They will keep touch with Post on either flank.

5. They will report to Officer i/c Post all rocket lights seen at sea, especially GREEN or GREEN and WHITE.

-------o-------

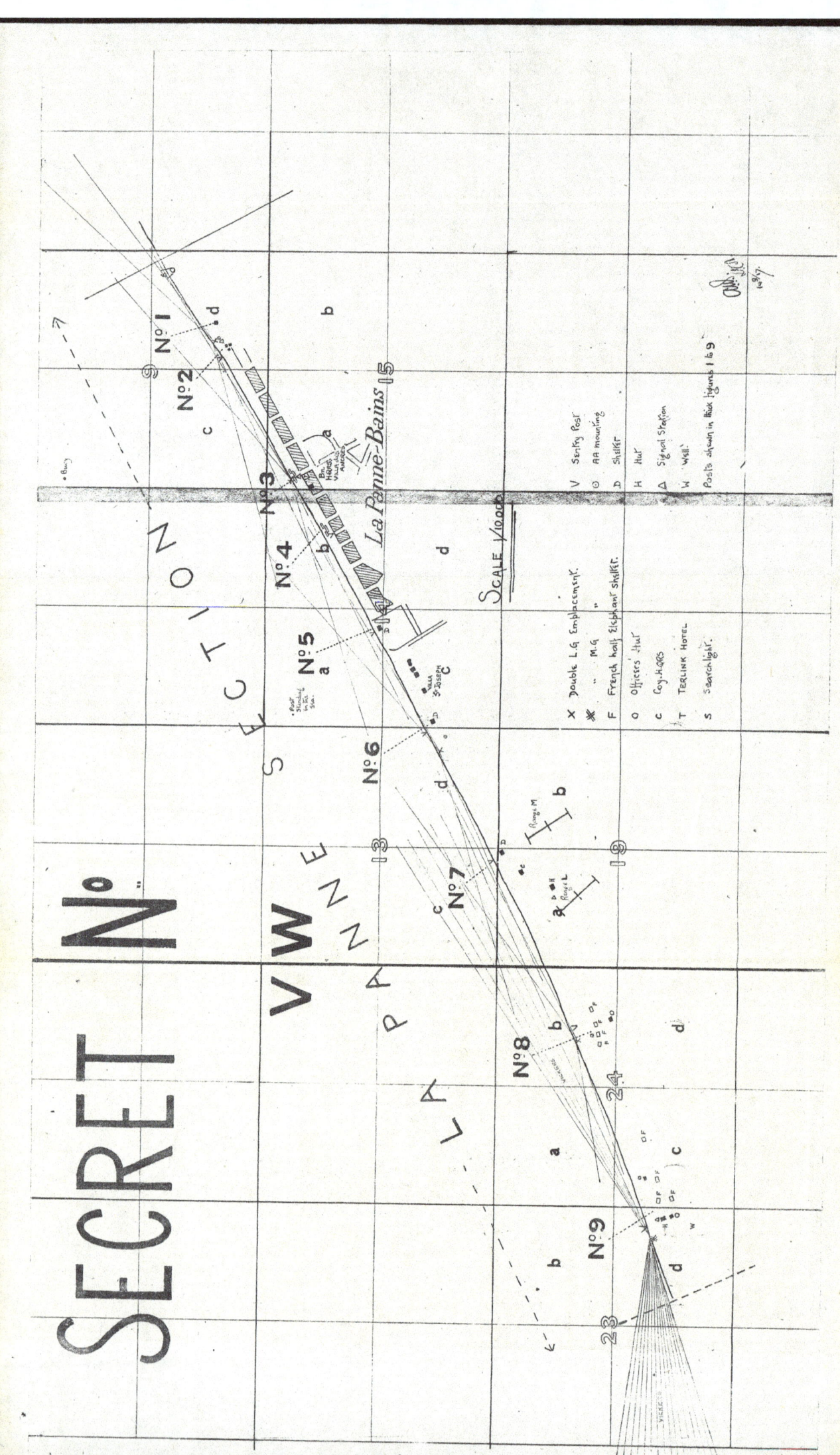

Subj:- Report on Defences.

From:- O.C.
       3/5th Bn. Lan. Fus.,

To :- Headquarters,
       197th Inf. Bde.,

Ref. Sheet 11 S.E. 1/20,000.

The Section is about 4,900 yards long extending from W.9.d.9.9. on the East to the Frontier at V.23.d.3.5. on the West.

<u>SYSTEM</u>. 1.   The general system consists of:-

  (a) Narrow band of barbed wire above high water mark.

  (b) Old trenches at various intervals along the Coast.

  (c) Posts and permanent garrisons are as follows:-

     No. 1. or "N" W.9.d.7.6. held by 1 section.
        2. or "O" W.9.c.9.2. .. .. 2 sections. (2 L.G's)
        3. or "P" W.15.a.45.80 .. .. 2 ..
        4. or "Q" W.15.a.00.75 .. .. 2 ..   (2 L.G's)
        5. or "R" W.14.b.2.2. .. .. 3 ..

     above are held by the Right front Company.

        6. or "S" W.14.b.25.75 held by 1 section.
        7. or "T" W.13.d.75.45 .. .. 2 sections. (2 L.G's)
        8. or "U" W.13.d.20.15 .. .. 2 ..
        9. or "V" V.23.d.95.75 .. .. 5 ..   (2 L.G's)

    The above four are held by Left front Company

  (d) Double M.G. post at No.9 or "V" enfilading the front of the wire to the West & East. A M.G. officer is permanently attached to Headquarters.

  (e) Dugouts for Reserve troops in rear of the front line of sand dunes. These are being repaired and cleared out and made habitable.

  (f) Officers huts at present in course of construction to accommodate the Officers of the left Company, none of whom at present live with, or in close proximity to their men.

  (g) Observation post in the HOTEL TERLINCK.

The scheme so far as the right Company is concerned is fairly satisfactory as the balance of the Company is near at hand in billets and can reinforce or counter attack without delay. So far, however, as concerns the left Company, the situation is unsatisfactory and will be so until the accommodation mentioned in para.1 (e) & (f) above is completed. When this is done the Company will be on the spot & the supporting platoons readily available. The C.R.E. has the matter in hand and I have an R.E. officer from 432nd Field Coy R.E. permanently attached to me to assist & coordinate the work of repair and construction.

TRAINING AREA

SCALE 1:10,000

ST IDESBALDE

DE ZEEPANNE

LA PANNE BAINS

SECRET. COAST DEFENCE ORDERS NO.1 COPY NO. 6
"QUARTIER DE MALO TERMINUS"
by Lt.Col.A.S.BATES,D.S.O.
Comdg. 1/5th.Bn.LAN.FUS.

Reference Sheet 1.

FRONT. 1. The Battalion is responsible for the coast defence from and
including the Centre of resistance No.3 at C.14.c.0.4 on the
West to midway between point d'appui "g" and the Centre of resistance No.
5, viz. about C.11.c.3.7.

DEFENCES. 2. Two well defined Centres of resistance Nos.3 & 4 and points
d'appui "d" & "e" (in 2 portions) "f" & "g" exist, with
certain other small sections of trench.

DISPOSITIONS IN CASE OF ALARM. 3.

Centre of Resistance	Points d'appui	Garrison	Coy.	In close support under O.C. Coy.	Approximate position.
3.		2 platoons	"A"	2 platoons less 1 L.G. section.	C.10.b.9.2
	"d"	1 L.G. section			
	"e"	1 L.G. section in each portion.	"D"	2 platoons less 1 L.G. section plus 1 sec.	C.15.b.1.3
	"f"	1 platoon & 1 section less 1 L.G.section.	"D"		
4.		1 platoon and 1 L.G.section.	"C"	2 platoons	C.15.d.9.2
	"g"	1 platoon less 1 L.G.section.	"C"		

Each Centre of resistance has a permanent garrison of 3 men as
a guard over ammunition etc.
In reserve "B" Coy at C.15.d.5.4.
Battle H.Qrs of Battalion and O.C.Sub-sector FORT DES DUNES.
Troops will be ready to move at 2 hours notice by day and at
immediate notice in foggy weather or at night.

ACTION. 4. Posts will be held at all costs. Should the enemy effect a
landing, immediate counter attacks will be made by the nearest
available troops to drive him back into the sea. Os.C. Centres of resistance, points d'appui, supports etc will make themselves acquainted with
the gaps in the wire which could be used for counterattacks. In all
cases fullest information must be sent to Battalion H.Qrs.

AMMUNITION. 5. See Appendix "A". The O.C. "C" Coy will detail 2 bombers
from a platoon in support to report immediately at Battn.
H.Qrs. for the purpose of detonating bombs. The limber loaded with S.A.A.
and 4 pack mules for point d'appui "g" will report at Battn. H.Qrs. to
load the boxes of detonated bombs. O.C. "C" Coy will arrange a guide for
the pack mules. These 2 bombers will rejoin their platoon on completion
of their work. L.G.limbers will report at once to their respective Coy.
H.Qrs. Balance of transport will remain at the Transport lines in reserve under the Regimental Sergt.Major.

RATIONS. 6. All available rations will be issued and carried.

-2-

WATER. 7. All water bottles will be filled. The water carts will take up the nearest possible positions to the 2 Centres of resistance and petrol tins will be distributed as follows. Carrying will be done by troops in support.

```
11 tins to Centre of resistance No.3
 3   ..   ..   ..   ..   ..   ..   ..   point d'appui "d"
 4   ..   ..   ..   ..   ..   ..   ..     "     "     "e"
 3   ..   ..   ..   ..   ..   ..   ..     "     "     "f"
12   ..   ..  Centre of resistance No.4
 6   ..   ..   ..   ..   ..   ..   ..     "     "     "g"
```

COMMUNICATION. 8. The Signalling Officer will distribute the Signallers so as best to assist in keeping telephonic communication open. He will also station signallers at the Barrage Battery at the Batterie de ZUYDCOOTE.

Runners from	Are to know the best route to
Coast garrisons	Posts on either flank & Battle H.QRS.
Supports	Above as well as own Coy. posts.
Battle Headquarters	All above as well as other Battalion Headquarters.

MEDICAL ARRANGEMENTS. 9. R.A.Ps will be established as follows.
    (a) Under canvas on the FORT DES DUNES—BATTERIE DE ZUYDCOOTE road North of the Railway.
    (b) In the corner house at C.30.b.2.4.

LIAISON. 10. Interpreters, if available, will be allotted as follows.
    (a) to the O.C. Left Coy. for liaison with the next allied post on the West.
    (b) To accompany the C.O. to Battle H.Qrs.

Distribution.
No.1 to C.O.
  2. "A" Coy.
  3. "C" Coy.
  4. "D" Coy.
  5. (Signalling Officer.
    (Adjutant & file.
    (Transport Officer.
  6. War diary.
  7. War diary.
  8. Colonel ARMITAGE, C.B.

Lieut. Colonel,
Commanding 3/9th. LAN. FUS.

Issued at 8 a.m.
24/8/17.

APPENDIX "A"

S.A.A. and Grenade Reserve.

The following boxes have been distributed.

Centre of Resistance.	Boxes S.A.A.	Boxes grenades. (detonated)	Remarks.
3	12	28	Garrison of Point d'appui "d" will fetch 4 boxes of S.A.A. & 6 boxes grenades from here on alarm.
4	11	24	

In event of alarm the following boxes of S.A.A. and detonated bombs will be taken by Companies as under.

Point d' appui.	Method.	Boxes S.A.A.	Boxes of grenades.	Remarks.
"e"	1 Limber	5	5	This limber will be taken as near to the posts as possible and the boxes carried by the garrison to their respective posts. O.C. "D" COY will detail an Officer to superintend the distribution.
"f"		6	6	
"g"	4 pack mules.	6	6	

Copy No. 7

G

Addition to COAST DEFENCE ORDERS No.1.
"QUARTIER DE MALO TERMINUS"
by
Lieut.- Colonel A.S.BATES D.S.O.
Commanding 3/5th Battalion LANCASHIRE FUSILIERS.

-----o-----

COMMUNICATIONS. 1. The Signalling Officer will make himself acquainted with Appendices "D" & "E" of Fourth Army Coast Defence Scheme 785/3(G) dated 1st August, 1917, kept at the Section Headquarters.

BARRAGE. 2. "Appendix B" attached.

LIASON. 3. Reference C.O. No.1. para.10 two French Interpreters are permanently attached to the Section.

Lieut.- Colonel.
Commdg 3/5th Bn. LANCASHIRE FUSILIERS.

DISTRIBUTION

Copy No.1. C.O.
2. "A" Coy
3. "C" Coy
4. "D" Coy
5. Signalling Officer
   Adjutant & File.
6. War Diary.
7. War Diary.
8. Colonel ARMITAGE, C.B.

25/9/17.

APPENDIX "B"

Barrage details so far as Battalion posts are concerned.

1. Barrage artillery is established at the BATTERIE DE ZUYDCOOTE.

2. After the alarm has been given, barrage can be called for as follows:-

    (a) By the Section Commander telephoning to the BATTERIE DE ZUYDCOOTE covering the coast between the latter and centre of resistance No.6.

    (b) By Centre 4 by night (by day calls are unnecessary) signalling to the BATTERIE DE ZUYDCOOTE by means of a signal lamp with a red light.

3. Lamp signals for barrage are made and received as follows.
    A succession of dots, coloured red, in the direction of the BATTERIE, sent at intervals, until the barrage is opened. Three discs, coloured red are provided for the purpose and are kept at Section Headquarters, being handed over on relief.
    O.C. Signals will provide a signal lamp for Centre No.4.

4. (a) On the alarm being given 2 signallers will be sent to receive Barrage calls at the BATTERIE DE ZUYDCOOTE.

    (b) These signallers, to gain entry, must be in possession of the pass provided for that purpose, which is kept at Section Headquarters. On the reverse side of the Pass are the numbers of the Centres from which the Signallers are responsible for receiving barrage calls.

    (c) On receipt of a signal for barrage, the recipient at the BATTERIE will immediately inform the French gunners by saying "Barrage" and pointing to the number on the card to indicate the centre which is calling. (Centre No.5 also uses a succession of red dots).

5. O.C. Signals of relieving Battalion must immediately test their barrage calls by day to ensure correct alignment.

3/5th BATTALION LANCASHIRE FUSILIERS.

CASUALTY LIST FOR MONTH OF SEPTEMBER, 1917.

Date.	KILLED		WOUNDED	
	Officers	Other Ranks.	Officers	Other Ranks.
1/9/17				39106 Pte WESTHEAD.J.
				203076 L/C KING.J.H.
4/9/17				205353 Pte STANSFIELD. M
5/9/17		3/16405 Pte WOOD.F.		3/16771 " CHADWICK.J.
				3/17152 " WARBURTON.T.
				205573 " GRIFFIN.J.
				203059 " ANDERTON.J.R.
				204463 " WOOLFENDEN.J
				202608 Sgt SUGDEN.T.
				203650 Pte JOHNS.W.J.
				204360 " HALES.H.W.

(signature)
Lieut.-Colonel.
Commanding 3/5th Battn. LANCASHIRE FUSILIERS.

30/9/1917.

197th Brigade.

66th Division.

3/5th BATTALION LANCASHIRE FUSILIERS OCTOBER 1917.

CONFIDENTIAL.

WAR DIARY

OF

3/5th BATTN. LANCASHIRE FUSILIERS

From:- 1/10/17.
To :- 31/10/17.

(VOLUME 9.)

Army Form C. 2118.

WAR DIARY
or
INTELLIGENCE SUMMARY.
(Erase heading not required.)

1/5th LANC[ASHIRE]

Place	Date	Hour	Summary of Events and Information	Remarks and references to Appendices
EECKE	1917 Oct. 3rd		On the 2nd Octbr the Batn left CAMPAGNE near ST OMER and marched to 6 FIELD into EECKE + Valmar Hutches.	
HALLEBAST (?A)			The day was very wet & the roads dusty notwithstanding the whole battalion arrived together with the exception of 2	
3rd			now suffering from foot stabs. These men joined the convoy from the 2/1st EAST LANC DIVISION FIELD AMBULANCE.	
MICKLEEGLE J 4.5	4th		Battalion left Eg. near EECKE for camp at J 4.6. about 1000 yds N of WINNIZEELE arriving there by 9 am.	
			Marching strength . 21 Officers including (M.O.) (who joined the strength + specialists) other ranks + O.R. as follows	

	H.Q.	A	B	C	D	Total
Officers	4	4	3	6	4	
O.R.	43	130	133	126	126	558
Total	104	2	2	2	2	112
	147	132	135	128	128	670

WAR DIARY

3/5 London R.F. Fusiliers

INTELLIGENCE SUMMARY.

(Erase heading not required.)

Army Form C. 2118.

Place	Date	Hour	Summary of Events and Information	Remarks and references to Appendices
WINNEZEELE	1917		He [reported?] me that there was 5.15. Up at 6am for C Coy. Reinforcement camp at Morbecque — Inspected by Major Capt. Crouch & tried to otherwise dispose of men. Lunch by Capt. HASTINGS (George Baron Staff) — Governor (on leave). A cold wind depressing they conversation on the scrap very fast & let the officers the CO had got equipment in 24 hours. to B.s.r. Dur. H.qrs at WINNEZEELE. Bur. H.qrs at J.16 b.4.4. Got up my recent telephone today. TTT the Battalion would entrain up my recent telephone today at J.14 b.94. Details unknown Left dump at 9am at J.14 b.94. Details unknown. The Bun took train to be at Dup of Coy ? This was almost impossible. Received the order that the Battalion would entrain at Capt. J.F. BRADDOCK Q.6 4.y... (totally unknown at 4pm. When entraining thinking that the Butts would finish the day easy journey. The buses were not at most Detailed as above. Marched to FREZENBERG RIDGE where the Batt. arrived at 6:30pm. Enroute the east extremely intemperate very wet all except C. Coy ~ 60 [under?] all others were with the
NEAR [FREZENBERG?]			

Army Form C. 2118.

WAR DIARY

2/5th Lancashire Fusiliers

INTELLIGENCE SUMMARY.

(Erase heading not required.)

Place	Date	Hour	Summary of Events and Information	Remarks and references to Appendices
FREZENBERG RIDGE	1917 Oct 5	(cont)	Battalion as the CO had no information as to the whereabouts of the Rest camp. About 9 P.M. Lts Thompson & Morley took 16 others down to BRAND HOEK where it was reported the Rest camp was situated. It was not in the actual position being about 1 mile WEST of YPRES ASYLUM, however, on the SOUTH side of the VLAMERTINGHE road. The Transport was instructed to proceed to G.6.d.4.1. (Sheet 28) where it would be met by a representative & guided to billets. The latter were entirely illusory imaginary & non-existent.	
FREZENBERG RIDGE		6"	Remained in bivouack with no real comfort, then in the pouring day - which incidentally had without any casualties the Company Commanders visited the assembly area. Received draft of 100 O.R. from the 19th LAN.FUS. to relieve Battalion here of the men who had been on the transfer. They looked to down along enough & were allotted as follows.	

Army Form C. 2118.

WAR DIARY
3rd HAMPSHIRE RIFLES
INTELLIGENCE SUMMARY.
(Erase heading not required.)

Instructions regarding War Diaries and Intelligence Summaries are contained in F. S. Regs., Part II. and the Staff Manual respectively. Title pages will be prepared in manuscript.

Place	Date	Hour	Summary of Events and Information	Remarks and references to Appendices
FREZENBERG RIDGE	1917 OCT.	6ᵗʰ (noon)	A Coy — 23 B Coy — 22 } 100 C Coy — 26 D Coy — 29 This made the attacking strength as follows:- H.Q. — 43 A — 153 Each Coy had probably one or two B — 155 casualties on the Ridge before C — 132 reaching off D — 135	
FREZENBERG RIDGE		7ᵗʰ	The C.O. went to Bde. H.Qrs. on the ZONNEBEKE – VAMPIRE HOUSE – road that the attack would take place early on the 9ᵗʰ. C.O. received final instructions	
		8ᵗʰ	Gough (?) shelled intermittently all day & aeroplane recompose	

WAR DIARY

3/5th BATT LANCASHIRE FUSILIERS
INTELLIGENCE SUMMARY.

(Erase heading not required.)

Army Form C. 2118.

Place	Date	Hour	Summary of Events and Information	Remarks and references to Appendices
FREZENBERG RIDGE	1917 OCT. 8th	(cont)	Casualties 2 Killed & 8 Wounded. Order to march at 6 p.m. queried by Aust/Canadian R.E. The Battalion had been instructed to give itself up entirely to recovery material. It was now ordered to get in at 3.45 p.m. in readiness. The C.O. signalled officer B/Maj of the Trenches at 3.45 p.m. to endeavour to see the ground. They left C.O. were sucessful enough [illegible] to meet etc. Both left at 6.30 p.m. under Capt LOUGHLIN. C.O.'s comments — worth to R — HAMBURG (by not attacking) between 8 - 9 p.m. after finding endeavours to find the C.O. 2/5 MANCHESTER REGT (who afterwards was found to be at Bn. H.Qr). The C.O. was in telephonic communication with Bde from Cole [illegible Strong] which was about 50x East of the R = HAMBURG. No troops had arrived by 1 a.m. on the 9th. Patrols & noted aft. at 6.30 p.m. Delayed by shelling & by Road blocked by Guide. Sec. Rear Coys the latter Battalion movements.	

Army Form C. 2118.

WAR DIARY

3/5th Batt. LANCASHIRE FUSILIERS.

INTELLIGENCE SUMMARY.

(Erase heading not required.)

Place	Date	Hour	Summary of Events and Information	Remarks and references to Appendices
FREZENBERG RIDGE	4/10	5:30	Enemy shelled the Ridge and the trenches & gullies near Potsdam at all	
		6:02	Close of firing	
			The Battalion reached assault near the end of Jack Track street 3	
		9:15	S.15.ag.	
		9:20	Capt. LAUGHLIN & the Adjutant were sent forward to the Company at and ordered to the attack, although the Barrage had been over 5.15 many K.D. and slows	
			On the Left. We arrived by S.m.d. CO = Lieut (2nd Lieut.) Knight that the attack safe as he title was consumed near of an officer	
			2Lt. PRESTON held his platoon at the end of Jack Track but never owns the Battle line	
			He C.O. Adiny reported by Clifford that to B" was not present & being to a certain extent compelled by the fact that no troops of the 16 197" or 196" Bde were on the left of Zero depth in the august. Hard hit and attack - Casualty not allotted.	

WAR DIARY
3/5th LANCASHIRE FUSILIERS
INTELLIGENCE SUMMARY.
(Erase heading not required.)

Army Form C. 2118.

Instructions regarding War Diaries and Intelligence Summaries are contained in F. S. Regs., Part II. and the Staff Manual respectively. Title pages will be prepared in manuscript.

Place	Date	Hour	Summary of Events and Information	Remarks and references to Appendices
	1917 Oct 7	9·"· (m)	Station in alarm	
			Lewis atacks	
		10"	Battalion in strive Hostilities attacked	
WINNIZEELE		11	Relief effected. 2 East Battalion assembled at M ASYLUM YPRES. Entrained at 8·PM for WINNIZEELE and marched to camp in afoo arrived 10 PM	
WINNIZEELE		12"	Bathing there. I commanded 2/6" Lan Fus Capt J.S. GILLAND assumed at 2·"· the command of the Battalion. Brigadier paid a surprise visit & to rack. The Battalion was mustered. He was not very sympathetic - verbs ad to the depression on the check - Red the Battn he had received general report of unsportmen form the Coy Commanders. He has cleaned him a being. At 2 PM. we marched back to Bygoho to proceed & rest of offes from all Battn. When he asked to bring to the beyelies etc.	

Army Form C. 2118.

WAR DIARY
or
INTELLIGENCE SUMMARY.
(Erase heading not required.)

Instructions regarding War Diaries and Intelligence Summaries are contained in F. S. Regs., Part II. and the Staff Manual respectively. Title pages will be prepared in manuscript.

Place	Date	Hour	Summary of Events and Information	Remarks and references to Appendices
WINNIZEELE	1917 Oct	13th	Orders received for Private officers to acting appointments as follows.	
			3/Lt LANCERS.	
			Capt. S.J. Cowans to be 2nd in Command	
			2/6 LANCERS.	
			Major H. WIKE to Command	
			Institution of Light infantry required before troops of higher rank arrived.	
WINNIZEELE		14th	During the remainder of the time at WINNIZEELE that such works were carried out under Company Commanders. The use of Lewis gun equipment although they were carried out	
WINNIZEELE		15th	The weather showing no signs of breaking the new Camp day been very plenty of accommodation for the men the battn. seemed quietly of its new abode and above all look happy.	
WINNIZEELE		16th	The Divisional Commander wished to battn on this day the weather spoiled all the display of the tops on the parade ground but he mentioned that the Division had been in the 9th Corps for 2 days the units were distributed	

3/7th WAR DIARY Fusiliers
INTELLIGENCE SUMMARY

Army Form C. 2118.

Place	Date	Hour	Summary of Events and Information	Remarks and references to Appendices
WINNIZEELE	9/10 Oct.	6th (a.m.)	Had a Section and GHEWVELT. O/C and 6 of the two Coys the Division were ordered to the II ANZAC CORPS, the Battalion this day received a draft of 10 Officers & 159 men. L.F. BRIGHT & 2 Lt SMITH from the 3/4 (Res) Bn LAN FUS. and 290 O.R. from 18th LAN FUS.	
WINNIZEELE		7	Lt WRIGHT was posted to B Coy. 2 Lt SMITH to D Coy. The following Officers are reported as Company Commanders. A Coy. Capt HASTINGS (on return from leave) B Coy. Lieut REID C Coy. Capt CROUCH D Coy. Capt ASHWORTH The following Officers will be stand in Command of Platoon Commanders until further Officers arrive:- A Coy. Lieut SENIOR B Coy. 2/Lt BELCHER C Coy. Lieut MORLEY in relieve of Capt ROUSE D Coy. 2/Lieut DUNN. All as ordered from 4th October 1917.	

Army Form C. 2118.

WAR DIARY
or
INTELLIGENCE SUMMARY.
(Erase heading not required.)

Instructions regarding War Diaries and Intelligence Summaries are contained in F. S. Regs., Part II. and the Staff Manual respectively. Title pages will be prepared in manuscript.

Place	Date	Hour	Summary of Events and Information	Remarks and references to Appendices
WINNEZEELE	1917 Oct	17th	LIEUT. C.H. TYE reported for duty from the 3rd AUSTRALIAN C.C.S. & was posted on 2nd Command of "D" Coy.	
WINNEZEELE		18th	CAPT. A. HASTINGS returned from leave & assumed Command of "A" Coy. Signalling & Lewis Gun classes were organised in order to complete the instruction of the portions of the Battalion which have not been instructed now in the 30th inst. to CAMPAGNE	
		19th	Receiving orders that the Battalion would move on the 20th inst. the C.O. issued Standing Orders referring to the same title in hopes the 20 mile Battalion journey to the Brigade train the 20 mile B.C. issued order that in full marching order everything was to be carried by motor lorry. The act was for the fitness & endurance of the men would exceedingly tell. The Battalion cleared the Brigade by the Brigade starting point at 9 a.m. & at 13.30 p.m. the Battalion bellies for whole time & the rest of the Brigade. Its its 3/6 "A" Coy the mostest kept Rebels arrived at its full Battalion in CAMPAGNE at 4.30 pm. Levery Medical Orders the whole Battalion arrived fittest.	
CAMPAGNE		20th	Lt. J.C. BYRNE reported for duty from hospital. 5.	

Army Form C. 2118.

WAR DIARY
of LANCASHIRE FUSILIERS
INTELLIGENCE SUMMARY.
(Erase heading not required.)

Instructions regarding War Diaries and Intelligence Summaries are contained in F. S. Regs., Part II. and the Staff Manual respectively. Title pages will be prepared in manuscript.

Place	Date	Hour	Summary of Events and Information	Remarks and references to Appendices
CAMPAGNE	1917 Oct. 21		Church parade 10th in field mass that 11.40	
CAMPAGNE	22		Training in Coy & Company movements. Res. moved out. Classes for Specialists. Revr. George & Stretcher Bearers were returned.	
CAMPAGNE	23		Training not finished. Classes continued	
CAMPAGNE	24		2/Lieut CARTER & Coy moved to 75th Bde L.M. G.S. with effect from 22.10.17. 2/Lieut A.B. CREILLIER proceded for duty from the 3rd Bn LAN FUS 22.10.17 and was posted to A Coy	
CAMPAGNE	25		5 Lt Horns of the Battalion were employed as Whitr Horses to the bde as STONER.	
CAMPAGNE	26		A Brigade tactical exercise was arranged for the day but owing to the inclement weather	

Army Form C. 2118.

WAR DIARY

3/5 — LANCASHIRE FUSILIERS

INTELLIGENCE SUMMARY.

(Erase heading not required.)

Place	Date	Hour	Summary of Events and Information	Remarks and references to Appendices
CAMPAGNE	1917 Oct.	27	The Battalion paraded in tents in a field near B Company's billet. The Brigadier presented the ribbons of medal ribbons to sixteen N.C.O. and men of the Battalion. The Chaplain then served in the Episcopacy of October 9th and 10th. 2/Lieut H.D. SMITH reported for duty (A) on 26th inst, from 3rd Bn (Rs) Lancers. He was posted to "D" Company.	
		28	The Battalion received a little ceremonial drill in preparation for the Commander-in-Chief's inspection on the 29th. A certain church parade of the 36th and 2/6th Lan: Fus Battalions was held on the full ton. B Coy's billet.	
		29	The Commander-in-Chief inspected the Brigade on the AIRE-ARQUES ROAD at 11am. The Brigade then marched past to Commander-in-Chief who expressed himself as pleased with the display and congratulated the Brigade on the Brigade's success of Order 9.	

Army Form C. 2118.

WAR DIARY
3/5 LANCASHIRE FUSILIERS
INTELLIGENCE SUMMARY
(Erase heading not required.)

Place	Date	Hour	Summary of Events and Information	Remarks and references to Appendices
CAMPAGNE	1917 Oct.	10	Slight shelling. The Battalion and 2/6th 8th Lancashire Fusiliers finished assembling in taped positions.	
	31st		Brigade Field Day.	
			The Brigade was practised in the attack on the T.3 area (Sect-27)	
			After the practice the Brigade assembled and General LAWRENCE the Divisional Commander showed the officers and other ranks of the Brigade. After the ceremony General LAWRENCE addressed the Brigade. He told the Brigade how pleased the Commander-in-Chief was with the Reputation on the 29th and with the march up to the present line. He told General HAIG's words "Every man he had seen something the proud of, and the fighting spirit shewn by the troops in the colour" Oct: 9th and 10th was such as affected by the Commander-in-Chief. General LAWRENCE said that on the night of the 6th Oct he was asked if he thought it would be possible for the Division to present to the attack on the 9th. He replied that if it were humanly possible the 66 Division	

Army Form C. 2118.

WAR DIARY
3/5 LANCASHIRE FUSILIERS
INTELLIGENCE SUMMARY.
(Erase heading not required.)

Place	Date	Hour	Summary of Events and Information	Remarks and references to Appendices
CAMP FACHE	1917 OCT. 31st	(Cont.)	would do it, and they did. The men were told that the higher authorities fully understood the great difficulties the Division had to put up with, and so the success was all the more remarkable and praiseworthy. In conclusion the General said that he had complete confidence in the Brigade, and if he had to take part in another fight this would be the Battalion that he would be proud of. He wished to see the best of luck during the coming winter.	

APPENDICES TO WAR DIARY FOR OCTOBER, 1917.

Appendices.

1. Battle Standing Orders, No. 10.
2. Officers in Action.
3. Detail Camp Narrative.
4. Diary of messages from Brigade H.Q. 8/10/17 to 10/10/17.
5. Operation Order 54 & amendment.
6. Operation Orders issued to Company Commanders.
7. ~~Army Barrage Map~~. *No duplicate copy available.*
8. C.O's account of action of Octr., 9th to 11th.
9. M.O's account of action of Octr., 9th to 11th.
10. Operation Order No. 55 (Relief)
11. Recommendations for Immediate Awards.
12. Battle Casualties by Coys & Ranks - Other Ranks only.
13. Casualties in Brigade.
14. Congratulatory Telegrams.
15. Special Order by C.O.
16. Gallant Conduct.
17. Honours & Awards - M.M's.
18. Honours & Awards, Division - D.S.O's - M.C's - D.C.M's.
19. Honours & Awards, Battalion.
20. Brigade Narrative of Battle of Octr. 9th.
21. Casualty Report of Officers of this Unit for Octr. 1917.
22. Casualty Report of Other Ranks of this Unit for Octr. 1917.

-------o-------

Appendix 1.

SECRET   BATTLE STANDING ORDERS   Copy No.
by
Lieut-Colonel A.S. BATES D.S.O.
Commanding "UNBEND"

1. The following orders published for the prospective operation in August are to be treated as Standing Orders for all operations & will not be republished in subsequent operation orders.
2. CASUALTIES:- Published in Instructions No.1. para.3, with the addition that any wounded NCO or man who is unable to advance or take any further part in the Action, will hand over his ammunition to the nearest soldier.
3. CODE NAMES:- Published in A.O.O.No.2 para.12 with the addition of the code names for other Battalions in the Brigade.
4. COMMUNICATIONS:- Published in O.O. No.1, para.8 & O.O. No.2 para. 17 (a) & (c)
5. CONSOLIDATION:- Published in Instructions No.1,para.6 with the addition that all ranks must be fully aware of the proced
6. COUNTER ATTACK:- Published in Instructions No.1,para.7.
7. ENEMY RUSES:- Published in O.O. No.2 para. 21.
8. ESCORTS:- Published in A.O.O. No.2 paras. 6 & 7.
9. GRENADES:- Published in Instructions No.1. para. 8, modified as may be necessary by altered conditions of warfare.
10. HINTS DURING AN ATTACK:- Published in Instructions No.1. para.13.
11. INFORMATION:- Published in Instructions No.1. para.11 & A.O.O. No.1 para.6
12. LEWIS GUNS:- Published in Instructions No.1 para.5.
13. LOOTING:- Published in A.O.O. No.1 para.8.
14. MESSAGES:- Published in A.O.O. No.2 para.9.
15. MISBEHAVIOUR:- Published in Instructions No.1 para.4
16. MOPPERS UP:- Published in Instructions No.1 para.10 with the addition that moppers up will be found by each Company unless otherwise definitely ordered.
17. NOTICE BOARDS:- Published in A.O.O. No.2 para.5
18. OFFICERS:- Published in A.O.O. No.2 para.11.
19. SIGNALLERS & PIGEON MEN:- Published in A.O.O. No.1 para.11.
20. PRISONERS:- Published in A.O.O. No.1 para.7 & A.O.O. No.2 paras. 6 & 7.
21. SALVAGE:- Published in A.O.O. No.2 para.4.
22. SANDBAGS:- Published in A.O.O. No.2 para.8.
23. STRONG POINTS:- A sketch of a strong point has been circulated to Os.C. Coys. If a strong point has to be constructed without R.E. supervision this pattern is to be adopted.
24. SYNCHRONISATION:- The system recently ordered is to be followed. The subject is one of the highest importance.
25. WHITE FLAGS:- Published in O.O. No.2, para.22

In addition to the following orders:-

26. S.A.A.:- Reference S.S. 143 Part I para.3 Riflebombers & Bombers will carry 75 rounds and not 50 as laid down.
27. RETIRE:- Serious consequences have arisen through the word "RETIRE" having been used by irresponsible people. The use of the word is absolutely forbidden at all times. Anyone making use of the word will be called upon to justify his conduct.
28. ORDERS:- Reference Orders which have been or will be issued in connection with forthcoming operations. Officers receiving copies are responsible that every Officer, NCO or man concerned with any portion of them is clearly warned of what does concern them. It will always be clearly stated at the foot what the exact distribution is. It is often impossible & always inadvisable to issue a large number of copies & the receipt signed by an Officer named in the table of Distribution will be taken to mean that all the necessary extracts have been communicated to all they may concern.

A.S.Bates
Lieut.-Colonel.
3/10/17.   Commanding "U N B E N D".

DISTRIBUTION.

Copy No.1 C.O.	Copy No.2. Adjutant	Copy No.3. 2nd in Command.
4. "A" Coy	5. "B" Coy	6. "C" Coy
7. "D" Coy	8. H.Q.Coy	9. Signalling Offcr
10/12. War Diary	13/14. Spare.	

Appendix 2.

OFFICERS.

The following Officers accompanied the Battalion into action.

Lieut.Colonel A.S.BATES, D.S.O.
Captain and Adjutant J.ROUSE.
Lieut.HOLDSWORTH. Signalling Officer.
Sec.Lieut.G.H.YAPP. Intelligence Officer.

"A" Company.   Captain C.G.STEVENS.
               Lieut.SENIOR.
               Sec.Lieut.BELL.
               Sec.Lieut.GLASS.

"B" Company.   Sec.Lieut.PICKETT.
               Sec.Lieut.TOWNSEND.
               Sec.Lieut.BARLOW.
               Sec.Lieut.BELCHER.

"C" Company.   Captain BENTLEY.
               Lieut.TWEEDY.
               Sec.Lieut.ALLEN.
               Sec.Lieut.HALSALL.

"D" Company.   Captain LAUGHLIN.
               Sec.Lieut.PRESTON.
               Sec.Lieut.BRIDGSTOCK.
               Lieut.TYE.

The following Officers did not go into action

Major WIKE, Second in Command at Corps Reinforcement Camp.
Captain CROUCH. . . . .
Lieut.REID. . . . .

Lieut.THOMPSON. . . . . with Battalion details.
Lieut. ~~HOLDSWORTH~~ MORLEY ..   ..   ..
Quartermaster . . . .
Transport Officer . . . .

Captain HASTINGS. . . . On leave.
Captain GOWLAND " . . . .

Sec.Lieut.HALL. . . . . On a course.
Sec.Lieut.WILSON. . . . .
Sec.Lieut.DUNN. . . . .

Above refers to the action of October 9th to 11th, 1917.

Appendix 3

DETAIL CAMP NARRATIVE.

October 5th.
On debussing the Battalion marched to the FREZENBURG RIDGE arriving there about 8.30 p.m.
At 8.30 p.m. Lieut. THOMPSON was ordered to collect all men for the detail camp, and having done so left with Lieut. MORLEY and 50 O.R. at 9 p.m. He was told to proceed to BRANDHOEK where the camp was said to be situated. The party marched back towards YPRES and were given a lift in empty lorries to BRANDHOEK. On arrival there application was made to the Area Commandant who was unable to give the location of the Brigade deatil camp. A similar application was then made to the Area Commandant at VLAMERTINGHE by other Officers of the Brigade, but with like results. The men were accommodated in an empty hut for the night and early the next morning Officers proceeded to search the area for the camp on both sides of the POPERINGHE - YPRES road. During this search a water cart belonging to the Brigade was met and the position of the camp obtained. The so called camp proved to be a very cramped and swampy field which was used as a horse watering point for all artillery horses in the district. The track to it led through the centre of the camp.
There was no shelter of any kind in the shape of tents or bivouacs and no accommodation for stores etc.
After occupying this ground for 24 hours the Brigade details were moved to better ground, but there was still no shelter although tents had been promised on the scale of 20 per Battalion.

October 7th.
On this date Lieut. THOMPSON was detailed for duty with the Division. No further shelter was obtained for the details during the whole time they were away from the Battalion. The weather throughout the whole period was very rough and wet.
Meanwhile Lieut. MORLEY was despatched by the O i/c Details (Major GELL) on the orders of the Brigade Major 197th.Inf.Bds. up the line to guard what proved to be a dump of 40 duck boards and 1500 sandbags. Four men and his servant went with him. No provisions were made for rationing these men.
This resulted in the Battalion detail camp being left without any Officers except the Transport Officer and Q-M, both of whom had their own work to do.
Lieut. MORLEY'S party was provided with shelter from the weather, not to mention shell fire, by the duck boards and sand bags under it's charge. Had orders been awaited from the usual source to come out with the Battalion this party would have still been there.

The details rejoined the Battalion at the ASYLUM YPRES at 1 p.m. 11/10/17.

DIARY OF MESSAGES

SENT AND RECEIVED TO AND FROM BRIGADE HEADQUARTERS

UNLESS OTHERWISE STATED - FROM 8/10/17 to 10/10/17.

MESSAGES SENT.

No.	Date	Sent	
ASB 1.	8/10	10.5 pm	If I am able to report the Battalion in position by telephone, I will use the code word "MANURE" which will signify that my Battalion is on the tape in attack formation less the posts in advance. I do not expect the Battalion to be in position till, possibly very late owing to the state of the track.
ASB 2.	9/10	3.15 am	Nothing to report.
ASB 3.	"	4.12 am	To 204 M.G.Coy & "A" Coy 2/7th Manch. There are no signs of my Battalion which ought to relieve you & attack at zero. I am hoping it will arrive. Pending other instructions you had better withdraw your men to the tape line at 4.30 am & if we do not attack then return to your trench at 5.40 am
ASB 4.	"	4.26 am	To O.C. "E" Coy, 2/7th Manch. For your information the barrage comes down at 5.20 am If you have not received any instructions you must withdraw your men to the tape line about 150 yards in rear by 5 am at latest. Keep a good lookout. If the 2/9th Manchesters do not attack you must resume your trench positions at 5.40 am. This must NOT be referred to on the telephone.
ASB 5.	"	6.5 am	No action took place on BULL front.

MESSAGES RECEIVED

No.	Date	Recd.	
BM761	Undated	–	On "X" day the artillery barrage will stop at Zero plus 214. On "Y" day a barrage will be put down at 4.45 am & continue till zero plus 33.

MESSAGES RECEIVED

No.	Date	Recd	
BM767	9/10	7 am 10/10	Push your Battn. on as units arrive & form strong fighting patrols & clear up the country - keeping touch between Australians & 198 I.B. You personally remain in front line & order other Bns of the Bde forward with all possible despatch. If no one else is available 2/7th Manchesters at present in front & support line may be of use.

MESSAGES SENT

No.	Date	Sent	
SB 6.	9/10	8.45 am	Your BM 767 received at 7 am. I found disjointed bodies of all Battalions arriving which were on their own initiative pushing on fast. I waited till it appeared no more troops were arriving & followed them up to get information. Think final objective has been occupied but dificult to ascertain strength of troops. Have sent all troops forward & am not attempting to consolidate red line. Will send reports as soon as runners are collected. Everybody very cheery & German prisoners coming in in large numbers.
SB 7	"	9.35am	Slight counterattack without artillery fire satisfactorily dealt with opposite centre of Brigade front. 2/6th L.F. does not appear to have turned up. No L.T.M.B's guns seen yet. 204 M.G.C. will have 4 guns about HILLSIDE in a couple of hours time for harassing fire on North of Railway. Am moving to AUGUSTUS dugouts.

MESSAGES SENT

No.	Date	Sent	
ASB 8	9/10	11.6 am	Nest of machine guns in DEADLINE COPSE on the Railway still holding out. I cannot get into touch with L.T.M.B. Am arranging to deal with it with rifle grenades. 1 Coy 2/6th has arrived. Have moved my HQ from AUGUSTUS DUGOUTS to dugouts immediately West of CEMETERY on Railway embankment & can get you visually if you will observe. Adjutant wounded.
ASB 9	"	12.35 pm	Cannot get touch on left with 198 Inf. Bde - men from their units are with us. Casualties believed slight but there must be a large number of men who never reached the tape line. I gather guides did not guide units right to the jumping off tape, but left them; the tape having been broken owing to the high wind made progress very difficult. Gunner Liason Officer has arrived. Still no signs of L.T.M.B. Hear Col. Roberts slightly wounded. No signs of my M.O. Intelligence Officer or carrying party. Have not seen either C.O. of 2/7th or 2/6th. Men very bucked but quite tired after last night.
ASB 10	"	1.6 pm	Your message received. All available men are sent up at once. Will SAA & water be sent to DASH crossing. I do not want to spare carrying parties longer away from the line than necessary.

MESSAGES RECEIVED

No.	Date Recd		
	9/10	11.45pm	From O.C."D" Coy"Final objective reached not yet in touch with 198 or Australians."
	Undated	1 p.m.	From E.G.C. Final objective captured. Push up ammunition via Railway track & any available men. S.A.A. can be sent up in bandoliers - it is being asked for.

MESSAGES SENT

No.	Date	Sent	
ASB 10 (cont)	9/10	1.6 pm	Heavy gunner liason officer has reported. *all in liaison by Suffolk*
ASB 11	"	3.5 pm	Unless otherwise ordered all troops will move forward to the final objective at 4.30 pm. An 18 pounder protective barrage will come down at that hour 200 yds beyond the final objective. It is essential that the line is reached & held at all costs. The barrage will last for 20 minutes. All men will be pushed forward & consolidation will be carried out in depth. Divisional Commander sends his congratulations to all ranks on their success.
ASB 12	"	3.45 pm	Orders have been issued as enclosed - Many thanks, on behalf of all ranks participating, for congratulations. Seldom I suppose has any attack been carried out under less favourable conditions.

MESSAGES RECEIVED.

No.	Date	Recd	
BM 776	9/10	3.40 pm	Hearty congratulations on the success But ALL men available & especially the 2/7th L.F. will be pushed forward at once to the final objective & hold it at all costs. Very urgent. The Divisnl commander adds his congratulations to all ranks on their splendid success.

MESSAGES SENT

No.	Date	Sent	
ASB 13	9/10	4.25 pm	Since writing previous message find that sniping & M.G. fire from left has driven line back to red line - 198th Bde does not appear to be assisting - my numbers are dwindling. Am trying to arrange get back to final objective at 5.15 with different artillery arrangements but fear even if successful that lack of co-operation on left & casualties will make holding on difficult.
ASB 14	"	11.20 pm	At between 5.45 & 5.30 pm at Bn.H.Q. behind the cemetery a stream of men was seen withdrawing on our left. The Adjutant, Lt.Holdsworth & myself immediately set out to endeavour to stay the rot. I regret to say this took some time but it was finally overcome & all men were sent back. Lt.Col.HOBBINS was in the red line at the time at my request & made every effort there to keep the men at their posts which they were leaving on the right of the line. He was not successful although he took extreme measures. I attribute this lack of discipline to:- 1. The mixture of the 3 units of the Brigade which took part in the action. Officers seldom commanded their own men. 2. The recent inclusion on the eve of action of drafts of apparently inexperienced men of a Labour Battalion. 3. The method of approach to the trenches last night when the guides did not lead the columns to the Assembly tape.

MESSAGES RECEIVED.

No.	Date Sent	

MESSAGES SENT

No.	Date	Sent
SB 14 (cont).	9/10	11.20 pm

4. The most uncomfortable circumstances of the 3 nights prior to the night of Assembly which did not add to moral.
Seeing how well the 3 Battalions did in attacking this morning, I feel that if the circumstances had been normal, the Brigade would have done itself credit. The line now held runs through Bn.H.Q. W.of the Cemetery. I apologise for delay in rendering this report but my Hdqrs shared with 202 MGC & Col. HOBBINS - situated at D.16.d.6.4. received 2 direct hits just outside the door causing 8 casualties which required attention inside the dugout. Reorganisation will not be possible tomorrow as the line is under observation & the enemy M.Gs are very active. No water has so far as I know arrived.

MESSAGES RECEIVED

No.	Date	Recd. Rank.
—	10/10	6.25 am

As soon as possible report ans.
1. If we hold the red line.
2. If we are in touch with 198 Bde on our left.
3. If 198 Bde are holding the red line.
4. If we have any troops in advance of the red line.
Report fully including action taken during action during the night. Divnl. Commander pressing for a reply.

| 1.04 | 9/10 | 6.40 am |

Corps Commander directs that all ground gained be retained & that foremost posts be line of resistance. Organize in depth at once & gain touch with units on flanks.

MESSAGES SENT

No.	Date Sent.		
ASB 15	1/10 7.5 am	Officers casualties unofficial. Killed. Captain Stevens. Wounded. Capt.Laughlin, Captn.Rouse (at duty) Lieut.Pickett; 2/Lt. Allen; Captn.Bentley; Lt. Tweedy; Lts.Senior & Tye; 2/Lt Glass; 2/Lt.Belcher; 2/Lt. Bridgstock. Known to be unwounded:- Self, Lt Holdsworth; Lt.Yapp; Lt.Bell; M.O. 2/Lt.Preston Three unaccounted for.		

ASB 16	1/10 7.10am	Message dated 2.50 am this morning received at 6.30 am Replies so far as can be made at present.
		  1. No.
		  4. No.
		  2 &3. Reports not yet in - will be sent as soon as received.
		My ASB 14 gives details of what happened when the Bde Major was here. The Germans are apparently in the Red line. We hold posts on East of CEMETERY.
		Your I.O.4 dated 4.35 pm 9th inst., received 6.40 am this morning.
		Water, 30 tins, just received 7 am, with Capt. Potter.
		Water, 20 tins, just received 7.6 am under 2/Lt. HERO, 2/7th		

MESSAGES RECEIVED

No.	Date Recd.	
B.O.1 10/10	7.44	From B.G.C. 198th Bde are sending two companies to close gap between 197 & 198 & protect 197 flank.
I.O.5 "	7.44	From B.G.C. Get touch with 5 Australians on your right & report when effected.

MESSAGES SENT

No.	Date Sent	
ASB 17	10/10 9.40 am	B.O.1 received 7.45 am have seen no traces of troops referred to. I.O.5 received 7.44 am have got int got into touch with 45 Bn 12 Bde 4 GW Australians who are now in line on our right about red line. BM 779 received 9.22 am today. Capt.POTTER has arrived. Cannot regain RED LINE on left owing to M.G. & sniping 198th Bde are not there -our line curves back from HILLS IDE FM to AUGUSTUS dugouts.

MESSAGES RECEIVED

No.	Date Rec'd	
BM 779	9/10 9.22 am	By daylight 10 Oct. you will be firmly established in the Red Line. With such troops of the Brigade as you have at your disposal. Captn POTTER is bringing up rations, water & solidified alcohol & SAA tonight to Bde Forward Station (where Lt. BRABY is) He & 70 O.R. & 2 other officers will remain up in the line under your orders. They will be available for stopping a counter attack & should man a definite line. RED LINE position will be established by sending out a succession of strong fighting p troops When RED LINE is established patrols will be pushed forward to find if BLUE LINE is held by the enemy. Captn.POTTER will act as your staff Officer.
BM 91	10/10 1.10 pm	Goddard returned. Your front line will be as Divisional Commander wishes provided Chesney fills gap to right of Augustus as he was directed to do by your last night. See that he does this at once & report completion. Col.Anderton is wounded. Capt.POTTER will take charge of 6th L.F. who are behind Capt. Chesney. Chesney was seen by Goddard

MESSAGES SENT

No.	Date	Sent	
ASB 101	10/10	5.30 pm	Line is outlined is held am in touch with Australians 198th Inf.Bde has not got into touch with me yet.
ASB 20	"	5.40 pm	Reference position ordered for Col. HOBBINS to put 600 men. It is quite open & under usual barrage line. I am of opinion very strongly that the men will be absolutely useless if required. We have been under continual harassing fire all day - casualties heavy, in fact I doubt our having 600 O.R. with Brigade.

MESSAGES RECEIVED

No.	Date	Recd.	
BM 91 (cont)	10/10	1.10 pm	on trench flanking on cemetery. Extending 45 degrees West of North.
BM 790	"	3.15 pm	The exact line which the Divisional Commander has ordered to be established is from railway crossing at D.17.b.30.28 - just W. of HILLSIDE FARM - AUGUSTUS at D.11.c.4.1. Reports already received state.we are already on or a part of this line - this is to be verified. Troops in front of the line will not be withdrawn but any front line posts in rear will be pished forward on to it. 3rd Aust. Div. report their left at D.17.b. 30.28 Touch is to be maintained with them 198 Inf. Bde are patrolling to obtain touch with this Bde every assistance will be given Report as soon as possible that above line is in our hands & that our right is in touch with the Australians. Report also when 198th I.B. have established touch with you.

APPENDIX S.

SECRET

197th INFANTRY BRIGADE OPERATION ORDER.
No. 54

Copy No. 7

Reference Edition 1A PASSCHENDAELE, 1/10,000   8/10/17.

1. INTENTION.   In conjunction with 2nd Australian Division on the Right and 49th Division on the Left, 66th Division will attack on "X" day. 197th Inf. Bde. on the Right, 198th Inf. Bde on the Left, 199th Inf. Bde Divisional Reserve. The two attacking Brigades relieving 199th Inf. Bde in the Line. The 199th Inf. Bde assembling in the present support position. Zero hour will be notified later.

2. BOUNDARIES.   On the Right, the YPRES - ROULERS railway exclusive to 66th Division.
On the Left D.10.c.7.5.; D.10.b.55.00: the RAVEBEEK.

3. OBJECTIVES.
(a) <u>First Objective</u>:- (RED LINE) D.17.b.63.37; D.17.b.35.75; HEINE HOUSE inclusive, AUGUSTUS WOOD inclusive; WATERFIELDS inclusive; D.10.b.60.05.

(b) <u>Final Objective</u>:-(BLUE LINE) D.18.b.05.85; VIENNA COT inclusive; D.12.a.45.00; D.12.a.30.20; D.12.a.0.4; HAALEN CORSE inclusive; D.11.a.9.9.

(c) Posts will be established approximately 100 yards in front of the Final Objective (BLUE LINE).

4. BRIGADE DIVIDING LINE   Road junction D.16.b.60.65 inclusive to 197th Inf. Bde. Group of dug-outs about the TUS of AUGUSTUS inclusive to 197th Inf. Bde DECK WOOD inclusive to 198th Inf. Bde.,
197th Inf. Bde will direct. 198th Inf. Bde will be prepared to fill any gap on the Right caused by the 197th Bde having to extend their front to keep on the YPRES-ROULERS railway.

5. BARRAGES.
(a) The <u>opening barrage Zero</u> to Zero plus 4 will be on a straight line D.17.a.6.0; D.10.c.93.67.
The Infantry tape line will be roughly 150 yards in rear of this line.
Infantry posts in advance of the Tape line being drawn to it before Zero.

(b) The moving barrage will be at the rate of 100 yards in 6 minutes.

(c) The RED and BLUE protective barrages are placed approximately 200 yards in advance of the objectives to be consolidated. All enemy strong points short of the protective barrage will be dealt with by the Infantry.

(d) The RED protective barrage will be stationery for one hour and will lift at Zero plus 106.

(e) As a signal to show when the barrage has become a protective barrage, a proportion of Smoke shell will be used.

(f) The barrage is divided into A,B,C, D & E.
The A barrage is an 18-pr barrage and this barrage only concerns the Infantry and their advance is controlled by it.

-2-

6. ACTION OF 197th INF. BDE.

The 3/5th Lan. Fus., attacking on a 4 Coy front of 1 platoon each Coy., will capture the 1st (RED) objective.

(2) The 2/6th Lan. Fus., and 2/8th on Left and 2/8th Lan. Fus., on right will closely support 3/5th Lan. Fus., - leading line 15 yards behind rear of 3/5th Lan. Fus., - and will capture the final (BLUE) objective; each Battalion attacking on a 2 Coy front of 2 Platoons each Coy.
Dividing line between Battalions HILLSIDE FARM - D.12.c.57.54.

(3) 2/7th Lan. Fus., will be in RESERVE and will cross 1st. objective at Zero plus 100.
1 Coy will be detailed to support closely RIGHT BATTALION (2/8th Lan. Fus.,) and will be responsible for capture of VIENNA COT.
Remainder of Battalion will thicken line of 2/8th Lan. Fus., where necessary owing to extension of front and will be prepared to repel counter attacks.

(4) 202 M.G. Coy will act under direct orders of the Brigade.
4 M.G's will move behind 2/6th Lan. Fus., and 2/8th Lan. Fus., and will establish themselves on RED (1st) objective and be prepared to assist the advance of Division on the Left.
4 M.G's will move with RESERVE battalion and will take up positions behind final objective to assist in repelling counter-attacks.

(5) 197th L.T.M.Battery.

2 guns with 39 rounds per gun will act as follows:-

(a) At Zero minus 120 to be in position to bombard cemetery at D.17.a.6.2. but not to open fire without orders from O.C. Right Company, 3/5th Lan. Fus.,

(b) At Zero plus 100 to report to O.C. 2/8th Lan. Fus., in RED objective.

7. ASSEMBLY.

On W/X night the 3/5th Lan. Fus. will relieve the 2/7th MANCHESTER REGT. in the line from RAILWAY to BDE BOUNDARY. Relief to commence as soon as possible after dark.
Battalion will be disposed along the Tape line, but posts in front will be held until withdrawn silently at Zero minus 60.

2 guns L.T.M.Battery will follow 3/5th Lan. Fus.,
2/6th Lan. Fus., will follow   3/5th Lan. Fus.,
2/8th Lan. Fus.,   "   "   2/6th Lan. Fus.,
2/7th Lan. Fus.,   "   "   2/8th Lan. Fus.,

All troops will be in position by Zero minus 120.

8. CONSOLIDATION.

The captured positions will be consolidated in depth and in such a manner as to form a good starting line for further operations.

9. COMMUNICATIONS. Instructions will be issued later

-3-

10. CONTACT AEROPLANES.

(a) 21st Squadron R.F.C. will furnish contact aeroplanes They are marked as follows, on both sides of the fusilage

    Large "A" in white.
    Dumbell painted white.

also one black streamer on each lower plane.

(b) Flares will be red and not more than one will be lit at the same time in the same place. They will be lit at the bottom of trenches or shell holes.
2 per man will be carried.
Only troops in the most advanced line will light flares.

(c) Aeroplanes will call for flares as follows:-

on RED LINE at Zero plus 60 minutes.
on BLUE LINE at Zero plus 170 minutes.
and will drop position map at D.H.Q. Dropping Station.

11. S.O.S.

Signal for Second Army front is,
Rifle Grenade signal parachute, three lights RED over GREEN over YELLOW.
At least 16 per company will be carried.

12. VERY PISTOLS.

Very Pistols 1" and at least 6 rounds ammunition will be carried; 1 pistol per platoon.

13. DUMPS.

A Brigade advanced dump will be formed at SPRINGFIELD D.16.c.1.1. to contain water, S.A.A., R.E. material, grenades, very lights S.O.S. rockets.

For position of other dumps, Dressing Stations, Battle Stragglers posts, etc., etc. see 66th Division Administrative Notes issued to units herewith.

14. PRISONERS OF WAR.

Will be sent to advanced Divisional post HILL COT 1.5.a. under an escort not exceeding 10% of the number of prisoners.

15. R.A.P.

For RIGHT sector is ALMA D.22.a.2.4.

16. CARRYING PARTIES.

Battalions will find their own ration parties. 3/5th Lan. Fus., will be prepared to act as carriers to forward positions after final objective has been obtained.

17. SYNCHRONISATION OF WATCHES.

Will take place at Brigade H.Q. D.26.a.Central at 2 p.m. 8th October and at advanced Brigade H.Q. at SPRINGFIELD, at 12 M/N 8/9th October.

18.   Advanced Brigade H.Q. will be at SPRINGFIELD DUG-OUTS D.16.c.11

19.   Units will report their arrival at position of assembly to advanced Brigade H.Q.

20.   A C K N O W L E D G E.

(sgd) J.M.MONK. Captn.
Brigade Major.,
197th Infantry Brigade

Issued at 5.0 a.m.

DISTRIBUTION

Copy No.:-
1 66th Division 'G'
2 66th Division 'G'
3 66th Division 'Q'
4 E.G.C.
5 Staff Captain
6 Bde Sig. Officer
7 3/5th Lan. Fus.,
8 2/6th Lan. Fus.,
9 2/7th Lan. Fus.,
10 2/8th Lan. Fus.,
11 202 M.G.Coy

Copy No. 12 197th L.T.M.Bty.
13 198th Inf. Bde.,
14 199th Inf. Bde.,
15 Art. Liason Officer.
16 11 Aus. F.O.R.E.
17 2nd Anzac Div.
18 147th Inf. Bde.
19 Div. Art. 3rd Aus. Div.
20 2/3rd Field Amb.
21 War Diary.
22 War Diary.
23 F I L E.

4 Battalions.　　　　　　　　　　　　　　　　　　　B.M. 755.
　　　　　　　　　　　　　　　　　　　　　　　　　　8.10.17.

Para. 7 O.O. 54 (order of march) is amended as follows:-

1. Tracing of tracks to be used as issued herewith for placing over GRAVENSTAFEL Sheet.

2. Lt. NORTON 11 Aust. F.C.R.E. will report to H.Q. 3/5th L.F. at 6 p.m. to-day and guide them up to Tape Line via JACK TAPE.

3. 197th L.T.M.B. will closely follow 3/5th L.F.

4. 2/8th to follow L.T.M. Bty.

5. 2/6th to follow 2/8th L.F. to Track junction and thence along JILL TRACK.

6. 2/7 L.F. follow 2/6 L.F. to Track junction and thence along JACK TRACK.

7. A Sgt from 11 F.C.R.E. (Aust) will report to LOW FARM H.Q. 2/6 L.F. at 7 p.m. to guide Bn along JILL TRACK.

8. Tracks will be marked by single tape thigh high - notice boards - and guides will carry luminous discs.

9. Men going to trenches take precedence of men coming from trenches who will be kept off the tracks and will on no account be allowed to break the up-going column.

10. Australian Traffic control men (shoulder patch oval purple with white border) will be at all doubtful places.

11. PACE DEAD SLOW.

12. TAPE LINES
　　　　for assembly positions will be put out tonight by 11 F.C.R.E. (Lt. MATTERS)

　A. For 3/5th L.F. a tape just behind present front line - tape marked with STRING TAILS.

　B. For 2/6 and 2/8 L.F. a Tape 130 yds behind front tape PLAIN TAPE will be used.

　C. A LEFT BOUNDARY TAPE marked with TAPE TAILS will also be put out.

　D. 1 Officer and 1 O.R. from each Bn will report to these H.Q. to-day at 2.45 p.m. to proceed with the Taping Officer to the position of assembly and be ready to guide their Battns into position on arrival.

　　　　　　　　　　　　　　　　　　　　(sgd) J. M. MONK, Captn.
197th I.B.　　　　　　　　　　　　　　　　Brigade Major.,
11.20 a.m.

APPENDIX 6.

Operation Orders issued to Company Commanders.

(Written on 3 sheets of message pad by the C.O.)

A.S.B.1. — 8/10/17 —— Reference PASSCHENDAELE sheet 1/10,900.

1. The 66th. Division will attack and capture the BLUE line, final objective, tomorrow.
   The 197th. Inf.Bde. will be on the right of the Div. with the 198th. Inf.Bde. on it's left. The 199th. Inf.Bde will be in Div. reserve. Australian troops will be attacking to the right of the 66th. Div.

2. The 3/5th. LAN.FUS. will take over the front line this evening from the 2/7th. MANCHESTERS from the YPRES ROULERS railway at about the A of DABBLE AVE on the right to the R of HAMBURG on the left, a distance of 600 yds.
   The 2/6th.L.F. on the left and 2/8th.L.F. on the right will leapfrog the Battalion and the 2/7th.L.F. will be in Brigade reserve.
   The 2/9th.MANCHESTERS will attack on the left of the 3/5th.L.F. (they wear yellow squares.) Post will be taken over as held but will be withdrawn at ZERO minus 1 hour. The remainder of the Battalion will assume attack formation on going into the line. "A", "B", "C" and "D" Companies from right to left, each Company in 2 lines at 15 yds. distance.
   The Battalion frontage is 600 yds for the attack. This will be taped. The right id bounded by the railway. The left by a line running 80 degrees magnetic from the G of HAMBURG to the H of HEINE HOUSE. The railway is exclusive to the Battalion.
   All movements in the line and behind it must be done without any noise or flashing of lamps which would indicate fresh troops being in the line.

3. ZERO hour will be notified later. (N.B. it was 5.20 a.m.)

4. The 3/5th.L.F. will advance at ZERO and will capture the first objective, the red line, which runs from the E of HEINE HOUSE to the EAST of the 3 concrete dugouts at HILLSIDE FM to the railway 175 yds EAST of the HALT at DEFY CROSSING.

5. The barrage will come down at ZERO 150 yds in front of the line and will remain there for 4 minutes. It will move thence at 100 yds. in 6 minutes and will cross the red line about ZERO plus 30 minutes. It will become a standing barrage 200 yds in front of the red line from ZERO plus 46 minutes to ZERO plus 106 minutes. Os.C.Coys will push out troops beyond the red line close up to the barrage until the 2/6th.L.F. and 2/8th.L.F. have come through and taken up their positions for the further advance when the troops pushed out can be withdrawn. The special role of these troops is to clear all ground up to within 40 yds of the barrage to facilitate the advance of the leapfrogging Battalions.

6. O.C."A" Coy. will pay special attention to the CEMETERY which must be rushed. The 2/8th.L.F. have been instructed to be ready to assist and 2 Stokes mortars will be available if required, but rush tactics will probably prove sufficient.

7. After capturing the red line each Company will construct 2 cunettes each in the front line, also 2 in the second line about 35 yds. in rear behind the intervals between those in the front line. In addition "B" and "D" Coys. will each construct a strong point of the sealed pattern if possible out of direct observation of the enemy on the reverse side of a slope close in rear of the line of cunettes.

8. Flares will be lit singly and not in groups of 3 when called for.

9. The greatest vigilance must be exercised after taking over the line and all Coys. will patrol carefully up to ZERO minus 1 hour.

10. When Coys. are in position, less advanced posts, reports will be sent at once to Battalion H.Qrs.

11. These orders will be destroyed prior to ZERO hour.

APPENDIX 8.

Subject. Action of October 9th - 11th. 1917.

Headquarters,
　197th. Infantry Brigade.

Reference Message map No.14 1/10,000.

1. Attached is a diary of messages sent and received to and from Brigade unless otherwise stated. The following notes are in amplification of it.

2. I went up on the afternoon of Oct.8th with Lt.HOLDSWORTH in an endeavour to see the ground by daylight. I could not get into touch with the H.Qrs. of the 2/7th.MANCHESTERS whom, prior to the attack, I was to relieve and finally took up my position in a shelter occupied by the 204 M.G.Coy. (Lt.WALLSGROVE) at the R in HAMBURG. This was close to Advanced Brigade Report Centre. Finding no troops of either this Brigade or the 198th. in position at 5 a.m. I left Lt.PRESTON at the head of JACK TRACK to report to me the moment any troops began to arrive. Just before ZERO I sent a telephone message to you that no troops had reached the tape line. My further action is set out in the copies of messages attached.

3. When I arrived at the tape line soon after 7 a.m. prisoners were on their way down unescorted and with every appearance of being beaten men. I feel sure that, with adequate support on the flanks, the Brigade could have held on to the BLUE line.

4. I never got into touch with the 198th. Inf. Bde. during the two days. I was in touch with the AUSTRALIANS across the cutting at the HALT and this was confirmed to me by the G.S.O.3 of their Division who visited me on the afternoon of the 10th.
I never saw any L.T.M. during the two days.
The 202 M.G.Coy did excellent work.

5. In the counter attack on the 9th. afternoon we, undoubtedly, killed a lot of Germans. One Company estimates that there were 75 - 100 bodies in front of them which were collected by the enemy under a Red cross flag on the afternoon of the 10th.

6. Enemy aeroplanes were very active on the morning of the 10th. as many as 16 being low in the air at once over our lines.

7. Early on the 10th. the enemy had the impudence to send over a note "Will you come over prisoners, we don't shoot". This was returned and the Sergeant taking it was instructed to try and find out what the enemy's dispositions were. He reported that they appeared to be entrenched about 150 yds in front, in strength probably less than our own. Neighbouring troops were warned in case the message was a ruse.

8. At about 9.30 p.m. 10th. two prisoners who were captured reported 2 Regiments to be lying in a copse to the S.E. across the road expecting an attack by us, but with no intention of attacking themselves. This report was sent down to me but never reached me.

9. Bombs were used as by night the enemy was able to creep from shell hole to shell hole without being seen.

10. I regret these notes are disjointed but my view of the Brigade front was very limited.

14/10/17

Lieut.Colonel,
Commanding 3/5th.LAN.FUS.

APPENDIX 9

MEDICAL OFFICER'S REPORT.

I pushed off from the FREZENBURG Ridge at about 7 p.m. on the evening of the 8th.Oct. in rear of the Battalion with a party carrying stretchers and medical stores. The Battalion was in single file, ploughing through mud. I had gone about 500 yds when an urgent call for the M.O. was passed down the line. I went forward to investigate, hurrying past the long winding column and collecting most of the FREZENBURG Ridge on the way, to find an exhausted soldier in a shell hole. I gave him some advice and halted there while the Battalion filed past. When my carrying party hove in sight I fell in line again. Had only proceeded about 50 yds further when another urgent message was received for the M.O. Nothing doing. I eventually overtook this second casualty, a L/Cpl stuck in the mud. My carrying party now proceeded to collapse and slowly settle down into the mud during the next 200 yds. I watched them whilst doing some heavy thinking. I decided to jettison the blankets & such kit as could be most conveniently spared. Did so. Finally got the carrying party on it's feet again, pushed on and found the Battn was out of sight. Although missing their cheery countenances and bright chatty conversation about the weather and mud I was greatly sustained by the thought that no more urgent messages were likely to get through for the M.O. We fought our way along "F" track slowly with the aid of an electric torch, following the tape, where it existed and looking for whitened props where it did not. (N.B. Why does somebody lay a tape across large shell holes containing water instead of round them?) Here I encountered Lt.TWEEDY and his runner who were looking for us and incidentally the track. Pushed on with a gentle rain falling. The carrying party were by this time

(1.) thoroughly tired and wet. Encountered the 2/6th. after some time and attempted to pass them on the track. Being numerically stronger they were able to hold the track so we left it and pushed up alongside until we passed all but the leading half company and reached a bridge crossing a large patch of water. Here we couldn't butt in for some considerable time but eventually succeeded and crossed in a gap between two companies. We overtook the 2/6th again when we came to the ZONNEBEKE road and were held up once more

(2.) where the track leaves the road. Here it was that the 2/7th. forged ahead and passed through the 2/6th, while we kept out of the way till the combatant troops had passed. Capt.HIGGINSON the M.O. of the 2/6th. appeared on the scene and volunteered to show me a way up the ZONNEBEKE road. He brought up his stretcher bearers and both parties proceeded up the ZONNEBEKE road and so got ahead of the 2/6th

(3.) on JACK track. We passed the 2/6th. apparently lining a ridge and pushed on up the track. Here we found some casualties and left Captain HIGGINSON and his bearers to attend to them and evacuate them, as he was then in advance of his own Unit.

(4.) I next saw the Adjutant on the railway and made my way across to him dodging crumps on the track. Ascertained that the "pillbox" on the railway was not Battalion H.Qrs and decided to form my R.A.P. there. Did so. The pillbox consisted of 2 strong dugouts not connected and each having a 2 foot square door near the floor on the HUN side. My Orderly explored these and subsequently they accommodated such slightly wounded cases as could crawl in to them. There was a lean to of wood against the HUN side of the pill box about 9 foot square feet floor space and on the British side was a narrow passage about 6 feet long by 5½ feet high and 2 feet wide. In these two places all the wounded were attended to. Actual protection on the German side was afforded by a mackintosh sheet but, fortunately, their shells came from the right and hit the end of the dugout. We had several direct hits which inconvenienced us by extinguishing the candles on each occasion. The lean to sustained a direct hit on the morning of relief and it is feared that the relieving M.O. has even less accommodation than I had. Stretcher cases could not be put under any cover. The M.O. 2/8th.L.F. estab-

(5.) lished his R.A.P. about 200 yds. in front and on the North of the railway and so out of the track of the wounded. This he closed on the morning of the 10th. The M.O. of the 2/6th. was hit and his relief appeared on the afternoon of the 10th. The M.O. of the 2/7th.

- 2 -

first appeared at the same time. They both sat in the dugout till
(6) night fall and then went up to Battalion H.Qrs. and were relieved
the same night. Cases were dressed in the open outside the pill box
in a shell hole. A very large number were so treated. On the first
(7) day the wounded were evacuated to an Australian dressing station
further down the railway, but no stretchers could be obtained to
replace ours. The Field Ambulance bearer sub-division did not get
into touch with ours until the 10th. when my Orderly Sergt. (Sergt.
(8) SUMMERSGILL) went down to the bearer post in charge of Capt. BERRY
and returned with 7 squads, coming up with them through a heavy
barrage to reach the R.A.P. On the night of the 9th. all cases
were evacuated. On the 10th. the bearer squads, above mentioned,
made 1 journey down but did not reappear so that at night some
cases were still at the R.A.P. The enemy shelled heavily during the
10th. from about 2 p.m. till 10 p.m. and again from midnight till
3 a.m. on the 11th. He obtained several direct hits on the end of
the pill box and unfortunately killed one or two of the wounded
lying outside.
(9) The H.Qrs. of the 2/8th., were in a shell hole opposite the R.A.P.
and stragglers persisted in collecting outside those H.Qrs and my
Aid post which constantly needed pushing on. A policeman would be
useful at the R.A.P. to move on loiterers.

My stretcher bearers worked magnificently. Six were killed and 4
wounded out of 16, and the medical orderlies worked very well.
I was impressed by the immense difficulty of transporting wounded
in the mud, and by the cheeriness and pluck of the wounded also by
the number of men who lost their false teeth.

I was relieved on the evening of the 10th./11th. and left the Aid
post at 6 a.m. on the 11th. arriving at the ASYLUM at YPRES about
9.30 a.m. (where I ought to have been admitted!)

H.M.Sandipow Capt R.A.M.C.
M.O. 3/5 Lon. Fus.

References to Trench Map ZONNEBEKE 28 N.E.1. Edition 7 A. 1/10,000

(1) Before reaching the ZONNEBEKE road.
(2) About on the ZONNEBEKE road.
(3) From abot D.21.c.4.1 round to D.21.c.5.7.
(4) About D.22.b.45.93.
(5) D.16.d.3.1.
(6) D.16.d.66.45.
(7) Somewhere in ZONNEBEKE.
(8) D.26.b.7.4.
(9) D.22.b.38.95.

APPENDIX 10

SECRET
Copy No.1.

OPERATION ORDER No. 55

3/5th Lan. Fus.,   B.M. 789   10.10.17.

1. The 197th Inf. Bde will be relieved in the line on night 10/11 Oct., by 11th Aust. Inf. Bde and will proceed to WINNEZEELE AREA by Bus from point West of YPRES, head of column at H.5.c.0.4. facing West at about 2 p.m. 11th Octr.,

2. The 44th Aust. Inf. Bn will relieve the FRONT LINE troops of the 197th Inf. Bde and the 43rd A.I. Bn the SUPPORT Troops.

3. Lieut.-Col. BATES D.S.O. will make all arrangements for the relief.

4. Lieut.-Col HOBBINS & Captn POTTER, Lt DICKINSON and 3 other Officers will remain behind with 600 O.R. from 2/6th L.F. and 2/7th L.F. and men of carrying party sent up last night and take up a position on RESERVE on approximate LINE DARING CROSSING - BEECHAM. This party under Col. HOBBINS will leave for the embussing point about 8 a.m. 11 Oct., withdrawing by small parties without further orders.

5. No troops of the 197th I.B. will withdraw tonight until relieved by the Australians and all parties

6. All parties will be marched back under an officer or NCO irrespective of their units.

7. Advance parties from 11 Aust. I.B. will report to Col. BATES to-day and arrange for guides.

8. Troops will not march at more than 1½ miles an hour and the Bde will assemble on main YPRES - VLAMERTINGHE road alongside the ASYLUM just West of YPRES.

9. All spare S.A.A. in boxes and bandoliers over and above 120 rounds per man will be handed over to incoming Bns. Also all bombs, flares, rifle grenades will be handed over. S.O.S. rockets will be personally handed over to officers. All shovels will be handed over.

10. EMPTY PETROL TINS will be invariably brought out and dumped at old Bde H.Q. at V.R. Dugout.

11. The 202 M.G. Coy will be relieved by the 11th Aust. M.G. Coy under arrangements to be made mutually.

12. All commanders who may have any stokes mortars or S.M. personnel will then belonging to the 197th L.T.M. Bty will bring them with them.

13. L.G. limbers will be on the YPRES - ZONNEBEKE road as far east as possible up to old Bde H.Q. (V.R. Dugout)

14. Completion of reliefs will be reported by the following.
    Lt.Col BATES FOR front and support lines troops.
    Lt.Col HOBBINS FOR Reserve troops.
    O.C. 202 M.G. and 197th L.T.M. Bty for their respective units.
Report to present H.Q. at LEVI HOUSE.

15. Transport will move on 11th Octr., to WINNEZEELE via POPERINGHE road junction L.13.d.6.0.- road junction K.5.b.0.9 - WATOE. Transport MUST halt for at least one hour about midday - but will not enter POPERINGHE till 12 noon.

16. At the ASYLUM there will be tea & biscuits for the troops & rations for the 11th at the embussing point.

17. Every man must know his destination and every effort will be made to bring along all stragglers.

18. ACKNOWLEDGE.

197th I.B.
1.55 p.m.
(sgd) J.M. MONK, Captn.
Brigade Major.,

Appendix II

APPENDIX

LIST OF NAMES OF OFFICERS AND OTHER RANKS
SUBMITTED TO BRIGADE FOR GALLANTRY AND
GOOD CONDUCT DURING THE OPERATIONS.

Captain HUGH ARTHUR SANDIFORD. R.A.M.C. attached

Captain C.W. LAUGHLIN.

Captain F.M. BENTLEY.

Lieut. J.A. HOLDSWORTH.

Sec. Lieut. S. BELCHER.

203252 Pte. J. ANYON.

235638 L/C. E. EDMONDSON.

201311 Sergt. H. SUMMERSGILL.

202654 L/C. E. KELSALL.

204495 Pte. T. HALL.

201952 Pte. J. O'HARA.

201978 Pte. E. EGERTON.

17296 L/C. J.H. POWER.

235312 Pte. R.W. JAMES.

201976 L/Sgt. A. DUXBURY.

3/18091 Pte. C. PICKTON.

200885 Pte. F. TOOLE.

202015 Cpl. W.J. SHARP.   203405 Pte. JOHN HOLT.

202118 Pte. T. FLETCHER.   36518 Pte. JOHN FREDERICK HERTWICK.

203219 Pte. W. CARMAN.

204370 Pte. G. THOMAS.   2/37809 Sergt. HARRY NICHOLS.

201207 Sergt. T. ENTWISTLE.   39105 Pte. PERCY UPHILL.

[signature]

Lieut. Colonel,
Commanding 3/5th. LAN. FUS.

Appendix 12

BATTLE CASUALTIES BY COMPANIES AND RANKS. OTHER RANKS ONLY.

Corrected up to 6 p.m. 16/10/17

	KILLED					WOUNDED						MISSING					TOTALS	
	Sgts	L/Sgts	Corporals	L/Cpls	Ptes	W.O.	S.gt.	L/Sgts	Corporals	L/Cpls	Ptes	Sgts	L/Sgts	Corporals	L/Cpls	Ptes		
A	1						3										4	
		1															1	
			.					1						.			1	
				.						7					2		9	
					8						40					17	65	80
B	1					1	3					1					6	
		.						2					.				2	
			1						4					2			7	
				1						5					.		6	
					7						48					10	65	86
C	.						3					.					3	
		.						2					.				2	
			1						6					.			7	
				.						1					2		3	
					9						35					11	55	70
D	3						1					.					4	
		.						.					.				.	
			1						3					.			4	
				2						3					2		7	
					6						30					17	53	68
	5	1	3	3	30	1	10	4	14	16	153	1	.	2	6	55	304	304

ANALYSIS BY RANKS ONLY

RANKS.	KILLED.	WOUNDED.	MISSING.	TOTAL
W.Os & Sergeants	6	11	1	17
Lance Sergeants.	1	4	.	5
Corporals.	3	14	2	19
Lance Corporals	3	16	6	25
Privates	30	153	55	234
	42	198	64	304

APPENDIX B.

CASUALTIES IN THE BRIGADE

13/10/17

OFFICERS.

Battalion.	Killed.	Wounded.	Wounded at duty.	Wounded & missing.	Missing.	Total
3/5th.	4.	5	1	1		11
2/6th.	2.	7			1	10
2/7th.	2.	6	2			10
2/8th.	3	8			1	12
202 M.G.Coy.		2				2
197th.L.T.M.B.	-	-	-	-	-	-
	11	28	3	1	2	45

Details of 3/5th. Officers.

    Killed. Captain BENTLE STEVENS.
          Lieut. TWEEDY.
          2/Lts. TOWNSEND and HALSALL.

    Wounded. Captains LAUGHLIN and BENTLEY.
          2/Lts ALLEN, BRIDGSTOCK and PICKETT.

    Wounded at duty. Captain ROUSE.

    Wounded and missing. 2/Lt. GLASS.

OTHER RANKS.

Battalion	Killed	Wounded	Missing	Total.
3/5th.	42	185	79	306
2/6th.	30	145	56	231
2/7th.	32	126	115	273
2/8th.	32	202	142	376
202 M.G.Coy.	10	36	8	54
197th L.T.M.B.	-	1	5	6
	146	695	405	1246

APPENDIX 14

CONGRATULATORY TELEGRAMS.

From the Lord Mayor of MANCHESTER.

To the C. in C.

"10th. October 1917. Manchester and the whole of East Lancashire have read with much pride and satisfaction magnificent achievements of Territorial Division comprising Manchesters, East Lancashires and Lancashire Fusiliers, and send grateful thanks and hearty congratulations to you and all gallant forces for brilliant and successful operations."

From the Headmaster BLACKLEY MUNICIPAL SCHOOL.

To the C. in C.

"10th. October 1917. Boys, Girls and teachers of Blackley Municipal School, Manchester, acknowledge debt of gratitude to Officers and men of Manchester, East Lancashire and Lancashire Fusiliers Regiments for brilliant advance and glorious victory. Union Jack flies on our flagstaff today."

From the East Lancashire Territorial Force Association

To the G.O.C. 66th (East Lancashire) Division.

12th. October 1917. The Chairman and members of the East Lancashire Territorial Force Association join with the Lord Lieutenant (Lord Shuttleworth) in the high appreciation of the splendid and indomitable achievement of the 66th. Divn. reported in Commander in Chief's despatch of October 9th."

From G.O.C. 66th. Divn.

To East Lancashire Territorial Force Association.

15th. October 1917. All ranks 66th. Division are grateful for and highly appreciate your message."

APPENDIX 15

SPECIAL ORDER BY
LT.COL.A.S.BATES, D.S.O.
Commanding 3/5th.LAN.FUS.

    The Brigade march tomorrow may be trying in view of the state of the roads and the physical condition of the Battalion.
    The Commanding Officer knows that the eyes of the Brigade will be on the Battalion, which will be leading most of the way, and he appeals to all ranks to do their utmost to assist him in keeping the good name of the 3/5th.LANCASHIRE FUSILIERS as a marching Unit up to the standard it has already earned as a fighting one.
    This can be accomplished if all ranks make up their minds to keep the strictest march discipline.
    On the last long march the Battalion made only two men were absent when the rear of the column reached it's billets, both being hospital cases.
    The Commanding Officer confidently expects this record can be improved upon.
    This Order will be read out on parade tonight and before starting tomorrow.

19/10/17

Capt.A/Adjutant,
3/5th.LAN.FUS.

Appendix 16

GALLANT CONDUCT.

Extract from ROUTINE ORDERS by General Sir HERBERT C O. PLUMER, G.C.M.G., G.C.V.O., K.C.B., A.D.C., Commanding Second Army.

Tuesday, 16th. October, 1917.

1932-- Gallant Conduct.

The Army Commander wishes to express his appreciation of the gallant conduct shown in the following cases:-

(2) .... No.203650, Private W.J.JOHNS, LAN.FUS.

Whilst themselves patients in hospital voluntarily acted as donors for blood transfusion with the object of saving the lives of comrades.

An entry of these actions will be made in the conduct sheets of these N.C.O.s and men in accordance with King's Regulations, para.1919 (XIV).

APPENDIX 17

HONOURS AND AWARDS

MILITARY MEDALS.

The following were awarded in SECOND ANZAC CORPS Routine Orders dated October 30th. 00th 1917.

```
            66th. Divisional Signal Company . . . . .  5

    127th. Inf.Bde.

    2/5th. Bn. LANCASHIRE FUSILIERS. . . . . 19
    2/6th. Bn. LANCASHIRE FUSILIERS. . . . . 13
    2/7th. Bn. LANCASHIRE FUSILIERS. . . . . 11
    2/8th. Bn. LANCASHIRE FUSILIERS. . . . . 12
    202 M.G.Company . . . . . . . . . . . .   6   61

    128th. Inf.Bde.

    2/4th. Bn. EAST LANCS . . . . . . . . .   3
    2/5th. Bn. EAST LANCS . . . . . . . . .  14
    2/9th. Bn. MANCHESTERS. . . . . . . . .   9
    2/10th.Bn. MANCHESTERS. . . . . . . . .  15   41

    125th. Inf.Bde.

    2/5th. Bn. MANCHESTERS . . . . . . . .   7
    2/6th. Bn. MANCHESTERS . . . . . . . .   6
    2/7th. Bn. MANCHESTERS . . . . . . . .  11
    2/8th. Bn. MANCHESTERS . . . . . . . .  12
    204 M.G.Company . . . . . . . . . . .    3   39

    2/2nd. EAST LANCS. FIELD AMBULANCE . .        2
    2/3rd. EAST LANCS. FIELD AMBULANCE . .        2
                                                150
```

Names of recipients in this Battalion.

201207 Sergt. T.ENTWISTLE.	36516 Private J.F.HERTWICK.
2/37809 Sergt. H.NICHOLLS.	202405 Private J.HOLT.
201511 Sergt. H.SUMMERSGILL.	202547 Private J.W.HUNT.
201936 L/Sgt. A.DUXBURY.	235312 Private R.W.JAMES.
202015 Corpl. W.J.SHARP.	3/18021 Private C.PICKTON.
202654 L/Cpl. J.E.KELSALL.	17296/L/Cpl
17296 L/Cpl. J.H.POWER.	201952 Private J.O'HARA.
201278 Private E.EGERTON.	200885 Private F.TOOLE.
202118 Private T.FLETCHER.	39096 Private M.TURNER.
204425 Private T.HALL.	39105 Private P.UPHILL.

Appendix 18

HONOURS AND AWARDS.

The following were notified in Divisional Routine Orders dated October 27th. 1917.

D.R.O.643.

Honour etc.	Our Brigade.	Rest of the Division.
D.S.O.	2 ※	2
Bar to M.C.	1	-
M.C.	9 ✕	17
Bar to D.C.M.	-	1
D.C.M.	7	7
M.M.	2	6
	21	33

※ Both to the 2/7th. LAN.FUS.

✕ Bde. Hqrs. 1
   2/5th. Bn. LAN.FUS. . . . . 3 (See previous sheet)
   2/6th. Bn. LAN.FUS. 1
   2/7th. Bn. LAN.FUS. 1
   2/8th. Bn. LAN.FUS. 2
   202. M.G.Coy 1

TOTAL HONOURS SO FAR PUBLISHED FOR THE ACTION OCT. 9/10th.

Honour etc.	Our Brigade.	Rest of the Division.	Total.
D.S.O.	2	2	4
Bar to M.C.	1	-	1
M.C.	9	17	26
Bar to D.C.M.	-	1	1
D.C.M.	7	7	14
M.M.	63	94	157
	82	121	203

29/10/17.

APPENDIX 19

HONOURS AND AWARDS.

The following were notified by the Brigadier 27/10/17.

MILITARY CROSS.
    Captain H.A.SANDIFORD, M.B., R.A.M.C. (T.F.) Attached
    Captain F.M.BENTLEY.
    Lieutenant J.A.HOLDSWORTH.

DISTINGUISHED CONDUCT MEDAL.
    303233 Private J.ANYON.
    235438 L/Corpl. E.EDMONDSON.

This brings the total Honours and Awards won by the Battalion to :-

    Military Crosses 3
    D.C.Ms. 2
    Military Medals 19

                   Total   24

APPENDIX 20

3/5th. LAN.FUS.
197th.Inf.Bde.S/909
dated 18/10/17.

1. Herewith Report on Operations of 8th.October and subsequent days, and a narrative of Operations.
2. These are sent you as they may be of interest for Regimental records.
3. They must be regarded as entirely Private and Confidential and must on no account be quoted as authority.
4. They are as accurate as it is possible to make them but their adduracy is not guaranteed.

(signed) C.GRAY, Lieut
B.H.Q.
18/10/17
for Captain.,
Brigade Major. 197th. Inf.Bde.

- -

Headquarters,
  66th. Division.

Report on operations on 8th.October and subsequent days.

In accordance with 66th.Division Operation Orders Nos. 46 and 47, and this Office Operation Order No.54 as amended by B.M./755, the 197th. Infantry Brigade advanced to the front line on the night 8/9th. October.
Units advanced in the following order:-
3/5th. LAN.FUS from FREZENBERG Ridge via JACK track at 6 p.m., followed by 197th. L.T.M.B. and 2/8th. Bn. LAN.FUS.
2/6th. Bn. LAN.FUS via JACK and JILL tracks followed by 2/7th Bn. LAN.FUS. and branched off at JACK track.
Some shelling of the FREZENBERG Ridge delayed the 3/5th. Bn. LAN.FUS. at the start.
JACK track had been used throughout the day by Pack animals for moving forward ammunition etc. Partly owing to this but chiefly owing to the appaling weather, the treck became exceedingly bad and where it crosses the ZONNEBEKE particularly, was well over the knees in mud of a very adhesive nature. Also a certain number of troops coming back along the track blocked the troops advancing.
At about 12.30 a.m. Oct.9th. it appeared that the Brigade would be late at the starting point. Division was informed and all available Staff Officers went out to assist in getting the Battalions forward with orders to push forward all men who were able to move quickly and leave those who were exhausted to come on later.
Men struggled through the night but were unable to get right up to the "tape line" by ZERO hour.
At ZERO hour the position of the Brigade was approximately as follows:-
  3/5th. Bn.LAN.FUS. head on Tape line.
  2/8th. Bn.LAN.FUS. about 400 yds. from Tape line.
  2/7th. Bn.LAN.FUS. topping Hill 40.
  2/6th. Bn.LAN.FUS. on West side of Hill behind LEVI House.
At 5.5 a.m. 2 Battalions of the 199th. Inf.Bde. were placed by Division at the disposal of B.G.C. 197th. Inf.Bde. Orders were immediately sent (subsequently confirmed by B.M.767) to Lt.Col. A.S.BATES, 3/5th. Bn. LAN.FUS at his Headquarters in the front line to take command of front line troops and send forward whatever troops of the 197th. Inf. Bde. were at hand, and, if necessary, to use the 2/7th. Bn. MANCHESTER Regt. who were holding the line.
Owing to the difficulty of communicating with the 199th. Inf. Bde., and the time available to take action, I anticipated the order of 2/7th. Bn. MANCHESTER Regt. being placed at my disposal, and issued orders without waiting for a message from the 199th. Inf. Bde.

As far as the two Battalions of the 199th. Inf. Bde. were concerned, one Battalion was not used - elements of the 2/7th. MANCHESTER Regt. went forward with the 197th. Inf. Bde as far as the CEMETERY. As soon as the 197th. Inf. Bde. came into action, these two Battalions automatically reverted to the command of the B.G.C. 199th. Inf. Bde.

At 7 a.m. 2/7th. Bn. LAN. FUS. were reported advancing over final objective.

At 7.50 a.m. Lt/Col/BATES 2/8th. Bn. LAN. FUS. reported first objective taken and many prisoners.

At 8.45 a.m. Lt.Col. BATES reported final objective taken and RED line being consolidated. (This was unconfirmed)

At 9.30 a.m. 2/8th. Bn. LAN. FUS. reported final objective taken and the enemy counter attacking.

At 9.40 a.m. the counter attack was driven off.

At 10.10 a.m. 2/8th. Bn. LAN. FUS. reported to be in position on final objective with right on VIENNA COT and left on D.12.a.1.4.

At 11.6 a.m. enemy machine guns were reported in the DECLINE COPSE, being dealt with.

At 11.45 a.m. orders were sent for all troops to push forward at all costs.

At 12.30 p.m. 2/6th. Bn. LAN. FUS. reported 3 companies to be at D.17.a.4.9.

At 1.35 p.m. 2/8th. Bn. LAN. FUS. reported front line withdrawn and that they were not in touch with the 198th. Inf. Bde. on the left.

During the time the Brigade was in the BLUE line the enemy shelling was fairly heavy on both flanks exposed. Two small counter attacks were beaten off, but owing to the fact that the flanks were in the air and a backward movement originated owing to the turning back on the left flank, the troops, through lack of Officers, thought a retirement was taking place, and withdrew to the RED line. The withdrawal was not caused by enemy counter attacks.

At 4 p.m. touch had not been gained with the 198th. Inf. Bde, and orders were sent out for patrols to go and search for them.

The B.G.C. also informed me he was sending 2 companies to fill the gap.

At 4.10 p.m. orders were sent that all ground gained was to be held and foremost posts was the line of resistance.

At 5.30 p.m. the enemy counter attacked with Infantry he was driven back by rifles fire and artillery. It was reported that his casualties were heavy.

At 12 midnight on the 9/10th. Oct. our line ran from RAILWAY CROSSING behind HILLSIDE FM to AUGUSTUS WOOD. (Note by A.S.B. the line certainly ran about 30 yds in front or to the East of HILLSIDE FM.)

Touch had been gained with the AUSTRALIANS on the right but not with the 198th. Inf. Bde on the left.

On the morning of the 10th. Lieut. GODDARD was sent to check the position of the front line and confirmed the fact that they were in the above mentioned positions. He also was unable to get in touch on the left.

At 10 a.m. the gap having been found in the line, a Company of the 2/6th. Bn. LAN. FUS behind HILLSIDE FM were pushed into the gap. Just before dusk on the evening of the 10th. an AUSTRALIAN Brigade moved up the front line to take over. From then until half an hour before dawn on the 11th., the enemy shelled area between Brigade H.Qrs. and front line considerably- the fire becoming intense about 11.30 p.m. and shortly before dawn.

The relief was complete at 6 a.m. and the ground was cleared of all wounded including a number of AUSTRALIANS.

CASUALTY REPORT OF OFFICERS OF THIS UNIT FOR THE MONTH OF OCTOBER, 1917.

Rank	Name & Initials	Nature of Casualty	Place	Date
Captain	G.G. STEVENS	Killed in Action	Belgium	9/10/17.
Lieut.	C.F. TWEEDY	-do-	-do-	-do-
2/Lieut.	J.L. TOWNSEND	-do-	-do-	-do-
2/Lieut.	D.C. HALSALL	-do-	-do-	-do-
Captain	C.W. LAUGHLIN	Wounded	-do-	-do-
Captain	F.M. BENTLEY	Wounded	-do-	-do-
2/Lieut.	G.R. ALLEN	Wounded	-do-	-do-
2/Lieut.	E.H. BRIDGSTOCK	Wounded	-do-	-do-
2/Lieut.	J.W. PICKETT	Wounded	-do-	-do-
2/Lieut.	L.G. GLASS	Wounded & Missing	-do-	-do-
Captn & Adjt	J. ROUSE	Wounded at duty	-do-	-do-

The undermentioned officers proceeded to Hospital "S" 8/10/17.
2/Lieut. C.H. TYE.
2/Lieut. J.C. BARLOW.

31.10.17.

Commanding 3/5th Battn. LANCASHIRE FUSILIERS.
Lieut.-Colonel.

--3--

The total casualties of the Brigade were as follows:-

	OFFICERS			O.R's			
	K.	W.	M.	K.	W.	M.	
3/5th. Bn. LAN.FUS.	4	5	1	42	185	79	= 316
2/6th. Bn. LAN.FUS.	3	7	1	30	145	56	= 242
2/7th. Bn. LAN.FUS.	1	7	0	32	126	115	= 281
2/8th. Bn. LAN.FUS.	3	9	1	32	202	142	= 389
202 M.G.Coy.	0	2	0	10	36	8	= 56
197th. L.T.M.B.	0	1	0	0	1	5	= 7
Brigade Signal Section	0	0	0	1	3	0	= 4
	11	31	3	147	698	405	=1295

B.H.Q.
15/10/17

(Signed) O.C.BORRETT
Brigadier General,
Commanding 197th. Infantry Brigade.

Appendix 22.

3/5th BATTALION LANCASHIRE FUSILIERS.

CASUALTY REPORT

OF

OTHER RANKS OF THIS UNIT

FOR MONTH OF

OCTOBER, 1917

CASUALTIES.

39297 Pte HEATH.M.   "B" Coy   Killed in Action   9/10/17.
         (Attached 202 M.G. Coy)

202567 Pte CHADWICK.G. "C" Coy   Killed in Action   9/10/17.
         (Attached 197th Inf. Bde Hdqrs)

13892 Pte GREENHALGH.R. "D" Coy   Wounded   9/10/17.
         (Attached 197th Inf. Bde Hdqrs)

WOUNDED AT DUTY.

201311 Sgt SUMMERSGILL.H. "A" Coy   Wounded at duty, 9/10/17.
36523 Pte FEELEY.R.   "A" Coy   Wounded at duty, 9/10/17.
36935 .. CHIPPENDALE.A. "D" Coy   Wounded at duty, 9/10/17.
202545 .. HADLEY.R.   "B" Coy   Wounded at duty, 9/10/17.

3/5th Bn. LANCASHIRE FUSILIERS.

CASUALTY REPORT

KILLED

"A" COMPANY:-   Date

| 202519 | Sgt | BROOKS.J. | 9/10/17 |
| 201068 | L/Sgt | HEATON... | 9/10/17 | 203080 L/C (u/A) FITZROY.H. 9/10/17
39283	Pte	CARTER.E.N.	9/10/17
203118	..	FOLEY.J.	9/10/17
202366	..	FORREST.F.	9/10/17
36495	..	FUDGE.T.	9/10/17
203125	..	KEWLEY.T.K.	9/10/17
203683	..	LIVESEY.C.	9/10/17
39117	..	WHALLEY.J.	9/10/17
203588	..	WHITE.H.B.	9/10/17
39108	..	WALKER J.B (DIED OF WOUNDS)	10/10/17

"B" COMPANY:-

202029	Sgt	SIMM.J.	9/10/17
201483	Cpl	WHITFORD.F.	9/10/17
204411	L/C (u/p)	LEE.W.	10/10/17
39279	Pte	ALLEN.G.	9/10/17
202461	..	BOARDMAN.F.W.	9/10/17
202454	..	BODDIS.F.	9/10/17
202428	..	DEWHURST.J.	9/10/17
39306	..	KIRKHAM.W.	9/10/17
39282	..	BOULTON C.	8/10/17
39075	..	ROSE W.	8/10/17

"C" COMPANY:-

202217	Cpl	CLOWES.F.L.D.	9/10/17
201159	Pte	DIGGLE.R.	9/10/17
202011	..	HOLT.W.S. (H.Q)	9/10/17
12547	..	LEVY.M.	8/10/17
202597	..	LORD.H.	9/10/17
202707	..	McCANN.T.	9/10/17
204415	..	McDERMOTT.E.	9/10/17
201236	..	NUTTALL.H.	9/10/17
39331	..	STEEL.J.	9/10/17
203266	..	TAYLOR.A.E.	9/10/17

"D" COMPANY:-

205347	Sgt	FERRINGTON.J.	9/10/17
202608	..	SUGDEN.T.	9/10/17
202033	A/Sgt	TAYLOR.F.	9/10/17
201315	Cpl	HASLAM.W.	9/10/17
235311	L/C (u/p)	FERGUSON.T.	9/10/17
235310	A/L/C	WILLIAMS.W.	9/10/17
202629	Pte	BRADSHAW.L.	9/10/17
201361	..	GREENWOOD.J.H.	8/10/17
202620	..	KITSON.W.	9/10/17
201996	..	RICHARDSON.F.	9/10/17
204481	..	SNELGROVE.E.	9/10/17
203666	..	ENTWISTLE R.	9/10/17
204459	..	WIGHTMAN R.	9/10/17

WOUNDED.

"A" COMPANY:-

		Date
202242 Sgt	BUTTERWORTH.J.E.	9/10/17.
201389 "	DAWSON.P.	9/10/17.
201192 "	GARLICK.G.	9/10/17.
201280 Cpl	REDFERN.P.	9/10/17.
202372 L/C	BOOTH.S.	9/10/17.
36953 A/L/C	BARTON.A.	9/10/17.
203656 L/C	BARNES.T.W.	9/10/17.
203116 L/C(u/p)	FENNER.J.	9/10/17.
203093 L/C(u/p)	HUGHES.O.	9/10/17.
203651 L/C	LIGHT.H.E.	9/10/17.
203104 L/C(u/p)	WILLIAMS.T.C.	10/10/17.
17564 Pte	BERRY.J.	9/10/17.
36957 "	BRIERLEY.J.	9/10/17.
201257 "	BROOKS.E.	9/10/17.
204447 "	BURROWS...	9/10/17.
203177 "	BUTTERWORTH.A.	9/10/17.
202698 "	BOWERS.J.	10/10/17.
39342 "	BUTCHER.F.J.	9/10/17.
36597 "	BRADLEY.W.	9/10/17.
203114 "	CRETNEY.J.T.	9/10/17. 36489 Pte CAPE W. 10/10/17
204409 "	CAWLEY.W.	10/10/17.
36485 "	DACK.J.W.	9/10/17.
17525 "	EVANS.J.	9/10/17.
204405 "	FENLON.A.	9/10/17.
39294 "	HALL.F.	9/10/17.
39293 "	HADDON.J.W.	9/10/17.
202705 "	HOLGATE.F.	9/10/17.
202227 "	JONES.S.	10/10/17.
203679 L/C(a/W)	LEEDHAM.A.S. (H.Q.)	9/10/17.
203678 Pte	LEADER.H.W.	9/10/17.
39308 "	LEGGOTT.E.	9/10/17.
203127 "	McHUGH.G.	9/10/17.
202370 "	MAY.J.	9/10/17.
203226 "	PEARCE.F.	9/10/17.
201212 "	POLLARD.E. (H.Q.)	10/10/17.
39320 "	RAITHBY.B.	9/10/17.
202369 "	ROWE.W.	9/10/17.
201387 "	SCOTSON.R.	9/10/17.
203100 "	STRONG.W.E.	9/10/17. 202540 Pte SHAW A 9/10/17.
39324 "	SAVAGE.P.	9/10/17.
202573 "	SUTCLIFFE.F.	9/10/17.
39334 "	TAYLOR.W.	9/10/17.
39113 "	WHITHEAD.J.	9/10/17.
39118 "	WHITFIELD.W.H.	10/10/17.
201337 "	WILLOUGHBY.J.	9/10/17.
39110 "	WINDLE.A.	10/10/17.
39122 "	WOODHOUSE.L.	10/10/17.
203107 "	WOODS.W.H.	9/10/17.
202717 "	WORMALL.T.W.	10/10/17.
204350 "	WOOD.E.T.	9/10/17.
39114 "	WALTON.F.	9/10/17.

"B" COMPANY:-

201185 C.S.M.	SMITH.S.	9/10/17.
201259 Sgt	BALDWIN.W.	9/10/17.
202243 A/Sgt	MICKLEWRAITH.W.	9/10/17.
201307 Sgt	RAMSDEN.H. (H.Q.)	9/10/17.
201298 L/Sgt	BURFOOT.E.	9/10/17.
201275 A/L/Sgt	YATES.D.	9/10/17.
203045 Cpl	BELL.E.B.	9/10/17.
202424 "	BRAMHALL.G.	9/10/17.
15099 A/Cpl	DAWSON.T.	9/10/17.
204381 "	LYON.J.J.	9/10/17.
202720 L/C	BRIERLEY.S.	9/10/17.
202530 L/C(u/p)	CORLETT.G.E.	9/10/17.
36676 L/C(u/p)	LINDSAY.G.	9/10/17.

```
202383 L/C(u/p) SMITH.J.T.           9/10/17.
202535 L/C WEST.J.C.                 9/10/17.
203247 Pte ASHILL.D.                 8/10/17.
 39280  ..  BALDOCK.F.                9/10/17.
 12458  ..  BEAMISH.G.                9/10/17.
203235  ..  BIRCHALL.P.               9/10/17.
 36841  ..  BRIERLEY.J.               9/10/17.
202411  ..  BURKE.W.                  8/10/17.
201217  ..  CHADWICK.J.               9/10/17.
202386  ..  CHAPMAN.H.                9/10/17.
203647  ..  CRAWLEY.J.V.              9/10/17.
202387  ..  FOSTER.H.                 8/10/17.
202457  ..  GREAVES.H.                9/10/17.
205356  ..  GEORGE.A.H.               9/10/17.
235439  ..  GODFREY.G.W.              9/10/17.
202403  ..  HILL.T.C.                 9/10/17.
203594  ..  HOWELLS.W.E.              9/10/17.
205142  ..  HOLT.M.                   9/10/17.
235442  ..  HADWIN.A.                 9/10/17.
202543  ..  HORSFALL.H.               9/10/17.
235443  ..  HALLWORTH.W.             10/10/17.
 30206  ..  HARLOCK.A.D.              9/10/17.
 36503  ..  HOLDEN.A.  (Accidental)   9/10/17.
 30303  ..  JACKSON.J.T.              9/10/17.
202544  ..  JOHNSON.J.                9/10/17.
202456  ..  JEBB.W.                   9/10/17.   36924 Pte JOHNSON S 9/10/17
 30300  ..  LEGGOTT.F.               10/10/17.
202253  ..  MANLEY.J.A.              10/10/17.
203506  ..  MASTERS.H.                8/10/17.
205351  ..  METCALFE.H.               9/10/17.
235318  ..  PATTISON.G.E.  (H.Q)      9/10/17.
202379  ..  PHILBIN.J.                9/10/17.
202398  ..  ROBINSON.A.    (H.Q)     10/10/17.
202448  ..  REES.A.                   9/10/17.
 39078  ..  ROBNETT.B.               10/10/17.
 39079  ..  ROBINSON.J.              10/10/17.
203241  ..  ROSCOE.H.                 8/10/17.
 39082  ..  SHUKER.S.                10/10/17.
 39080  ..  STANISTREET.A.           10/10/17.
 30329  ..  SMITH.F.                 10/10/17.
202414  ..  TATTERSALL.H.             9/10/17.
203638  ..  TUNSTILL.A.              10/10/17.
202439  ..  TURTON.T.                 9/10/17.
202533  ..  WARD.T.                  10/10/17.
 36747  ..  WILLIAMS.G.               9/10/17.
201362  ..  WARBURTON.G.              8/10/17.
203244  ..  WARHURST.G.              10/10/17.
203246  ..  WHITEHEAD.S.              9/10/17.
 39341  ..  WOODS.J.H.                9/10/17.
235297  ..  BROWN J.D. (HQ)          10/10/17.
```

"C" COMPANY:-

```
 17897 Sgt DICKENSON.A.              9/10/17.
202013  ..  ROSCOE.G.                10/10/17.
202525 A/Sgt SMITH.J.E.               9/10/17.
 36623 A/L/Sgt DAWSON.W.              9/10/17.
202603         SANDERSON.J.L.         9/10/17.
 17806 A/Cpl BARNES.H.                9/10/17.
202600 Cpl BRIGGS.H.                 10/10/17.
202598 A/Cpl HOLT.R.H.               10/10/17.
204419 Cpl MARSDEN.R.                 9/10/17.
201376  ..  MOORE.E.  (H.Q.)          8/10/17.
202566  ..  WOOD.G.                  10/10/17.
203280 L/C JONES.P.                  10/10/17.
201160 Pte BAILEY.T.H.               10/10/17.
202426  ..  BALL.E.                  10/10/17.
3/17091 ..  BOARDMAN.H.               9/10/17.
 39285  ..  COULING.F.                9/10/17.
201394  ..  CHADWICK.T. (H.Q)        10/10/17.
203256  ..  DUDLEY.H.                 9/10/17.
202591  ..  FLETCHER.L.               9/10/17.
```

- 4 -

203619	Pte GRAHAM.G.	9/10/17.	
202582	.. HARRISON.A.H.	9/10/17.	
203632	.. HAYES.J.H.	9/10/17.	
202563	.. HEALEY.J.P.	10/10/17.	
203624	.. HOPWOOD.J.H.	10/10/17.	
27354	.. JENKINSON.H.	9/10/17.	
39301	.. HURT.G.E.	9/10/17.	
202688	.. LAMB.T.	9/10/17.	
18459	.. LONG.W.	9/10/17.	
204464	.. McALLISTER.A.	10/10/17.	
202689	.. MURPHY.G.	10/10/17.	
204403	.. MURRAY.J.	10/10/17.	
202709	.. NUTTALL.J.	10/10/17.	
36044	.. NORBURY.F.	9/10/17.	29622 Pte ORRELL W 10/10/17
202429	.. PARKER.E.	9/10/17.	
204356	.. PASHLEY.W.R.	9/10/17.	
36708	.. PEASE.H.	8/10/17.	
36712	.. REED.W.A.	9/10/17.	
36715	.. RIGBY.J.	9/10/17.	
36710	.. ROGERS.G.E.	10/10/17	36716 Pte ROBERTS A 9/10/17
15161	.. SIDDONS.W.	9/10/17.	
39086	.. SMITH.J.W.	10/10/17.	
36507	.. SCOWLER.G.W.	9/10/17.	
39093	.. STEEL.G.	9/10/17.	
39090	.. STEPHENSON.W.	9/10/17.	
202716	.. TIMMS.J.W. (H.Q)	8/10/17.	
203251	.. THOMAS.D.	10/10/17.	
203253	.. WILLIAMS.D.R.	9/10/17.	

"D" COMPANY:-

18104	Sgt RAGAN.T.	9/10/17.	
202613	Cpl EVANS.T.	9/10/17.	
202038	.. LAW.E.	8/10/17.	
202585	.. TICKNER.J.	9/10/17.	
203028	L/C(u/p) AKISTER.E.A.	8/10/17.	
202640	L/C FINCH.P.	9/10/17.	
17274	L/C(u/p) RYAN.E.	9/10/17.	
202487	Pte BUTTERWORTH.R.	8/10/17.	
203611	.. BREEZE.H. (H.Q)	9/10/17.	
203029	.. BROWN.J.	8/10/17.	
201715	.. BIRTWISTLE.G. (H.Q.)	10/10/17	
235297	.. BROWN.J.D. (H.Q.)	10/10/17	
3/19029	.. COLCLOUGH.T.	10/10/17	
235437	.. COOK.W.	9/10/17.	
201247	.. COWBURN.F. (H.Q.)	10/10/17.	
202433	.. DEWHURST.A.	9/10/17.	
35436	.. DYKES.F.	10/10/17.	
203025	.. HEMMINGS.A.	9/10/17.	
203051	.. HOYLE.R.	9/10/17.	
203671	.. HOWORTH.C.	9/10/17.	
203650	.. JOHNS.W.J.	9/10/17.	
202660	.. LILLEY.T.	10/10/17.	DIED OF WOUNDS 11/10/17.
203052	.. LEE.F.	9/10/17.	
201372	.. LOMAX.J.	9/10/17.	
202661	.. LITTLER.J.	10/10/17.	
202618	.. MACKIE.J.	9/10/17.	
203133	.. ROBERTS.A.	10/10/17.	
204453	.. ROBINSON.T.	9/10/17.	
203066	.. STOREY.H.	10/10/17.	
36926	.. SCOTT.J.	9/10/17.	
36950	.. STOWE.S.	9/10/17.	
36516	.. TEAL.G.W.	9/10/17.	
202472	.. TAYLOR.F.	9/10/17.	
204372	.. WISE.T.	8/10/17.	
203581	.. WILLIAMS.D.R.	9/10/17.	
17689	.. WILSON.W.	9/10/17.	
27320	.. WITHNELL.F.(self inflicted)	8/10/17.	
36928	.. WATERWORTH.J.	9/10/17.	
17819	.. WEAVER.J.	9/10/17.	
18886	.. RILEY.W. (SHELL SHOCK)	9/10/17.	

MISSING.

"A" COMPANY

203645 L/C	WOODHALL.W.	203680 L/C(u/p)	FITZROY.H.
36484 Pte	ARMSTRONG.T.	~~36527 Pte~~	~~BLENKHORN.J.~~
36481 ,,	COATES.A.	36482 ,,	COWE.R.H.
17597 ,,	CORRISTINE.J.B.	~~36489~~ ,,	~~CAPE.W.~~
203115 ,,	EWBANK.R.J.	203081 ,,	FRANCIS.G.H.
203094 ,,	GAFFNEY.J.	203089 ,,	HALL.T.G.
203649 ,,	HANDLEY.F.	202096 ,,	HORROCKS.J.H.
202241 ,,	JORDAN.J.	202221 ,,	JAMES.R.
203185 ,,	SMITH.J.	~~39108~~ ,,	~~WALKER.J.B.~~
~~39119~~ ,,	~~WHITE.N.J.~~ (H.4)		

"B" COMPANY

201329 Sgt	KIRKMAN.G.	200945 Cpl	HOWARTH.E.
204457 Cpl	KNIGHT.W.H.	202388 Pte	DANIELS.W.
235445 Pte	HILL.C.J.	202524 ,,	OPENSHAW.A.B.
39319 ,,	PRESCOTT.H.	~~202540~~ ,,	~~SHAW.A.~~
39335 ,,	THORNLEY.G.R.	202430 ,,	WOOLF.R.
202718 ,,	WHITLEY.W.A. (H.4)	~~235380~~ ,,	~~NICHOLLS.A.W.~~
		39077 ,,	REID.W.

"C" COMPANY.

202685 L/C	CRANE.H.	203295 A/L/C	KNIGHT.T.
203657 Pte	BARNES.W.E.	202631 Pte	CASEY.M.
203618 ,,	GELDARD.E.	202593 ,,	HARRISON.J.
17377 ,,	KELLY.C.	36678 ,,	LEDWARD.C.P.
36498 ,,	MILLAR.A.	~~29622~~ ,,	~~ORRELL.W.~~
~~36716~~ ,,	~~ROBERTS.A.~~	~~39093~~ ,,	~~STEAD.J.~~
39101 ,,	TIDY.C.		

"D" COMPANY.

202641 L/C(u/p)	FITTON.F.	202659 L/C	LEE.J.
203061 Pte	DONALDSON.C. (H.4)	203572 Pte	EDWARDS.W.
~~203666~~ ,,	~~ENTWISTLE.R.~~	235301 ,,	FIELL.G.
~~235362~~ ,,	~~GIBNEY.A.~~	~~235363~~ ,,	~~HALL.G.~~
202649 ,,	HEATON.J.	202651 ,,	HOWARTH.A.
3/14459 ,,	INGHAM.T.	3/16446 ,,	MELLOR.T.
3/17070 ,,	ROBINSON.H.	204472 ,,	SMITH.A.
202463 ,,	STRINGER.W.	36823 ,,	TAYLOR.E.
15240 ,,	TRAVIS.T.	202672 ,,	WALDRON.J.
~~204450~~ ,,	~~WIGHTMAN.R.~~		

ALL THE ABOVE MEN ARE MISSING AS AND FROM 10/10/1917.

3/5th Bn. LANCASHIRE FUSILIERS.

LIST OF OFFICERS WHO HAVE JOINED THE BATTALION
DURING THE MONTH OF OCTOBER, 1917.

Rank	Name & Initials	From	Date.
2/Lieut.	L.F. WRIGHT	3rd Bn (Res) LAN. FUS.	16/10/17.
"	L. FORSHAW	-do-	16/10/17.
"	A.E. GRELLIER	-do-	22/10/17.
"	H.D. SMITH	-do-	26/10/17.
"	J. CROSBIE	5th (Res) Bn. LAN.FUS.	30/10/17.
"	C.J. LEWIS	-do-	30/10/17.
"	H. ROSS	-do-	30/10/17.
"	A.J. LEWIS	3rd Bn (Res) LAN. FUS.	31/10/17.
"	T.W. QUARMBY	5th (Res) Bn. LAN. FUS.	31/10/17.
"	H.W. SMITH	-do-	31/10/17.
"	A.A. SIMPSON	-do-	31/10/17.
"	H.G. SIMPSON	-do-	31/10/17.
"	E.C. LOVELL	-do-	31/10/17.

Lieut.- Colonel.

31.10.17.   Commanding 3/5th Bn. LANCASHIRE FUSILIERS.

197th Brigade.

66th Division.

3/5th BATTALION LANCASHIRE FUSILIERS NOVEMBER 1917.

CONFIDENTIAL

WAR DIARY

OF

3/5th BATTALION LANCASHIRE FUSILIERS

From:- 1st November, 1917   To:- 30th November, 1917.

(VOLUME 10)

Army Form C. 2118.

WAR DIARY
3/5th LANCASHIRE FUSILIERS
INTELLIGENCE SUMMARY
(Erase heading not required.)

Instructions regarding War Diaries and Intelligence Summaries are contained in F. S. Regs., Part II, and the Staff Manual respectively. Title pages will be prepared in manuscript.

Place	Date	Hour	Summary of Events and Information	Remarks and references to Appendices
	1917			
CAMPAGNE	Nov. 1		A, B, C and H.Q. Companies went for a route march. The remaining Coys were left on the range.	
		2	The Commanding Officer received a letter from the O.C. 1/5th Bn Lanc Fus in which Major Winter regretted him to convey to officers and other Ranks of the Battalion the best wishes recently received during the season of furlough of parties of the 1/5 Bn who contact from London Gazette. Summary 29.9.17. LAN. FUS Lieut to have pay and allowance as from July 1st. T.R. BLAKE D.R. TWEEDY (since killed in action) P.D. UREN. the Lieuts to be Lieuts from June 1st 1916 also E.H.C. TOWLER. G.H. YARD (July 1) Lieut 2/Lt W. HALL granted leave 29.10.17 to 3.4.17 for completion of Course of Instruction	

WAR DIARY
3/5th LANCASHIRE FUSILIERS
INTELLIGENCE SUMMARY

Army Form C. 2118.

Place	Date	Hour	Summary of Events and Information	Remarks and references to Appendices
CAMPAGNE	1917 Nov 1	3	Officers returned to Lewis Gun Instruction course at Lt.R. of Scottish Rifles	
			Afternoon various contests at Baths at Argues were attend	
		4	Lieut T. Myers granted Retainer of leave to U.K. B.E.F.	
		5	Battalion Route March Route — CAMPAGNE — ARQUES — ST OMER — WIZERNES — BLENDECQUES — CAMPAGNE	
		6	Brigade on the march. The Brigade carried out a route march at	apps I
			to HOCQUET	
			Monthly Returns — Acting offr. having been kept W. wire 3/5th Bn. LANCS FUS. to command 2/6 Bn Lan Fus. was appt (A/Lt.Col.) H.L. ANDERTON wounded	
			9.10.17.	
			Leave Lt J.R. HOLDSWORTH D.C. Granted leave S.H.D 6 to 16.11.17	

WAR DIARY
INTELLIGENCE SUMMARY

Army Form C. 2118.

Place	Date	Hour	Summary of Events and Information	Remarks and references to Appendices
CAMPAGNE	1917 Nov. 7		Orders received to move next day by train from to WESTOUTRE Area – Horses of Transport	
			Left by road. Capt Sandiford R.A.M.C. Officer Coyt. Deepens reported in his place	APP^x II
	8		Entrained at 4.30 p.m. at EBLINGHEM Station. Train under Lt.Col. A.S. Bates D.S.O. also held 2/6 Som F.LI. – 436 Field Coy R.E. + 2/1 East Lancs Field Ambce. Arrived at	
			OUDERDOM 7.30pm – Marched to York Camp – arrived 9.15 p.m. – Remainder of Transport had proceeded by road	
WESTOUTRE	9		At 5 a.m. received orders to march at 9 p.m. to YPRES – to relieve the 3rd Australian Brigade. Guides met the Battn and it spent the night in the Infantry Barracks	
			YPRES – The Transport took new lines from the 12th Australian Battn. 2/Lieut Dunn	
			and 1 N.C.O. per platoon proceeded by bus and went into the line.	
YPRES	10		The Battn marched to HELL-FIRE Corner and was met at 11 p.m. by guides from the 2nd Australian Battn whom it relieved – No casualties during relief – The Relief complete 2.45 P.M.	APP^s II
			position taken up was that of the Left Support Battn – Relief complete 2.45 P.M.	
			Went into line – 23 officers – 533 O.R. – Distribution of Officers of the Battn attached as APP^x III (a)	
	11		In support. Reconnaissance very bad.	

Army Form C. 2118.

WAR DIARY
3/5 Lan. or Fus.

INTELLIGENCE SUMMARY.
(Erase heading not required.)

Instructions regarding War Diaries and Intelligence Summaries are contained in F. S. Regs., Part II, and the Staff Manual respectively. Title pages will be prepared in manuscript.

Place	Date	Hour	Summary of Events and Information	Remarks and references to Appendices
YPRES	Nov.	12	In support.	
		13	do. S.O.S went up off PASCHENDAELE at 4.30 p.m.	
		14	Sentence of death passed by F.G.C.M on No. 20445 Private Smith for desertion from the FREZENBURG RIDGE on 9/10/17. carried out by firing party under 2/Lieut Dunn this morning. Relieved the 2/7 Lan.Fus. in front line Batten. on the left of the Divisional Line. D. Coy had gone in the previous night – relief complete 1-7 am. 13/11/17	
		15	S.O.S. went up off PASCHENDAELE about 6.30 p.m.	
		16	Actual Strength return 17 officers – 307 O.R.	
		17	1 Coy 2/8. Lan.Fus. relieved D. Coy. 3/5 Lan.Fus + came under command of O.C. 3/5 Fus. – D. Coy 3/5 Lan.Fus joined 2/8 Bn. in Reserve and came under command of O.C. 2/8 Lan.Fus.	
		18	Still in front line. Much Shelling.	
		19	Relieved by 2/10 Manchester Regt. – Relief complete 12.30 am. 20/11/17	
		20	Arrived at CANAL DUGOUTS – YPRES – Moved to CANAL AREA – KRUISSTRAAT according IV Casualties for the tour in Support and front line as follows :– See App. V	

WAR DIARY
3 Leinster or Fus
INTELLIGENCE SUMMARY

Army Form C. 2118.

Place	Date	Hour	Summary of Events and Information	Remarks and references to Appendices
YPRES	Nov.	21	Distribution of officers as at 6 P.M. attached.	App.ᵈˣ VI
	22		Lieut. Col. A.S. Bates D.S.O. proceeded on leave - Major T.J. Biddulph 2/3. Lan. Fus. took over command during the absence on leave of Lt. Col. Bates.	
			The Batt⁹ moved to the BERTHEN Area by march Route. O.O. attached.	App.ᵈˢ VII
BERTHEN	23		The Batt⁹ moved to the STAPLE area by bus. Billets very scattered. Capt. and Adjutant J. Rowe returned from leave. Batt⁹ in rear - O.O. attached	App.ᵈˢ VIII
STAPLE	24		Draft of 2 officers (2/Lt Wilson & 2/Lt Dickins) and 37. O.R. reported - Coys. spent day cleaning up - inspections - Capt. Sandiford M.C. R.A.M.C. returned to duty. Capt. Deeping R.A.M.C. returned to Field Ambulance.	
	25		Church Parade - The Corps Commander, Lt. General Sir A.J. Godley, K.C.B., K.C.M.G., attended - 2/Lieut Ball returned from Hospital.	
	26		Batt⁹ commenced Platoon Training - Lewis Guns, Signalling, Young Officers and N.C.O.'s classes commenced - Batt⁹ parade for Amalgamation of Court Martial sentences on nos. 204957 Private Smith, 203578 Private North, 203046 Private Brokes. The two latter reviewed to 15 years penal servitude - sentence to Lewis Gun Course. 2/Lieut. Belcher returned from Course. 2/Lieut Brooke proceeded to Lewis Gun Course.	

Army Form C. 2118.

WAR DIARY
3/5 Bn. of Fus.
INTELLIGENCE SUMMARY.
(Erase heading not required.)

Instructions regarding War Diaries and Intelligence Summaries are contained in F. S. Regs., Part II. and the Staff Manual respectively. Title pages will be prepared in manuscript.

Place	Date	Hour	Summary of Events and Information	Remarks and references to Appendices
STAPLE	Nov.	28	Capt. Lewis proceeded on leave. 27/11/17. – 2/Lieut Smith H.D. proceeded to office of A.P.M. 66th Division for 10 days tour of duty there. Training classes continued.	
		29	Capt. Read returned from leave. Training classes continued. No 3/19026 Private Wilkinson. O.W. awarded Military Medal by Corps Commander	App^x IX
			26-11-17	
		30	Training classes continued. Roll of Officers to date attached. Strength of Batt^n on this date. 34 Officers. 683 O.R. Roll of officers att^d as app^x X	

D.J. Russell Capt
Comdg 3/5 N.F.B

App^x I.

BRIGADE TACTICAL EXERCISE No.5.   Copy No. 10

INTENTION.
1. (a) The Brigade will carry out a practice attack on the LE HOCQUET Area tomorrow. A contact aeroplane will be in the air.
(b) The Brigade will attack on a 2 Battalion front - the 3/5th LAN. FUS., on the left & the 2/6th LAN. FUS., on the right - 8 platoons of the 2/8th LAN. FUS., will "mop up" behind each Battln.
(c) Frontage per Battalion about 225 yards.

ASSEMBLY TAPE
2. (a) will run from the cottage at A.17.a.4.4. in a S.W. direction on a bearing of 232 degrees grid.
(b) Lieut. N.D. THOMPSON will arrange to lay this tape, for the Brigade, out by 10.15 a.m. He will utilise Battn. runners for this purpose. Approach tapes 200 yards long will be laid out in the centre of each Battalion front.
(c) 2/Lieuts. WRIGHT & A.A. SIMPSON, plus 1 guide per platoon will parade at the entrance to the area at 10.00 a.m. as guides to the approach tape. Os.C. "A" & "B" Coys will each detail one man to report to above officers at the same time and at the same place to act as left & right flank markers respectively.
(d) 2/Lieuts. H.G. SIMPSON & QUARMBY will be at Point X on approach tape at 10.00 a.m.
(e) 2/Lieuts. CROSBIE & ROSS will be at Point Y, at junction of approach & assembly tape at 10.0 a.m.
(f) The Battalion will arrive "A", "B", "C", "D", "H.Q".

FORMATION:
3. (a) The Battalion will be in position by 11.00 a.m.
(b) The formations will be as if the hour was dawn and the assembly took place during the hours of darkness. i.e. Two Companies in front, "A" on the left, "B" on the right with "C" on left in rear of "A" and "D" on right in rear of "B" - each Company being in line of Sections, in file covering the Company frontage.
(c) Formation for the attack - Each Company on a 2 Platoon frontage - each Platoon with 2 Sections in each line, i.e. each Company will move in 4 lines of 4 Sections in file. Distance between lines - 15 yards.

OBJECTIVE.
4. The Blue line running from A.10.d.2.3. in a S.W. direction to A.16.a.6.7. This line will not be marked by flags. The distance from the assembly tape to the Blue line is 700 yards.

HEADQUARTERS
5. Battalion Headquarters on the road 250 yards in rear of the left of the Battalion front A.17.d.6.1.
Brigade Headquarters - A.17.d.8.4.

ATTACK.
6. The 3/5th & 2/6th L.F. will capture the Blue line and consolidate thereon in depth. The 8 platoons of the 2/8th Lan. Fus., "mopping up" behind the Battalion will establish strong points about 300 yards in rear of the Final objective.

BARRAGE
7. Represented by the drums of the attacking Battalions will come down at Zero hour 125 yards in front of the assembly tape and will stand for 4 minutes. Thereafter it will move forward for 200 yards at the rate of 100 yards per minute and will stand at every 200 yards for 10 minutes to enable the infantry to clear the ground & move up under it again. On reaching the final objective the barrage will stand 200 yards in front & become a protective barrage. The Barrage will be actually on the Blue line from Zero plus 30 to Zero plus 40.

ZERO HOUR
8. Zero hour will be 11.30 am which will be presumed to be dawn.

-2-

SYNCHRONISATION. 9. Watches will be synchronised by Lieut. YAPP at Brigade Headquarters at 10.45 a.m. with the Brigade Signalling Officer. He will then take the time to Company Commanders in the front line.

INSTRUCTIONS 10.
(a) At zero minus 10 the contact aeroplane will call up both Battalion Headquarters and receive "O.K" from each Battalion.
(b) During the attack flares will be lighted by the front line troops if called for by the Aeroplane. On reaching the final objective, flares will be lit by the front line troops and all signallers throughout the Brigade will signal their position by shutters.
(c) The aeroplane will call as usual by the KLAXON HORN and if that fails, by white Very lights.
(d) The aeroplane will fire several green Very Lights as a signal to the Infantry in the event of an enemy counter attack being observed developing.
(e) In event of a counter attack S.O.S. Signals will be sent up and action taken by troops in reserve to repel the attack.
(f) The "enemy" will consist of 2 Coys of the 2/7th Lan. Fus., under Lieut.- Col. HOBBINS, D.S.O.
(g) Messages will be sent to the contact aeroplane in accordance with S.S. 135 p.71 if the situation calls for them.
(h) Coys will endeavour to establish visual communication with Battalion Headquarters.
(i) "A" & "B" Coys will each draw 75 flares and 1 S.O.S. Signal from Battalion Headquarters tonight.

(sgd) A. S. BATES,

Lieut.- Colonel.
5.11.17.   Commanding 3/5th Bn. LANCASHIRE FUSILIERS

DISTRIBUTION

Copy No. 1. C.O.
2. 2nd in Command
3. Adjutant.
4. "A"
5. "B"
6. "C"
7. "D"
8. H.Q.
9. Lieut. YAPP.
10/12. War Diary.

BRIGADE TACTICAL EXERCISE No. 5.   Copy No.10

Ref. para. 6.

(a) The direction of the attack is 310 degrees grid, i.e. not exactly at right angles to the assembly tape but 12 degrees to the East of a right angle. The left is bounded by the road.

(b) The front line will be in charge of Captn. GOWLAND after the Blue line has been captured.

                              (sgd) A.S. BATES,
                                     Lieut.-Col.
5.11.17.   Commanding 3/5th Battn. LAN. FUS.,

Distribution

Copies 1-12. As per orders.

APPX II

SECRET   3/5th Bn. LANCASHIRE FUSILIERS   Copy No. 10
             Operation Order 23.   7.11.17.

1. The Battalion will move tomorrow to the WESTOUTRE Area.

2. It will entrain at EBBLINGHEM Station at 3.25 p.m. and will reach the station at 3.10 p.m.

3. An officer from each of "H.Q." "A" "B" "C" & "D" Coys will meet the C.O. at Hdqrs at 1.15 p.m. and proceed with him to the Station. Each Officer will have correct strength return of his Company and will be accompanied by an Orderly.

4. The Battalion will parade in the order "H.Q." "A" "B" "C" "D" facing East with the head of H.Q. Coy opposite the Gateway of Battn. Headquarters ready to move off at 1.25 p.m.

5. Breakfast will be issued at an hour to allow the cookers to be ready to move at 7.45 a.m.

6. Two lorries will report before noon. Two cooks per Company will travel on these lorries i.e. 8 men in all and will probably be the loading party. They will take camp kettles etc., in order to prepare tea for troops on arrival in WESTOUTRE.
Personnel of H.Q. Coy will take tea from their Company dixies on arrival at WESTOUTRE.

7. Blankets will be neatly & tightly rolled in bundles of ten and taken to the Q.M. Stores by 11.0 a.m.

8. Officers valises will be taken to the Q.M. Stores by 11.0 a.m.

9. Lorries will proceed independantly and will report to Lieut. CHRISTELOW, 2/7th Lan. Fus., at Area Commandant's Office, WESTOUTRE on arrival unless otherwise ordered.

10. Bicycles will proceed by road, those riding them being detailed by Sgt CALVERT.

                                         (sgd) R.S. MORLEY.
                                                     Captn.
                             A/Adjutant, 3/5th Lan. Fus.

             Distribution

             Copy No. 1. C.O.
                     2. 2nd in Commd.
                     3. Adjt & File.
                     4. "A"
                     5. "B"
                     6. "C"
                     7. "D"
                     8. H.Q.
                     9. Q.M.
                  10/12. War Diary

APPX III

SECRET   "COW" OPERATION ORDERS   Copy No. 12
9/11/17.

1. The Battalion will relieve the 2nd AUSTRALIAN BATTALION in the ZONNEBEKE Sector tomorrow.

2. It will take over the Support Battalion position.

3. Battalion will move in the order H.Q. - "A" - "B" - "C" - "D" Coys and proceed to HELL FIRE CORNER where guides from the Battalion to be relieved will meet their opposite Companies of the Battalion and guide them to their new positions.

4. H.Q. Coy will be ready to move at 9.0 a.m. and be at HELL FIRE CORNER at 10.0 a.m. Coys following at usual distances.

5. All secret maps, aeroplane photographs, trench stores, etc., will be handed over and a return rendered of each to Hdqrs as soon as possible.

6. Relief complete to be telephoned or conveyed by runner by code word "MINDEN".

7. ACKNOWLEDGE.

(sgd) R.S. MORLEY, Captn.
A/Adjutant.,

DISTRIBUTION

Copy No. 1. C.O.
2. 2nd in Commd.
3. Adjt & File.
4. "A"
5. "B"
6. "C"
7. "D"
8. H.Q.
9. T.O. & Q.M.
10/12. War Diary.

DISTRIBUTION OF OFFICERS AS AT 10/11/17.

APPENDIX

APPX III (a)

With Battalion. (23)

Lt.Col. A.S. BATES, D.S.O.
Captn. GOWLAND. S.J.
 " R.S. MORLEY.
Lieut. N.D. THOMPSON.
 " G.H. YAPP.
Captn. G.W. DEEPING,
 R.A.M.C.

Leave (2)

Capt. J. ROUSE.
Lt. MOLDSWORTH.
 J.H.

Courses (3)

Capt. H. HASTINGS.
A.B. GRELLIER
S. BELCHER.

Sick. (1)

T.G. PRESTON.
Capt. H. A. SANDIFORD.

"A" Coy

Captn. A.F. SENIOR.
Lieut. P.D. UREN.
 W. HALL.
 J. CROSBIE.

"B" Coy.

Captn. S.E. REID.
 J.C. BARLOW.
 L.F. WRIGHT.
 C.J. LEWIS.
 M.G. SIMPSON.

"C" Coy.

Captn. F.H. CROUCH.
 G.L.F. FORSHAW.
 H. ROSS.
 E.C. LOVELL.

"D" Coy.

Captn. R.S. ASHWORTH.
 E.J. DUNN.
 F.W. BELL.
 H.W. SMITH.

At Transport Lines. (6)

Lieut. A.F. ANONI.
Lt. & Qr.Mr. J.W. STEPTOE.
 A.A. SIMPSON.
 M.D. SMITH.
 A.J. LEWIS.
 T.W. QUARMBY.

All 2nd Lieuts unless otherwise stated.

30.11.17.

Major,
Commanding 3/5th Battn. LAN. FUS.

Appx IV.
Copy. No. 11.

"COW" OPERATION ORDERS

20.11.17.

1. The Battalion will move from CANAL DUGOUTS to CANAL AREA KRUISSTRAAT to-day.

2. It will occupy the billets vacated by the 2/6th MANCHESTER REGIMENT who will furnish 1 guide per Company & 1 for H.Q. Coy, to lead the Coys to their new area.

3. Guides will report to Headquarters at 1.0 p.m. and be taken to their opposite Companies by H.Q Runners

4. The Transport lines will not move.

5. ACKNOWLEDGE.

(sgd) R.S. MORLEY
Captain,
A/Adjutant.,

DISTRIBUTION

Copy No.1. C.O.
    2. 2nd in Commd.
    3. Adjt & File.
    4. "A"
    5. "B"
    6. "C"
    7. "D"
    8. T.O. & Q.M.
9/12. War Diary.

APPENDIX

CASUALTIES 10/11/17 - 19/11/17
3/5th BATTALION LANCASHIRE FUSILIERS.

OFFICERS:- 2 Killed.   2/Lts. E.C.LOVELL & G.L.F. FORSHAW.
            1 Wounded.   2/Lts. H.G. SIMPSON.
            1 Gassed.   2/Lt. L.F. WRIGHT.
            3 Sick.   Lt. P.D.UREN, 2/Lts. J.C.BARLOW
                                              F.W. BELL.
            ─
            7

OTHER RANKS:-

	H.Q.	"A"	"B"	"C"	"D"	Total
Killed	1	9	2	6	2	20
Wounded	3	12	10	6	8	39
Missing	-	3	4	-	-	7
Battle Casualties	4	24	16	12	10	66
Sick in Hospital	2	20	16	11	21	70
Losses from all causes	6	44	32	23	31	136

Biddulph Major
Comdg. 3/5 Lan.Fus.

APP^x VI

APPENDIX

DISTRIBUTION OF OFFICERS REFERRED TO IN APPENDIX AS AT 21/11/17.

DUTY (20)	LEAVE (4)	COURSES (2)	SICK (6)
Lt.Col.A.S. BATES D.S.O.		Capt.H. HASTINGS	Captn.S.J. GOWLAND.
Capt. R.S. MORLEY.	Capt. J. ROUSE.	S. BELCHER.	Lt. P.D. UREN.
Lieut.G.H. YAPP.	Lieut.J.A. HOLDSWORTH		J.C. BARLOW.
Capt. G.W. DEEPING. (R.A.M.C.)	Captn.S.E. REID.		F.W. BELL.
Lieut.A.F. ANONI.	Lt. N.D. THOMPSON.		T.G. PRESTON.
" J.W. STEPTOE.			Capt. H.A. SANDIFORD. (R.A.M.C.)

◊◊◊◊◊◊◊◊

"A" Coy.

Captn. A.F. SENIOR.
    A.J. LEWIS.
    A.A. SIMPSON.
    J. CROSBIE.

"B" Coy

    E.J. DUNN
    C.J. LEWIS.
    W. HALL.

"C" Coy.

Captn. F.H. CROUCH.
    H. ROSS.
    A.E. GRELLIER.

"D" Coy.

Captn. R.S. ASHWORTH.
    H.D. SMITH.
    H.W. SMITH.
    T.W. QUARMBY.

WOUNDED (2)	KILLED (2)
H.G. SIMPSON	G.L.F. FORSHAW.
L.F. WRIGHT.	E.C. LOVELL.

30.11.17.

J. Rudolph
Major,
Commanding 3/5th Battn. LAN. FUS.

APPX VII

SECRET.   "COW" OPERATION ORDER 23.   Copy No.12
                                                    21.11.17.

1. The Battalion will move to the STAPLE Area by stages. It will move to the BERTHEN Area tomorrow.
2. Parade on YPRES - BELGIAN BATTERY CORNER - BELGIAN CHATEAU road facing West, ready to move off at 7.55 a.m. Order of march - "H.Q." - "A" - "B" - "C" - "D", head of H.Q. Coy at BELGIAN BATTERY CORNER, remaining Coys closed up.
3. The Battalion will move in threes & Os.C. Coys will be careful that the pace is never hurried. They will be mounted and ride in rear of their Coys. Strict march discipline will be maintained and no one will fall out without a chit from his Company Commander.
4. Lorries on a scale of 3½ for the Unit will be at Brigade Headquarters at 7.0 a.m.
5. Drums will be distributed by Cpl DUCKWORTH throughout the Coys which will march with usual distances.
6. Blankets rolled in neat bundles of 10 will be in the Signallers Hut by 6.30 a.m. packs stacked on the road opposite the dump on route for place of parade in time to collect the Coys and fall them in ready to move off at the scheduled time. One guide per Coy will report to Sgt HALLIWELL at 6.0 a.m. when he will show them the spot where packs will be dumped.
    Officers valises will be in the Signallers Hut by 7.15 a.m.
7. Three men per Coy, 2 per H.Q. Coy and Pte A. WRIGHT will be detailed as loading party. These men will travel on the lorries and should be those who are unlikely to be able to complete the march. They will be under Lieut. YAPP & Sgt HALLIWELL. They will parade at Bn. H.Q. in full marching order at 7.0 a.m. Lieut. YAPP will be in charge of, and travel on the motor bus.
8. The following certified as unfit for marching tomorrow will parade at Battn. Hdqrs at 7.0 a.m. in full marching order:-

Hdqrs:- Regtl Sgt Major.

"A" Coy:- 203112 Pte CONVERY   47912 Pte GOULD.
           202376 Sgt BOWERS   205360 .. TRICKETT
"B" Coy:-   47931 Pte HAMMOND   22769 .. CAMPBELL
            24887 .. IDLE.H.   47825 .. JOHNSON.J.
           202453 .. DAVENPORT.W.
"C" Coy:-   47831 .. BALAAM.A.   202552 .. SANDERSON
           203187 .. DUKE   47853 .. ADAMS.
            47934 .. HOWARD.H.J.   203265 .. STEWART
           201975 .. HARRISON.J.   201952 L/C O'HARA
                     CSM DODDSON.
"D" Coy   202508 .. COCKROFT.A.   18145 L/C BOND.

9. A rear party of 1 NCO and 12 men from "A" Coy under 2/Lieut. SIMPSON.A.A. will remain behind to see that all billets and environments occupied by the Battalion are left clean & tidy for the incoming unit. This party will follow on to the BERTHEN Area (R.27) as soon as everything is left to 2/Lt's SIMPSON'S satisfaction and to that of the incoming Battalion.
10. ROUTE:- Radd junction R.14.b.5.8. - OUDERDOM - road junction R.29.b / central - RENINGHELST - WESTOUTRE - BERTHEN.

                                    (sgd) R. S. MORLEY. Captn.
            Distribution   A/Adjutant, "COW".

        1. C.O.   2. Adjt & File   3. "A" Coy
        4. "B" Coy   5. "C" Coy   6. "D" Coy
        7. H.Q.   8. T.O.   9. Q.M.
       10. M.O.   11. Major BIDDOLPH 12/14. War Diary.

ROUTINE ORDERS
by
Lieutenant-General Sir A.J.GODLEY, K.C.B., K.C.M.G.
Commanding 2nd ANZAC CORPS.

Headquarters,
26.11.1917.

G E N E R A L   S T A F F

N I L.

ADJUTANT & QUARTERMASTER GENERAL'S BRANCH

1435. MILITARY MEDAL:-

The Corps Commander under authority delegated to him has awarded the MILITARY MEDAL to the undermentioned man:-

Dated 25th November 1917.

3/5th Lanc. Fusiliers. (T.F). No. 3/19026 Pte C. U. WILKINSON.

"Certified true extract"

J. Biddulph
Major
Comdg. 3/5 Lanc. Fus.

SECRET   "COW" OPERATION ORDER - G. 24   Copy No.13
22.11.17.

1. The Battalion will move by 'bus to the STAPLE AREA tomorrow. It will embus at Crossroads X.4.c.3.4. at 10.0 am.

2. Coys will parade ready to move off with the head of "D" Coy at road junction R.33.a.4.2. at 9.15 a.m.

3. Order of march - "D" "C" "B" "A" "H.Q".

4. The one blanket per man issued tonight will be carried tomorrow, rolled & strapped to the back of the belt.

5. Indiscriminate carrying of unauthorised parcels is sandbags, etc., is forbidden.

6. All valises, Mess boxes, etc., drawn tonight must be ready packed at 6.30 a.m.
The T.O. will arrange for collection of these in sufficient time to be able to move his Transport at 7.30 a.m. He will also call for Water Carts, Field Kitchens, Mess Cart & Maltese Cart at 7.0 a.m. at which hour they will be ready.

7. A loading party will report at H.Q. tomorrow at 8.30 a.m. consisting of 1 N.C.O. and 8 men from "A" Coy. This party will travel on the lorries and will be in charge of the Q.M.

8. Os.C. Coys will be responsible for the leaving of their billets in a satisfactory condition.

                                       (sgd) R. S. MORLEY,
                                                Captain,
                                   A/Adjutant, "COW".

              Distribution

          Copy No.1. C.O.
                 2. 2nd in Commd.
                 3. "A"
                 4. "B"
                 5. "C"
                 6. "D"
                 7. H.Q.
                 8. T.O.
                 9. Q.M.
               10. Adjt.
               11. File.
               12. R.S.Major.
           13/15. War Diary.

Subj:- <u>Immediate Honours & Awards.</u>

Headquarters,
    197th Infantry Brigade.

I wish to bring to your notice the undermentioned man of this Battalion with a view, if possible, of his being awarded the MILITARY MEDAL for the reasons stated.

<u>3/19026 Private CHARLES ULRIC WILKINSON</u>

A Battalion runner. He behaved with the utmost gallantry, resource and coolness throughout the 6 days the Battalion was in the front line. He always made two trips per night to the front line, each taking 3 to 4 hours. On the day of relief, when there was still some question as to whether the tape lines were still in existence, he volunteered to lay an additional tape before dusk to ensure the route being well marked. This he did although HILLSIDE FARM, from which point he had to start and the ground beyond it was under hostile observation and heavy shell fire all the time. He subsequently led up the first reliefs and it was very largely owing to his work that the relief was so satisfactorily carried out. He set a splendid example to the other runners during the whole time.

(sgd) ARTHUR. S. BATES.
Lieut.-Col.
21.11.17. Commanding 3/5th Bn. LAN.FUS.

Appx X

NOMINAL ROLL OF OFFICERS
3/5th BATTALION LANCASHIRE FUSILIERS.

	Name	Perm. Rank	Temp. Rank	Act. Rank	How employed.
	BATES.A.S.	Major	Lieut.-Col	—	Leave.
£	GOWLAND.S.J.	Lieut.		Captain	Hospital
	ASHWORTH.R.S.	Captain			Coy Commander
	HASTINGS.H.	Lieut.		Captain	Course.
	CROUCH.F.H.	Lieut.		Captain	Coy Commander
	REID.S.E.	~~Lieut.~~	Lieut.	Captain	Coy Commander
	ROUSE.J.	Lieut.		Captain	Adjutant.
	MORLEY.R.S.	Lieut.		ø Captain	Coy Commander
	SENIOR.A.F. (13th E.Surrey.R)	Lieut.		ø Captain	Leave
	McARA.T.	Lieut.			Leave
	THOMPSON.N.D.	Lieut.			Leave
	HOLDSWORTH.J.A.	Lieut.			Signalling Off.
	ANONI.A.F.	Lieut.			Transport Off.
	BLAKE.T.R.	Lieut.			Att. 197th LTMB.
	UREN.P.D.	Lieut.			Hospital
	YAFP.G.H.	Lieut.			Att.197th Bde H.Q. (Intell.Off)
	BELL.F.W. (6th London R.)	2/Lieut.			Platoon Commdr.
øø	DUNN.E.J.		2/Lieut.		Platoon Commdr & 2nd in Commd of Company
øø	BELCHER.S.		2/Lieut.		Platoon Commdr & 2nd in Commd of Company
øø	PRESTON.T.G.		2/Lieut.		Hospital
øø	BARLOW.J.C.		2/Lieut.		Hospital
	HALL.W.	2/Lieut.			Platoon Commdr.
	WILSON.E.J. (A.L.in error)	2/Lieut.			Platoon Commdr.
@	GRELLIER.A.E.		2/Lieut.		Platoon Commdr.
@	SMITH.H.D.		2/Lieut.		Course (Traffic Control)
	CROSBIE.J.	2/Lieut.			Course
	LEWIS.C.J.	2/Lieut.			Platoon Commdr.
	ROSS.H.	2/Lieut.			Platoon Commdr.
@	LEWIS.A.J.		2/Lieut.		Platoon Commdr.
	SMITH.H.W.	2/Lieut.			Platoon Commdr.
	QUARMBY.T.W.	2/Lieut.			Platoon Commdr.
	SIMPSON.A.A.	2/Lieut.			Platoon Commdr.
@	DICKENS.W.C.		2/Lieut.		Platoon Commdr.
	STEPTOE.J.W.	Hon. Lieut. & QuarterMaster			Quarter Master
	SANDIFORD.H.A.	Captain (R.A.M.C.(T).)			Medical Officer

£ - 6th Lan. Fus.,
øø - 1st & 2nd Bns. Lan.Fus.(attached 3/5th Lan.Fus)
@ - 3rd Bn.(Res) Lan.Fus.(attached 3/5th Lan. Fus)
ø - Additional Captain.

A.Biddulph Major,
Commanding 3/5th Battn. LAN. FUS.

30.11.17.

197th Brigade.
66th Division.

3/5th BATTALION LANCASHIRE FUSILIERS DECEMBER 1917.

CONFIDENTIAL

WAR DIARY

of

3/5th Battalion, LANCASHIRE FUSILIERS

From :- 1.12.17

To :- 31.12.17.

VOLUME 10.

Army Form C. 2118.

WAR DIARY
3/5 LANCASHIRE (ENGINEER)
INTELLIGENCE SUMMARY.
(Erase heading not required.)

Place	Date	Hour	Summary of Events and Information	Remarks and references to Appendices
STAPLE	1917 DEC	5	DUTY:-	
			LIEUT. N.D. THOMPSON rejoined from leave	
			2/LIEUT. J. CROSBIE rejoined from Course of Instruction on Lewis Gun	
			(Course "A" G.H.Q. Small Arms School)	
			2/LIEUT. J.C. BARLOW rejoined from Hospital "S"	
			(LT.-COL. A.S. BATES D.S.O. rejoined from Leave 8/12/17)	
			2/LIEUT. C.J. LEWIS proceeded on Course of Instruction to I ANZAC CORPS	
			SCHOOL (TRENCH MORTAR (V. RSE)	
			Court-Martial:-	
			20443S PTE W. SMYTH 3/5th L.F. was tried by FIELD GENERAL COURT-MARTIAL	
			on the following charge. "When on active service deserting his majesty's service"	
			The accused having been warned to proceed to the trenches absented	
			himself with two others and remained absent until he surrendered himself	
			at a BASE DEPOT 3 days later. The sentence of the Court was "To suffer death	
			by being shot". Sentence was duly carried out at 6.30 AM	
		6	2/LIEUT. T.W. QUARMBY to Course B G.H.Q. Small Arms School Lewis Gun	

Army Form C. 2118.

WAR DIARY
3/5th LANCASHIRE FUSILIERS
INTELLIGENCE SUMMARY.
(Erase heading not required.)

Instructions regarding War Diaries and Intelligence Summaries are contained in F. S. Regs., Part II. and the Staff Manual respectively. Title pages will be prepared in manuscript.

Place	Date	Hour	Summary of Events and Information	Remarks and references to Appendices
STAPLE	1917 Dec			
		7	STRENGTH – REINFORCEMENT. – Draft of 14 N.C.O.s joined the Battalion.	
			MILITARY MEDAL – PRESENTATION. Major T.T. BIDDULPH presented the Military Medal to 3/19026 Pte. WILKINSON V.C.	
			ROUTE MARCH. (Ref: Sheet 28) Route:- U.11.a.8.2 – LONGUE CROIX – Road junction U.5.n.4.6 – CROSS ROADS O.28.a.4.7. – CROSS ROADS O.26.a.3.2. – MANOIR BLANCHE – CROSS ROADS N.23.d.8.4. – CROSS ROADS T.6.c.6.9. – Road junction T.12.a.5.7. – ROAD junction U.20.a.9.3. – CROSS ROAD U.22.a. 50.95. – BILLETS	
		8	LEAVE. Lieut. A.F. ANONI granted leave to 22/12/17	
			STRENGTH – INCREASE. 2/Lieuts. A.G. CRUMP and N.T. GIBSON from 6th (R) Bn Lanc. Fus. } joined 2/Lieuts. J.C. ANDERSON and N. BRAMWELL from 7th Lanc. Fus. } Battalion 2/Lieut. W.E. BELL from 8th Lanc. Fus.	

Army Form C. 2118.

WAR DIARY
3/5TH LANCASHIRE FUSILIERS
INTELLIGENCE SUMMARY.
(Erase heading not required.)

Place	Date	Hour	Summary of Events and Information	Remarks and references to Appendices
STAPLE	1917 DEC.	8	Lt. Col. A.S. BATES D.S.O. rejoined from leave 8/12/17 and assumed Command of the Battalion.	
		12	The undermentioned officers are appointed 2nd in Command of Companies as and from 12.12.17.	
			2/LIEUT S. BELCHER 'A' Coy	
			2/LIEUT E.J. DUNN 'B' Coy	
			2/LIEUT H. ROSS 'C' Coy	
			2/LIEUT H.W. SMITH 'D' Coy	
		14	A/CAPT. R.S. MORLEY 'A' Coy granted leave 14.12.17 to 26.12.17.	
			Christmas Celebrations. In order to minimise as far as possible the risk of Christmas Celebrations being disturbed by hostile moves the Major General Commanding approves of all celebrations taking place on WED. 19th inst.), which will be observed as a whole holiday throughout the Division.	
			LEAVE: LIEUT T. McARA 'C' Coy granted extension of leave to 13.12.18.	
			(Granada - Argenteuil)	
			LIEUT (A/CAPT. A.K. SENIOR 13TH E. SURREY REGT. a/tach 3/5TH LAN FUS granted	

WAR DIARY

3/5TH LANCASHIRE FUSILIERS

INTELLIGENCE SUMMARY

(Erase heading not required.)

Army Form C. 2118.

Place	Date	Hour	Summary of Events and Information	Remarks and references to Appendices
STAPLE	1917 DEC. 14		(cont.) Exclusion of leave to 1.1.16.	
	15		ROUTE MARCH - ROUTE - CROSS ROADS LONGDE CROIX V.5.C. - CROSS ROADS T.6.5. CROSS ROADS T.9.C.4.0 - RENESCURE - CROSS ROADS V.22a.8.0 - Cross Roads Staple.	
	16		DUTY:- LIEUT. (A/MAJOR) S.J.GOWLAND rejoined from sick leave.	
	19		Christmas celebrations were held throughout the Division. Divine Services were held in the morning. The N.C.O's and men thoroughly enjoyed the excellent dinner provided for them. The Commanding Officer visited all the Companies during the dinner-hour and wished to officers, N.C.O's and men the compliments of the season and the best of luck in the New Year. Football matches were played in the afternoon and Company held concerts in the evening.	
	21		Route March: ROUTE :- Road Junc. U.16.6.80. - LA BELLE HOTESSE - LYNDE - CROSS RDS V.19.a.6.2. - CROSS RDS T.18.a.9.0. - ROAD JUNC V.7.C.1.3 - LONGUE	

Army Form C. 2118.

WAR DIARY
5/6th LANCASHIRE FUSILIERS
INTELLIGENCE SUMMARY.

(Erase heading not required.)

Instructions regarding War Diaries and Intelligence Summaries are contained in F. S. Regs., Part II. and the Staff Manual respectively. Title pages will be prepared in manuscript.

Place	Date	Hour	Summary of Events and Information	Remarks and references to Appendices
STAPLE CROSS Rds	1917 DEC 21st (cont)		BILLETS.	
		22	STRENGTH — DECREASE.	
			2/Lieut. T.W. QUARMBY transferred to Machine Gun Corps, GRANTHAM 18/12/17 and struck off strength accordingly.	
			Extract from Supplement 6 London Gazette 18/12/17.	
			Mentioned in Despatches 7/11/17.	
			Lan. Fus: Major W. NIKE	
			Temp Sec. Lt. S. BELCHER 203678 Pte. H.W. LEADER (killed in action)	
	23		Extract from Supplement to London Gazette 21/12/17.	
			Mentioned in despatches 7/11/17.	
			SHROPS. LIGHT INF.	
			T/2nd Lt. (acting Lt. A/Capt.) S.E. REID Shropshire Light Inf.	
			allotted 3/5th LAN. FUS.	
	24		STRENGTH — DECREASE. — Lieut. T. McARA "C" Coy Struck off strength 15/12/17	
			2/Lt. L.K. WRIGHT B Coy to U.K. S. O. 12/12/17	
			DUTY — LIEUT. A.F. AVON — From leave.	

Army Form C. 2118.

WAR DIARY
3/5th LANCASHIRE FUSILIERS
INTELLIGENCE SUMMARY.

(Erase heading not required.)

Instructions regarding War Diaries and Intelligence Summaries are contained in F. S. Regs., Part II, and the Staff Manual respectively. Title pages will be prepared in manuscript.

Place	Date	Hour	Summary of Events and Information	Remarks and references to Appendices
STAPLE	1917 DEC 25		Xmas Day. Divine Service was held during the morning. No training was done.	
	28		LEAVE:- LIEUT. J.H. STEPTOE granted leave 26.12.17 to 9.1.18.	
	29		COMMAND:- LT-COL A.S. BATES D.S.O relinquishes command of the Battalion as such from 29.12.17 and assumes temporary command of the Brigade during the absence on leave of BRIG-GEN. O.C. BORRETT, D.S.O. MAJOR T.J. BIDDULPH 2/8th LAN. FUS. assumes command of the Battalion during the temporary absence of LT-COL A.S. BATES D.S.O. Extract from London Gazette – Supplement – Dated 24/12/17: mentioned in Despatches :- 7.11.17 CAPTAIN R.A. SANDFORD, M.C., R.A.M.C. (T.F.)	
	30		DUTY:- CAPTAIN R.S. MORLEY "A" Coy. from leave 30/12/17 MOVE:- The Transport moved to GODENAERSVELDE, SOUTH AREA (OPERATION ORDERS G30)	

Army Form C. 2118.

WAR DIARY
3/5" LANCASHIRE FUSILIERS
INTELLIGENCE SUMMARY.
(Erase heading not required.)

Instructions regarding War Diaries and Intelligence Summaries are contained in F. S. Regs., Part II. and the Staff Manual respectively. Title pages will be prepared in manuscript.

Place	Date	Hour	Summary of Events and Information	Remarks and references to Appendices
STAPLE	1917 DEC 30		(contd.) the transport rested at this place for the night	
			An advance party of 5 officers left STAPLE for BUSSEBOOM to take over details of work on the CORPS SUPPORT LINE from the 2/5th Bn MANC. REGT.	
		31	Moved the Battalion entrained at O.34.6.33 and proceeded to BUSSEBOOM and relieved the 2/5th Bn MANC. REGT in DEVONSHIRE CAMP	See O.063.
BUSSEBOOM				

SECRET   OPERATION ORDERS G. 30.   Copy No 5.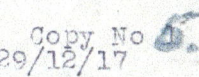
                                            29/12/17

1. The Transport will move to BUSSEBOOM by stages. O.C. 542 Coy. A.S.C. will be in charge.

2. It will move to GODEWAERSVELDE, South Area, tomorrow, and on 31/12/17 to BUSSEBOOM, arriving there by 3.00 p.m.

3. Starting point LONGUE CROIX at 9.15 a.m. 30/12/17.

     N.B. (1)   2/Lieut. DICKENS, A/Q.M. (Mounted) and 2 O.Rs,. on bicycles will report to an officer detailed by O.C. 542 Coy A.S.C. at Area Commandant's Office, GODEWAERSVELDE at 11.00 a 30/12/17. This Officer will allot him a billeting area for the night 30th/ 31st December 1917.
         (11)   Any route may be taken.

4. ORDNANCE:-   The Brigade Ordnance Dump will be at H.16.d.2.2. on and after 1st January.

5. BAGGAGE WAGONS:- will report to this Unit at 4.00 pm on 29/12/17. They will move with the Transport and remain with them until arrival in the new area.

6. 1. Wagon G.S. will be detailed from Train Coy to report to this Unit on 29/12/17 to carry second days supplies for transport and personnel moving by road. This wagon will march with the Transport and report to Train Coy immediately on arrival in new area.
        Only supplies will be loaded on this Wagon.

7. The Transport Officer will arrange for horses for Comapny L.G. Limbers and Field Kitchens to be at respective Company Headquarters as under:-

            "A" & "D" Coys   7.45 a.m. 30/12/17
            "B" & "C" Coys   8.00 a.m.   ..

8. Train Transport will deliver rations direct to units on 31st Decr & 1st January respectively for consumption on 1st & 2nd January respectively.
On and after 2nd January supplies will be drawn by 1st Line Transport at refilling point.

Issued at 4 pm.   Captain,
                            Adjutant, 3/5th Battn, LANCASHIRE FUSILRS

                   Distribution
          Copy No.1. Adjt & File
                2. Transport Officer
                3. Quartermaster
                4. War Diary
                5. .. ..

SECRET
Copy No. 10.
30/12/1917

OPERATION ORDER G.31.

Map reference:- Sheets 27 & 28, 1/40,000.

1. The Battalion will proceed to BUSSEBOOM (O.22.b.8.7.) tomorrow 31/12/17 by 'bus and relieve the 2/5th MANCHESTER REGIMENT.

2. Coys will parade in sufficient time to enable them to pass the LONGUE CROIX Crossroads as follows:-

   "A" Coy   9.50 a.m.
   "B" Coy   9.51 a.m.
   "C" Coy   9.52 a.m.
   "D" Coy   9.53 a.m.
   H.Q Coy   9.54 a.m.

   They will form up 110 yards S. of 2/8th Lan. Fus., on road from U.5.a.4.6. to O.34.b.3.7.

3. DRESS:- Full marching order, including 2 blankets - greatcoats will be worn. Unconsumed portion of rations for 31/12/17 to be carried on the man.

4. EMBUSSING POINT:- On road from U.5.a.4.6. to O.34.b.3.7.
   Time:- 10.30 a.m.   Debus at O.22.b.5.4.

5. Officers Valises, Mess Boxes, etc., must be ready packed and dumped at 8.15 a.m. 31/12/17 at the following places:-

   "A" Coy
   "B" "C" & "D" Coys   Road junction U.16.b.9.4.
                                        U.11.a.2.3.
   H.Q. Coy.   Crossroads U.9.c.9.5.

   R.Q.M.S BERRY will arrange to collect in a lorry.
   Any kits, etc., not there to time will be brought to new area under Company arrangements.

6. The following will parade at the Orderly Room at 7.45 a.m. 31/12/17 and work under R.Q.M.S BERRY as loading and unloading party.

   201193 R.Q.M.S BERRY   203084 Cpl GOWLAND, "H.Q"
   200872 Pte WALSH.A."B"   201290 Pte ASHWORTH "H.Q"
                     Pte REDFERN (2/8th L.F)

   In addition, 1 man from each Company who would be useful for preparing for the arrival of Coys in the new area.

7. Os.C. Coys will see that all instructions in Warning Order dated 25/12/17 and amendment dated 29/12/17 are fully complied with before leaving this area.

8. All billet and Area stores (including gum boots, thigh) now held by the 2/5th MANCHESTER REGIMENT in the forward area will be taken over and receipts obtained.

9. ACKNOWLEDGE.

Issued at 12.50 p.m.

Captain,
Adjutant, 2/8th Bn. LAN. FUS.

DISTRIBUTION

Copy No.1.   C.O.   Copy No.2.   Adjt & File.
        3.   "A" Coy   4.   "B" Coy.
        5.   "C" Coy   6.   "D" Coy.
        7.   H.Q. Coy   8.   M.Os & R.S.M.
        9.   War Diary   10.   War Diary.

CONFIDENTIAL.

WAR DIARY
OF
3/5TH BATTALION LANCASHIRE FUSILIERS
FROM:- 1.1.18.   TO:- 31.1.18.

(VOLUME. 11.)

Army Form C. 2118.

WAR DIARY
3/5th LANCASHIRE FUSILIERS
INTELLIGENCE SUMMARY.
(Erase heading not required.)

Instructions regarding War Diaries and Intelligence Summaries are contained in F. S. Regs., Part II. and the Staff Manual respectively. Title pages will be prepared in manuscript.

Place	Date	Hour	Summary of Events and Information	Remarks and references to Appendices
Bussebeom	1918 Jan.	1	Commencing on this day the Battalion sent two kinds of to trench strength	(APPENDIX I.)
(Nr.) BELGIUM			to work daily on the CORPS SUPPORT LINE (POSTS 1.2 and 3 and C.T.)	APPENDIX E
AND FRANCE			for details of the work and arrangements see APPENDICES I, II & III	APPENDIX III
SHEET 28			COMPANY TRANSFER :-	
EDITION 3			2/Lieut. S. BELCHER 'A' Coy transferred to 'B' Coy as from 1.1.18	
G.22.C.8.6.)		2	Usual work on CORPS SUPPORT LINE (maps referred):- No1. POST at J.14.b.3.3.-	
			No 2. POST J.14.6.8.9. - No 3 POST J.9.c.3.3)	
			STRENGTH - INCREASE :-	
			LIEUT. E.H. PARSONS (8th LAN. Fus.) transferred from 2/6"	
			Bn LAN. FUS. and taken on strength of the Battalion with effect from	
			28th Dec. 1917.	
			APPOINTMENTS :-	
			CAPTn J.A. HOLDSWORTH relinquishes the appointment of	
			Signalling Officer as of from 28.12.17.	
			LIEUT. E.H. PARSONS appointed Signalling Officer as and from	
			26.12.17	

Army Form C. 2118.

WAR DIARY
3/5th LANCASHIRE FUSILIERS
INTELLIGENCE SUMMARY.
(Erase heading not required.)

Place	Date	Hour	Summary of Events and Information	Remarks and references to Appendices
BUSSEBOOM	1916 JAN	2	(CONT.) CAPT. R.S. MORLEY "A" COY relinquishes the appointment of ASST. ADJUTANT as of from 28.12.17. CAPT. J.A. HUDSWORTH appointed ASST. ADJUTANT as of from 28.12.17.	
		3	Usual work on CORPS LINE. The ARMY COMMANDER and CORPS COMMANDER inspected the CORPS SUPPORT LINE and the former expressed his appreciation of the work done. SICK LEAVE:- 2/LIEUT. T.G. PRESTON "C" COY granted 8 weeks sick leave to U.K. 22.12.17.	
		4	Usual work on CORPS SUPPORT LINE. AWARD:- Extract from LONDON GAZETTE SUPPLEMENT dated 1.1.1918 for distinguished conduct in the Field: Awarded the MILITARY CROSS. LT. (A/CAPT.) FRANCIS HARRIE CROUCH. PROMOTION:- Extract from LONDON GAZETTE SUPPLEMENT dated 2.1.1918 LAN. FUS: LT. N.D. THOMPSON to be CAPTAIN. NOV. 15. 1917.	
		5	Usual work on CORPS SUPPORT LINE.	

Army Form C. 2118.

WAR DIARY
3/5TH LANCASHIRE FUSILIERS
INTELLIGENCE SUMMARY.
(Erase heading not required.)

Place	Date	Hour	Summary of Events and Information	Remarks and references to Appendices
	1918			
BUSSEBOOM	JAN 6		Usual work on CORPS SUPPORT LINE.	
	7		Work on CORPS LINE	
			DUTY:- 2/Lt. E.T. DUNN B' Coy rejoined from leave 7.1.18.	
			STRENGTH:- DECREASE:- Lt.Col. A.S. BATES D.S.O. to U.K. 7.1.18. (Auth. W.O.L. 76/FRANCE/1937(M.S.1.a) dated 13.8.17) 2/Lt T.J. BIDDULPH to U.K. 7.1.18. (Auth M.S.1.a) dated 13.8.17) 2/Lt.M.Fox attached Command of Battalion assumed from 7.1.18	
	8.		Work on CORPS LINE.	
	9.		Work on CORPS LINE	
	10.		Work on CORPS LINE.	
HALIFAX CAMP (H.14.c.3.5.)	11		Move to new area, the Battalion moved to Halifax Camp and relieved 1/5 Bn. WEST RIDING REGT. the 197th Inf. Bde the 147th Bde in Divisional (OPERATION ORDER No C.3) Reserve. The Battalion had to march a distance of 3 miles only to the (INDENT NOT ATTACHED) Camp. (MSIVE) ONE	
	12		Following parties were found daily for work with H20 & Coy R.E. (REF:U.O.C.2) No.1. Party working on SLAB ROAD (50 workers) No.3. " " " "K" TRACK (20 workers)	
	13.		Working Parties as on 12th inst.,	

Army Form C. 2118.

WAR DIARY
3/5th Bn LANCASHIRE FUSILIERS
INTELLIGENCE SUMMARY.
(Erase heading not required.)

Place	Date	Hour	Summary of Events and Information	Remarks and references to Appendices
HALIFAX CAMP (H.14.C.3.5) SHEET 28.	1918 JAN. 14.		Working parties found as on 13th inst.	
	15		Working parties found as on 14th inst.	
			Attachment :- 2/Lt. H.D. SMITH "D" Coy attached to A.P.M. 66th Div. for Traffic Control Duties.	
			Duty :- 2/Lt. F.W. BELL "D" Coy from 430th FIELD Coy R.E. 11.1.18	
			2/Lt. A.J. LEWIS "A" Coy to 4th ARMY ANTIGAS SCHOOL 13.1.18	
			Course of Instruction :-	
			Award :- Extract from Battalion orders part 1. dated 14.1.18	
			"The Commanding Officer wishes to congratulate the undermentioned N.C.O. who has been awarded the DISTINGUISHED CONDUCT MEDAL Extract from LONDON GAZETTE SUPPLEMENT d/a 1.1.18 For distinguished conduct in the field"	
			204360 A/SGT. SEED. R. "D" Coy.	
			Extract from LONDON GAZETTE SUPPLEMENT d/a JAN.9.1918. Lancs. Fus :- Lt. (A/Capt) (additional) F.H. CROUCH retains the acting rank	

Army Form C. 2118.

WAR DIARY
3/5th LANCASHIRE FUSILIERS
INTELLIGENCE SUMMARY.

(Erase heading not required.)

Instructions regarding War Diaries and Intelligence Summaries are contained in F. S. Regs., Part II. and the Staff Manual respectively. Title pages will be prepared in manuscript.

Place	Date	Hour	Summary of Events and Information	Remarks and references to Appendices
HALIFAX	1918 JAN. 15		A/Capt. whilst comdg. a Co. (Oct. G.1917)	(See APPENDIX I)
CAMP			Extract from London Gazette Supplement d/d Jan.10.1918. Lancs. Fus:- Temp. Lt. S.E. REID SHROP. L.I. to be actg. Capt. whilst comdg. a Co.	
			To be actg. Capt. (acting) - Lt. R.J. TURLEY	
			TEMP. LT. A.F. SENIOR E.SUR.R (Oct.26.1917)	
LINE	16.		The Battalion relieved the 2/4th Bn. E. Lan. Regt. in the Line	SEE OPERATION ORDER G.33 (APPENDIX II)
H.O. D.16.d.8.2.				
LINE	17		Battalion in the line. Detail camp at HALIFAX CAMP. Extract from London Gazette Supplement d/d Jan.12.1918. Lancs. Fus:- Lt. J. ROWSE to be A/Capt. with pay allowances of a Lt. whilst empld. as ADJT.	APPENDIX III APPENDIX IV APPENDIX V APPENDIX VI
			Sick Leave:- Lieut. P.D. UREN "A" Coy to U.K. (sick leave) 29.12.17 G.T.P.116.	
			Course of Instruction:- 2/Lt. H. ROSS "C" Coy to 22nd CORPS GENERAL SCHOOL 15.1.18	

Army Form C. 2118.

WAR DIARY
2/5 LANCASHIRE FUSILIERS
INTELLIGENCE SUMMARY.
(Erase heading not required.)

Place	Date	Hour	Summary of Events and Information	Remarks and references to Appendices
HALIFAX (CAMP)	1918 JAN	18	Duty :- 2/Lt. W.E. BELL B Coy. from Course of Instruction 2.1.18	
LINE		20	A composite company being required by the 2/6th Lan. Fus. for duty in the line the Battalion detailed 2 Platoons under 2/Lt W.E. BELL for duty with above. These Platoons were found from the "Details" Camp. STRENGTH - INCREASE :- Lieut. (A/CAPT) A.F. SENIOR 'A' Coy awaiting trial. Board in U.K. under instruction from War Office. Extract from List No. 170 d/d 13.1.18 :- The undermentioned relinquish the pay of Tem. acting rank under the terms of A.R.O. 2678 d/d.9 Oct 1917. Temp Lt. (A/CAPT.) A.F. SENIOR 13th Bn. E. SURREY R. on ceasing to be Acting Capt. (additional) 12th DEC. 1917	
LINE		21	Duty :- 2/Lieut A.J. LEWIS A Coy from Course of Instruction 20.1.18 2/Lieut A.R. SIMPSON A Coy from Course of Instruction 21.1.18	
SUPPORT T.3 a.4.u SUPPORT		22	Battalion relieved by 2/7th LAN. Fus and moved into SUPPORT at ANZAC HOUSE	APPENDIX X
		23	STRENGTH - DECREASE :- 2/Lt. T.G. PRESTON D Coy Medical Board Ordered (U.K.) War Office List d/d 15.1.18.	

Army Form C. 2118.

WAR DIARY
3/5th LANCASHIRE FUSILIERS
INTELLIGENCE SUMMARY.
(Erase heading not required.)

Instructions regarding War Diaries and Intelligence Summaries are contained in F.S. Regs., Part II. and the Staff Manual respectively. Title pages will be prepared in manuscript.

Place	Date	Hour	Summary of Events and Information	Remarks and references to Appendices
	1918			
SUPPORT	JAN 24		Strength decreased:- Lt. QM. T.W. STOPPOE - Recent Board ordered Was Office Lout.	
T.3.a.4.2			A/ad 17.1.18	
SUPPORT	26.		Leave:- 2/Lt. J.C. BARLOW 'B' Coy GRANTED Leave to U.K. 27.1.18 to 10.2.18.	
			Hospital:- 2/Lt. A.G. CRUMP 'D' Coy to Hospital Sick 25.1.18	
SUPPORT	27		Course of Instruction:- 2/Lt. N. HALL 'B' Coy to 22nd Bspn Gas School MONTECQUE 22nd	
HALIFAX CAMP	28		Battalion relieved by 2/7th MANCHESTER R. and moved to HALIFAX CAMP. APPENDIX A.	
	29		A working party of 2 officers and 100 workers was found for salvage work on CAMBRIDGE ROAD.	
	30		Working party found for Salvage work on CAMBRIDGE ROAD	
	31		HOSPITAL:- LIEUT. A.F. ANONI to HOSPITAL Dental Treatment 26.1.18	
			Duty:- 2/Lt. F.W. BELL from leave 29.1.18	
			LIEUT. A.F. ANONI from HOSPITAL (Dentist) 29.1.18	
			Leave:- LIEUT. E.H. PARSONS GRANTED Leave 1.2.18 to 15.2.18.	

31/1/18

APPENDIX 1.

S E C R E T

WORK ON CORPS LINE:-

In continuation of notes issued 2/1/18.

9. Hours of work:- All parties must work within 1¼ hours of detraining, and must not stop work till 1¼ hours before their train goes. Should any party NOT commence work within the above limits, a report will be rendered to Battn. H.Q. explaining the reason.

10. Dress:- Skeleton drill order - i.e. Rifle, Bayonet, 120 rounds S.A.A. filled waterbottle, haversack containing iron ration complete & haversack ration. NO pack and NO entrenching tool.

11. Points to be noted by all Officers:-

(1) The same Unit should always be kept on the same work, i.e. reliefs should be arranged by withdrawing so many men from each platoon and NOT by withdrawing a whole platoon at a time.

(2) When digging breastworks, borrow pits should seldom be nearer than ten feet to the front of the firing trench.

(3) Always draw or pump water out of a shell hole before filling it up.

(4) Until the ground is entirely thawed no earth will be put on top of filled gabions. The parapet can be built up except that the top of the gabions will be left clear so that when the earth sinks owing to the thaw, more earth can be put in and so prevent the gabions telescoping.

(sgd) T.J. BIDDOLPH.
Major.
3.1.18　　　　　　　　Commanding 3/5th Bn. LANCASHIRE FUSILIERS.

APPENDIX II

WORK ON CORPS LINE

The following arrangements will come into force at once and will be STRICTLY COMPLIED WITH.

1. 2/Lieut. F.W. BELL will act as Liason Officer between the R.E. and the Battalion & will visit works daily, will ensure that all stores are available, & that the Officers are fully acquainted with details of the work allotted to them. He will meet the train each morning & will accompany the C.O. (or 2nd in Command) to the work. He will bring to the notice of the C.O. and to the notice of the O.C. Field Coy R.E. any difficulties which Officers in charge may have. ~~Cancelled~~

2. All Officers & superintending N.C.O's are to be provided at once with working drawings of the work for which they are responsible.

3. Two thirds of the working strength of the Battalion to be turned out daily, so that each man gets one day's rest in three.

4. Daily tasks are to be arranged for in consultation with R.E. Officers concerned and where such tasks are not completed, men concerned are to be turned out for work on their resting day.

5. The work for ensuing day must be laid out & tasks allotted on the previous day by superintending officers & NCOs.

6. Stretcher Bearers to be given half tasks.

7. Two Company Commanders will proceed with the parties daily. They will be responsible for same sections of the work & will relieve each other as follows:-

   O.C. "A" & "B" Coys work together & relieve each other.
   .. "C" & "D" ..   ..

   O.C. "A" & "B" repensible for supervising of No.1 post & Support line
   .. "C" & "D" responsible for Nos. 2 & 3 posts

8. All Officers will make full use of the ~~Liason Officer~~ R.E. Officers on the work so that the work will always be making satisfactory progress & material will never be lacking.

         (sgd) T. J. BIDDULPH.,
              Major.
2.1.18.   Commanding 3/5th Battn. LAN. FUS.,

SECRET.

APPENDIX III

Copy No.
3.1.18.

3/5th Bn. LANCASHIRE FUSILIERS.

INSTRUCTIONS FOR WORKING PARTIES IN CASE OF ATTACK.

1. In case of enemy attack during working hours, working parties on the CORPS LINE SYSTEM will come under orders of B.G.C's Brigades in the line as under:-

2. Working parties of this Battalion will come under the tactical command of B.G.C. Right Brigade, New Zealand Division, H.Q. HOOGE CRATER (I.18.b.0.5.) and will rendezvous at GLENCORSE WOOD, J.14.b.2.9. in conjunction with "A" Company, 2/6th L.F.

3. Rendezvous will be marked by a board.
    (For 3/5th L.F. & "A" Coy 2/6th L.F)   GLENCORSE AREA.

4. Communication will be maintained as under:-
    3/5th Lan. Fus.   )
    2/6th Lan. Fus. "A" Coy) Test Point F.F. J.14.b.3.3.
    The S.O. will arrange to reconnoitre the above TEST POINTS and every day sufficient signallers with the necessary instruments will parade with the working parties to establish communication if necessary.

5. The Officer i/c the Battalion Party will report DAILY to the Brigade H.Q. under whose command they will be in case of attack.

6. In case of alarm or very heavy shelling the Officer i/c the Battalion Party will send an Officer and 2 Runners to report to the Brigade H.Q. as above.

7. In the event of the enemy breaking through, working parties in the absence of other orders will fight on their own initiative on or near the ground where they are working.

8. In the event of "Battle Precautions" being ordered working parties will rendezvous as above, and at once establish communication with their different Brigade H.Q.

9. No working party will be withdrawn without orders from the B.G.C. responsible for the Sector.

10. AMMUNITION:- An extra supply of 100 boxes S.A.A. is being maintained at GARTER POINT, J.3.a.1.4.

11. HOSTILE AEROPLANES:- Each party will post an aeroplane sentry. On the approach of a hostile aeroplane all ranks will take cover or lie down and remain motionless and NOT look up.

12. All working parties will be armed. During work arms will be piled or laid on the ground in the immediate vicinity of the owner.

13. ACKNOWLEDGE.

    Issued at. 6.30 p.m.

(sgd) T.J. BIDDOLPH.
Major,
Commanding 3/5th Bn. Lan. Fus.,

DISTRIBUTION

Copy No.1.	C.O.	Copy No.2.	2nd in Command.
3.	O.C. "A" Coy	4.	O.C. "B" Coy
5.	O.C. "C" Coy	6.	O.C. "D" Coy
7.	Signalling Offr.	8.	File.
9.	War Diary	10.	War Diary.

NOT TO BE TAKEN INTO FRONT LINE IN ACTION.　　APPENDIX IV

Page No. 9

EXTRACTS FROM PRELIMINARY INSTRUCTIONS ISSUED BY
197th INFANTRY BRIGADE FOR THE RELIEF OF THE
147th INFANTRY BRIGADE
----

1. RELIEF. The 66th Division (less Artillery) will relieve the 49th Division in the line between the 10th & 13th January.

2. DEFENCE SCHEME. The line will be taken over exactly in accordance with the scHEME of the 49th Division.

3. DISPOSITIONS ON RELIEF. The 197th Infantry Brigade will relieve the 147th Infantry Brigade in Divisional Reserve. Instructions as to relief to be carried out by this Battalion will be issued later.

4. WORK ON CORPS LINE. The 197th Infantry Brigade will cease work on the Corps Line on evening of January 11th. Four Battalions of the 49th Division will take over the work on January 13th. No work on Jany. 12th.

5. PRINCIPLES OF DEFENCE. (a) The extreme importance of the position which the Division is about to take over & the necessity for the most vigorous action in the event of a temporary hostile success must be impressed on all ranks.
(b) The whole of the front line system is to be held at all costs. If the enemy does succeed in penetrating into any part of our position, he is to be ejected at once by immediate local counter-attack.

6. ACTION IN CASE OF ATTACK. (i) <u>Probable forms of attack</u>. The enemy is not likely to attack the Divisional front as an isolated operation.
His most probable lines of advance are:-
(a) By the GRAVENSTAFEL and POELCAPPELLE Spurs parallel to the YPRES-ROULERS Road.
(b) By the BELLEVUE Spur towards MOSSELMARKT and KERSELAAR.
(c) By the WALLEMOLEN Spur towards the main BROODSEINDE - PASSCHENDAELE RIDGE.
An attack under (a) would fall on the Corps on our Right but success there would immediately threaten our gun positions & communication. A successful attack under (c) would threaten our possession of PASSCHENDAELE which must be looked upon as a position of the utmost importance.
(ii) <u>Action of Divisional Reserve</u>. As soon as it is evident that a serious attack is being made on our front, the following Urgent Operation Priority message will be sent to all concerned:-
MAN DIVISIONAL RESERVE
on receipt of which, action will be taken at once in accordance with this scheme.
The Reserve Brigade will be moved by the undermentioned routes to positions of assembly (to be reconnoitred by officers of the Reserve Brigade) in the POTIJZE Area.
ROUTES:- (i) VLAMERTINGHE - YPRES - BANKS WALK.
(ii) OUDERDOM - H.14.b.5.7. - H.16.c.1.1. - ASYLUMSTRAAT INFANTRY BARRACKS - LILLE GATE - BUNDEL Road.
R.E. Companies and Pioneer Battalion of 49th Division will assemble in POTIJZE Area.
NOTE:- Reconnaissance of all tracks & approaches to positions of assembly & from the Reserve Brigade area to all parts of the front line will be made by all officers of the Brigade in reserve. In addition all officers of the Brigade in reserve will make themselves acquainted with the tracks & with the positions of Brigade & Battalion Hdqrs. in the area of the Divisions on their flanks.
(iii) <u>Action of Detached Units</u>
(a) All parties temporarily detached from their units for work, etc. which at the time of alarm are east of the WESTHOEK LINE will be at the tactical disposal of the G.O.C. Inf. Bdes. in the line.
(b) In the event of the enemy breaking through before other orders can reach them, working parties will fight on the initiative of

-2-

7.
LOCATIONS OF HDQRS. A location list of Hdqrs. of Units of the 49th Division is attached to copies Nos. 1 to 6 only.

8. Further details as to moves and reliefs will be issued later.

9. ACKNOWLEDGE.

[signature]
Captain,
Adjutant, 2/5th Bn. D.L.I.

Issued at 8pm 8/1/18.

DISTRIBUTION

```
Copy No. 1.    C.O.
        2.    2nd in Command.
        3.    O.C. "A" Coy
        4.    O.C. "B" Coy
        5.    O.C. "C" Coy
        6.    O.C. "D" Coy
        7.    Q.M.
        8.    T.O.
        9.    War Diary.
       10.    War Diary.
       11.    File.
```

SECRET   Copy No. 12

APPENDIX V

3/5th BATT. LANCASHIRE FUSILIERS.

OPERATION ORDER No. G.32

Map reference   11th Jan.1918.
Sheet 28, 1/40,000

1. The 197th Infantry Brigade will relieve the 147th Infantry Brigade in DIVISIONAL RESERVE.
Relief to be complete by 2 p.m.
2. The Battalion will relieve the 5th West Riding Regt. at HALIFAX CAMP (H.14.c.3.5) tomorrow, the 12th inst., It will be relieved in this Camp by the 4th West Riding Regt.
3. INSTRUCTIONS:-

    (a) <u>Order of March</u> - Band & H.Q. "A", "B", "C", "D", Transport.
    (b) <u>Starting point</u> - Crossroads at G.23.c.7.5.
    (c) <u>Time</u> - 10.15 a.m.
    (d) <u>Route</u> - X roads G.23.c.7.5. - OUDERDOM - left to X roads G.30.b.1.9 - HALIFAX CAMP (H.14.c.3.5)
    (e) <u>Baggage</u> - All Officers kits, Mess boxes, etc., to be stacked by Transport Lines opposite DEVONSHIRE CAMP Notice Board by 8.00 a.m. 12.1.18 Lewis gun limbers, Field Kitchens, etc., to be ready loaded under Company arrangements by 9.15 a.m 12.1.18
    (f) <u>Loading Party</u> - O.C. "C" Coy will detail a loading party consisting of 1 NCO and 10 men to report to Q.M. Stores at 8.00 a.m. 12.1.18
    (g) <u>Blankets</u> - One will be carried by the man and the other by the Transport. The latter to be rolled in bundles of 9 with a tenth rolled round them and stacked at the corner of the Farm nearest the Transport Lines at 8.00 a.m.
    (h) <u>March discipline</u> - Strict march discipline will be maintained and distances in accordance with Fourth Army No. G.S. 148 issued to O.C. Coys.

4. ADVANCE PARTY:-
consisting of Captain THOMPSON and 1 NCO per Coy including H.Q. Coy, will proceed to HALIFAX CAMP this afternoon to take over everything in connection with the Camp, including A.A. mountings, code names & station calls, &c (if any)
This party will parade at the Orderly Room at 3.00 p.m. 11.1.18
Dress, Full marching order, 1 blanket and rations for 12.1.18.

5. REAR PARTY:-
consisting of Captn. MORLEY, 1 Senior NCO and 20 men of "A" Coy will remain behind to complete cleaning up the Camp, and will ensure same being left in a satisfactory condition. This party will not leave until the arrival of the incoming Battalion, and Capt. MORLEY will, before leaving, obtain a certificate to the effect that the Camp has been handed over in a clean, sanitary and satisfactory condition.

6. ACKNOWLEDGE.

                                                                                     J. House
                                                                                       Captain,

Issued at 1 p.m.   Adjutant, 3/5th Bn. LANCS. FUSLRS.
11.1.18.

                                          DISTRIBUTION

Copy No.1. C.O.   Copy No.2. Second in Command.   Copy No.3. O.C. "A" Coy
      4. O.C. "B" Coy   5. O.C. "C" Coy   6. O.C. "D" Coy
      7. Q.M.   8. T.O.   9. Sig. Offcr
      10. Capt. THOMPSON   11. Capt. MORLEY   12. War Diary
      13. War Diary   14. File.

SECRET.   Copy No. 12

APPENDIX VI

W.D.

ADMINISTRATIVE INSTRUCTIONS issued with reference to 3/5th Bn. LANCASHIRE FUSILIERS. O.O. G.32

oooooooooooooooooooooooooo

1. TRENCH STORES & AREA STORES in 49TH DIVISIONAL AREA:-

    (a) Area Stores in Camps at present occupied will be handed over and receipts obtained.

    (b) All reserve supplies, ammunition, trench and area stores, will be carefully checked before being taken over and receipts will be given. Duplicate receipts will be forwarded to Battalion H.Q. by 12th instant.

    (c) Packsaddlery as under will be handed over by 147th INFANTRY BRIGADE H.Q.:-

72 sets	(Inf. Bde H.Q............ 4 sets
	(Each Inf. Battalion.....17 sets

2. TRENCH FOOT:-

    (a) Attention is called to 66th Divn. letter No. 2341/A dated 13th Decbr. 1917 issued to all Officers on 15.12.17.
    It is most important that every man's feet are carefully washed and treated as laid down in the above quoted letter before going into the trenches.

    (b) Socks:-

    Every man going into the trenches must be in possession of two pairs of socks in addition to those he is wearing.
    The 49th Division have agreed to units of this Division in the line exchanging socks at the 49th Divn. Baths, YPRES, in a similar manner to their own units.
    The following procedure adopted by 49th Division will be carried out by Units of this Division until other arrangements can be made.
    Every day the socks of all men in the line will be changed, the discarded socks being put into sand-bags - one sandbag to each Platoon.
    One man per platoon (or an equivalent number of men per Battalion) will carry the sandbags of dirty socks to the 49th Divn. Baths, YPRES, and there receive a similar number of clean dry socks.

    (c) Foot troughs:-

    In the camps occupied by the 4 Battalions of the Reserve Brigade and the Reserve Battalions of the Brigade in the line, there are two troughs for foot washing and two Soyer stoves.
    These will be taken over and used.

    (d) Preparation and issue of anti-trench foot mixture:-

    On and after 9th inst., 2/1st Field Ambulance will prepare the camphor mixture for the whole Division.
    Next week's supply will be at the Advanced Ordnance Dump, H.16.d.2.2. by noon on 10th inst.,
    Units will draw from this Dump, as required, bringing their own tins or other receptacles.

3. ORDNANCE:-

    From 9th - 13th Jany, 197th Inf. Bde. Group will draw from the Dump at H.16.d.8.2. (Sheet 28)
    On and after 13th Jany. the Brigade Group (less Field Coy R.E.) will draw from D...D.O.S. Store, RENINGHELST.

-2-

4. New Refilling Point for 197th Inf. Bde Group will be H.13.d.8.2. (date of taking over will be notified later)

5. Instructions with regard to Medical arrangements, water supply, baths, laundries, etc., are being issued separately.

6. BAGGAGE WAGONS:- will report to this Unit at 4 p.m. 11th inst.,   No further transport is available. Wagons will be returned to the Train Company immediately after completion of move.

7. ACKNOWLEDGE

J. House

Captain,

Issued at 1.15 pm   Adjutant, 3/5th Battn. LAN.FUS.,
11.1.18.

Copies to all recipients of O.O. G.32

SECRET   Copy No......12..

                            WARNING ORDER
                    -.-.-.-.-.-.-.-.-.-.-.-.

Map reference Sheet 28, 1/40,000.

1. The 197th INFANTRY BRIGADE will relieve the 198th INFANTRY
   BRIGADE in the Left Sector on 16th/17th January.

   3/5th Lan. Fus.,   Right Front Battalion.
                                       H.Q. D.16.d.7.2.

2. Units will take over the line exactly as held by the 198th
   Inf. Bde.

3. The following will reconnoitre the line tomorrow, 14th January.

   Os.C. "A", "B" and "D" Companies, and 2nd in Command of
                                           "C" Coy.

   These Officers will take with them one other Officer from their
   Company and also one runner.

   Lieut. K.H. PARSONS and one Battalion H.Q. Runner.
   Runners will be instructed to take in as much as possible of
   all routes, tracks, etc.,

4. Attention is drawn to circular issued to all Officers on 10.1.18
   "Points on taking over Line"

5. Above Officers and runners will go up the line with working
   parties tomorrow by the train leaving H.14.b.4.8. at 8.30 a.m.

Issued at 7 pm
13.1.1918.
                                                        Captain,
                                   Adjutant, 3/5th Battn. LAN. FUS,

                            Distribution

                Copy No.1.   C.O.
                       2.   Second in Command.
                       3.   Adjt & File.
                       4.   S.O.
                       5.   O.C. "A" Coy
                       6.   O.C. "B" Coy
                       7.   O.C. "C" Coy
                       8.   O.C. "D" Coy
                       9.   O.C. H.Q Coy
                      10.   Transport Officer.
                      11.   Quarter Master
                      12.   War Diary.
                      13.   War Diary.

SECRET APPENDIX VIII
Copy No. 13

3/5th Battn. LANCASHIRE FUSILIERS.

Administrative Instructions issued with reference to Operation Order G.33

1. FOOD:-

Rations. Units will take over from outgoing units the present system of delivery of rations, etc., to the line.

Supplies are delivered by Train transport to the Q.M. stores of the two front Battalions.

Pack Transport dump rations for the two front line Battalions and the two forward companies of the Support Battalion at SEINE DUMP. Rations for the remaining two companies of the SUPPORT Battalion are taken by limber to GARTER POINT.

Forward Pack Transport Lines, POTIJZE, I.3.d.5.4. to which point rations are delivered by limbers.

3/5th and 2/8th LANCASHIRE FUSILIERS will detail 1 Sergeant and 1 corporal respectively, with 20 pack animals and complement of 12 men from both battalions to report at POTIJZE I.3.d.5.4. at 3.00 pm 16th instant, when they will come under charge of the Brigade Transport Officer.

Pack animals will be changed over on inter-Battalion relief.

Water.- There are wells at the following points:-
D.16.d.9.9.   D.16.d.6.1. (3 wells)

There are also two wells close to the Soda Factory, ZONNEBEKE. The water in one is good, but that of the other is bad. Water tanks are being placed at all Battalion H.Q.

2. SOLIDIFIED ALCOHOL:-

Solidified alcohol will be drawn daily from Brigade Q.M. Stores as under:-

Front line Battalions ... ... 39 tins.

3. Drinking water is obtained by boiling water at B.H.Q. in Soyers Stoves. Number of petrol tins needed 108
Distribution   54 at B.H.Q. at the Stoves.
               12 at "A" Coy, including 2 for officers.
               11 at "B"   ..   ..   ..
               11 at "C" Coy
               12 at "D" Coy
                8 at H.Q.Coy   ..   3 for officers

Method of Supply - Daily.
(1) Officers messes will send batmen to B.H.Q. to draw water for their officers, bringing 2 empty petrol tins per Officers mess for "A" "B" "C" & "D" Coys & 3 empty tins for H.Q. Mess. They will receive an equal number of full tins from B.H.Q.
(2) Support Coy, Reserve Coy & H.Q.Coy will return empty tins to the numbers as above less those for officers messes & will receive an equal number of full ones at B.H.Q.
(3) Reserve Coy will supply 10 men for carrying 10 tins to "A" Coy and 9 men for carrying 9 tins to "C" Coy. These men must return an equal number of empty tins to B.H.Q. from those Coys each night.
N.B.(a) 1 full petrol tin weighs 20 lbs.
    (b) The filled petrol tins at B.H.Q. will not be available until 6 pm daily.
    (c) By this scheme each officer will get 1 gall. of water per diem for cooking & drinking and each O.R. 1 quart for drinking.

ACKNOWLEDGE.

Issued at 7 pm 15.1.18.

Capt.
Adjutant, 3/5th Bn.Lan.Fus.

Copies to all recipients of O.O. G.33

SECRET   Copy No. 13.
                                                                    APPENDIX IX

3/5th Battn. LANCASHIRE FUSILIERS.

Operation Order G.33

1. The 197th Infantry Brigade will relieve the 198th Infantry Brigade in the LEFT SECTOR of LEFT DIVISIONAL FRONT of XXII Corps Front on 16th January, 1918.

2. The 3/5th LAN. FUS., will relieve the 2/4th East Lancs. Regt. in the Right Front Line of the Left Sector.

3. INSTRUCTIONS:-

    (a) The Battalion will move forward by train from VLAMERTINGHE at 11.00 a.m. and detrain at GORDON HOUSE SPUR (I.16.a) at 11.30 a.m. The Battalion will entrain at the rear end of the train & in the following order:- "C", "A", "B", "D" & "H.Q. Coys. Two Field Kitchens will be at GORDON HOUSE SPUR by 12.30 p.m. with hot food for the Battalion. The Transport Officer will arrange and must also accompany these field kitchens.
    The Battalion will commence moving from GORDON HOUSE in sufficient time to enable the first party of the leading Coy ("C" Coy) to reach the Junction of CAMBRIDGE ROAD and F TRACK by 3.00 p.m.
    (b) Coys will relieve Coys of 2/4th East Lancs. in the line as follows:-   "C" Coy relieve Right Coy.
                    "A" Coy relieve Left Coy
                    "B" Coy relieve Support Coy
                    "D" Coy relieve Reserve Coy
    (c) Guides from 2/4th East Lancs. Regt will meet parties at Junction of CAMBRIDGE ROAD and F TRACK at 3.00 p.m. Coys should be split up into parties as discussed at Coy Commanders conference to-day (i.e. by posts, &c) and should move in complete small parties from GORDON HOUSE.
    (d) All Trench and Camp stores, air photos, maps, S.A.A. and Grenades and A.A. Mountings will be handed and taken over, and duplicate receipts made out and rendered to Battalion Hdqrs as soon as possible after taking over.

4. The Defence Scheme as handed over by Units in the Line will became operative for the 197th Infantry Brigade and local schemes will be submitted in by Coys to Battalion H.Q. at once.

5. The S.O.S. Signal in use is a Rifle Grenade bursting into coloured stars, RED over GREEN over YELLOW.

6. REPORTS will be rendered to reach Battn. H.Q. as under:-
            (a) Situation Report   3.30 a.m.   3.30 p.m.
            (b) Intelligence & Patrol   7.00 a.m.

7. Transport Lines will NOT be moved.
8. Completion of relief will be reported by the word "MUD".
9. ACKNOWLEDGE.

                                                                    Capt.
Issued at 6.15 pm 15.1.18.   Adjutant, 3/5th Bn. LAN.FUS.
                        DISTRIBUTION
Copy No.1. C.O.   Copy No.2. Second in Commd Copy No.3 "A" Coy
        4. O.C."B" Coy   5. O.C. "C" Coy   6."D" Coy
        7. O.C.H.Q.Coy   8. Sig. Off.   9.I.O.
       10. T.O.   11. Q.M.   12.File
       13. War Diary   14. War Diary.

SECRET   3/5th Bn LANCASHIRE FUSILIERS   Copy No.

APPENDIX X

OPERATION ORDER No 35

Map Ref:
    Zonnebeke 1/10,000 Ed 9a
    Sheet 28, 1/40,000   21 Jany 1918

1. Inter Battalion Reliefs will take place on 22/23 Jan: throughout the Brigade.

2. The Battalion will be relieved in the Right Front Line by 2/7th Lancs. Fusiliers. On relief the Battalion will withdraw to Support.

3. INSTRUCTIONS.
    (a) Coys will relieve as follows:-
        "A" Coy will relieve "A" Coy 2/7 Lan Fus @ THAMES
        "B"   "   "   "B"   ALBANIA nr ANZAC
        "C"   "   "   "C"   In Rly Cutting
        "D"   "   "   "D"   ANZAC
        "HQ"   "   "   "H.Q."   Anzac House.
    (b) On relief "A" Coy will come under the Tactical Command of O.C. 2/7th Lan Fus. (Right Front Bn). On relief "C" Coy will come under the Tactical Command of O.C. 2/6th Lan. Fus. (Left Front Bn)
    (c) "A"&"C" Coys will commence relief of their opposite numbers at 2.0 pm, 22/1/18.
    (d) O.C. "B" "D" & "H.Q" Coys will send guides as follows to meet their opposite numbers at THAMES ("H.Q" attached Coy) at 4.30 pm.
        1. Guide per front line post
        1.   "   "   Coy H.Q.
        1.   "   "   Batt H.Q.
    These guides will report to Adjutant before proceeding to THAMES.
    Guides as follows from 2/7th LAN.FUS. will report to Bn H.Q. by 5.0 pm. where they will wait for and conduct "B"&"D"&"H.Q" Companies back to their respective positions in Support.
        1. Guide per Coy ("B"&"D")
        1. Guide for Bn H.Q..
    (e) All maps, air photos, defence schemes, trench stores, S.O.S. Rockets, etc, will be carefully handed over and receipts in duplicate sent to B.H.Q. by 6.0 pm 23/1/18.
    (f) All work in progress will be handed over in exact detail to incoming units. Company Commanders will please be most particular on this point.
    (g) Front line companies should not commence Relief before 5.0 pm.
    (h) Completion of Relief to be notified to B.H.Q by word BON

4. WORKING PARTIES. (Battalion in Support)
Found at present by 2/7 LAN FUS will be found by this Battalion on and after 23rd inst, whilst in Support.

5. RATIONS.
"A"&"C" Coys rations as before, draw their own at SEINE DUMP each evening. "B","D",&"H.Q" rations brought up to ANZAC HOUSE by limber. Coys draw their own.

(2)

6. **GUM BOOTS.**

   Arrangements for handing over issued separately.
   Copies to all recipients of O.O. 35

7. **ACKNOWLEDGE.**

Issued at 12 p.m.

                                            Captain
                              Adjutant 3/5th Bn LANCS.FUS.

                    DISTRIBUTION.

         Copy No 1.....................C.O.
           "   2.....................O.C. "A" Coy
           "   3.....................O.C. "B" Coy
           "   4.....................O.C. "C" "
           "   5.....................O.C. "D" "
           "   6.....................O.C. "H.Q".
           "   7.....................2/7th L.F.
           "   8.....................T.O..Q.M..& O.C.Details
                                      All to initial.
           "   9.....................Spare.
           "   10.....................War Diary.
           "   11.....................War Diary.

SECRET.   Copy No 10.

To be attached to O.O.35

Relief 22/23/1/18
            Instructions re Gum-Boots - Vide O.O. 35.

1. No Gum-boots will be changed tomorrow morning. It is suggested that after the morning foot-rubbing, massage and change of socks, that all men put on their ordinary boots.
   In any case all men in front posts must change into their ordinary boots and sandbags (or putties if without sandbags) before being relieved. These men will bring down their gum-boots with them out of the line and dump them at junction of ZONNEBEKE TRACK and the cutting (near B.H.Q). No gum-boots from any Coys will be dumped at this point before 6 pm 22/1/18.

2. O.C."C"Coy, will arrange for supervision of this dumping at 6 pm 22/1/18, as above and will be responsible for transferring these gum-boots to Mules at SEINE DUMP before they are returned to Staff Captain YPRES. He will at the same time obtain a receipt from O.C. RATION PARTY for all gum-boots handed over.

                                                                    Captain
21.1.18.   Adjutant, 3/5th Bn LANCS FUS.

SECRET.   Copy No 8

APPENDIX X

3/5th Bn LANCASHIRE FUSILIERS

OPERATION ORDER No 36

Map Ref.- Zonnebeeke 1/10,000 Sheet 28 1/40,000.   27th Jan 1918

1. The 197th Infantry Brigade will be relieved in the LEFT sub-sector by the 199th Infantry Brigade on 28th Jan.1918.
The 3/5th Lancs. Fusiliers will be relieved in support by the 2/7th Manchester Regt.

2. On relief the Brigade will be in Divisional Reserve. The Battalion will be in reserve at HALIFAX CAMP.

3. INSTRUCTIONS.
(a) GUIDES. 1 per Company & Batt H.Q. will meet incoming Coys & H.Q. at the junction of Zonnebeke Road and X track.
These guides will be provided by BATTALION. H.Q. and Coys need not send any.
(b) All air photos, Map defence schemes, Trench Stores, S.A.A. etc, will be carefully handed over and receipts given. Receipts in duplicate will be sent to Battalion H.Q. by 10 am 29th Jany 1918.
(c) The Battalion will entrain at BIRR X Roads at 4.30 pm.
Detrain VANCOUVER 5.30 pm.
(d) Companies will use following routes on coming out of Trenches:-
"A" & "C" Companies:- ZONNEBEKE TRACK - CORDUROY TRACK - MOLE TRACK - BIRR X ROADS
Batt H.Q. "C"&"D" Coys:- MOLE TRACK - BIRR X ROADS.
(e) Completion of Relief will be notified by wire by code numeral 53.

4. WORKING PARTIES.
Present parties will be explained and details handed over carefully to incoming units. All working parties tomorrow will cease work early enough to be back at ANZAC by 1.30 pm

5. TRENCH FOOT.
As there is certain to be a wait at the entraining station in order to minimise the chance of TRENCH FOOT, all ranks will as far as possible March out of Trenches with dry socks on. Tea will be provided in the vicinity of BIRR X ROADS. The Q.M. & T.O., will arrange for same to be ready waiting in the Field Kitchens at or near BIRR X ROADS by 3.15 pm. The T.O will accompany the Kitchens to BIRR X ROADS and remain in order to obtain a site suitable to comply with Traffic Regulations as before.

6. TRANSPORT.
One (1) limber will report to ANZAC HOUSE to collect petrol tins, camp kettles &c. Coys will dump their camp kettles &c at ANZAC HOUSE, the rear Coys before leaving, the forward Coys as they pass
Above limber will report at 2.00 pm.

7. The Q.M. will arrange for a hot meal for the men on their arrival in camp about 5.30 pm.

8. O.i/c.Details will arrange for the taking over tomorrow of HALIFAX CAMP from the 2/6th MANCHESTER REGT. Usual instructions as regards receipts clean certificates &c to be followed to the letter. He will so arrange matters that the men can be billetted and fed quickly and as soon as

(2)

possible after arrival.

9. ACKNOWLEDGE.

        Issued at 3.00 pm.

                                            Captain & Adjutant
                                      3/5th Bn LANCS.FUSILIERS.

DISTRIBUTION.

```
Copy No 1...........C.O.
   "    2...........O.i/cDetails (for information
                                 (and instruction
                                 (of T.O.&.Q.M)
   "    3...........O.C."A"Coy
   "    4................"B" .
   "    5................"C" .
   "    6................"D" .
   "    7...............2/7th Manchester Regt.
   "    8...............War Diary.
   "    9...............War Diary.
   "   10...............File.
```

NOTES TO ACCOMPANY OPERATION ORDERS No 36 d/d 27/1/18

SALVAGE.
Every man will bring down some form of salvage out of the line.

WORKING PARTIES.
During Reserve as follows:-

200 men daily for salvage
CAMBRIDGE ROAD - entrain by light railway at VANCOUVER. Only 100 men required for 29th January only. Further details later.

TRENCH FEET.
Every Officer's attention is directed to O.O. 36 para.5. This is highly important.

[signature]
Captain,
Adjutant, 3/5th Bn LANCS FUSILIERS.

NOMINAL ROLL OF OFFICERS
3/5th BATTALION LANCASHIRE FUSILIERS.

	Name	Perm.Rank	Temp.Rank	Act.Rank	How employed
	BIDDULPH T.J. (2/8th Lan Fus)	Captain		Lt-Col	Commanding
	GOWLAND S.J. (6th Lan Fus)	~~Captain~~ Lieut.		Major	2nd in Command
	Ashworth R.S.	Captain			Coy Commander
	THOMPSON N.D.	Captain			L.G.O.
	HASTINGS H.	Lieut.		Captain	Coy Commander
	CROUCH F.H.	Lieut.		Captain	" "
	REID S.E. (6th Shrops L.I)		Lieut.	Captain	" "
	ROUSE J.	Lieut.		Captain	Adjutant
	MORLEY R.S.	Lieut.		ø Captain	2nd in Comd Coy
	HOLDSWORTH J.A	Lieut.			Course
	ANONI A.F.	Lieut.			Transport Off.
	BLAKE T.R.	Lieut.			197th L.T.M.B.
	UREN P.D.	Lieut.			Sick Leave
	YAPP G.H.	Lieut.			I.O.&Snipe.Off
	PARSONS E.H.	Lieut.			Sig. Officer
	BELL F.W. (6th LondonRegt)	2/Lieut			Platoon Comdr
øø	DUNN E.J.		2/Lieut		" "
øø	BELCHER S.		" "		" "
	BARLOW J.C.		" "		Leave
	HALL W.	2/Lieut.			Course
	WILSON E.J. (A.L. in error)	2/Lieut.			Platoon Comdr
@	GRELLIER A.B.		2/Lieut		" "
@	SMITH H.D.		" "		A.P.M. 66th Div
	CROSBIE J.	2/Lieut			Platoon Comdr
	LEWIS C.J.	2/Lieut			197th L.T.M.B.
	ROSS H.	2/Lieut			Course
@	LEWIS A.J.		2/Lieut		Platoon Comdr
	SMITH H.W.	2/Lieut			" "
	SIMPSON A.A.	2/Lieut			" "
@	DICKENS W.C.		2/Lieut		A/ Q.M.
ƒ	Crump A.G.		2/Lieut		Hospital
ƒ	GIBSON N.J.		" "		Platoon Comdr
	ANDERSON J.G.		" "		" "
	BRAMWELL N.		" "		" "
K	BELL W.E.		" "		" "
ƒ	WILSON A.		" "		" "
	SANDIFORD H.A.	Captain R.A.M.C.T.			Medical Off.
	FOSTER E.(C.F)	Captain			Wesleyan Chapln

ø Additional Captain
K 8th Bn Lan.Fus.
øø 1st & 2nd Bns Lan.Fus.
@ 3rd Bn (Res) Lan.Fus.
ƒ 6th Bn Lan.Fus.
ƒ 7th Bn Lan.Fus.

31.1.18

T.J.Biddulph
Lieut.-Colonel
Comdg 3/5th Bn Lancashire Fusiliers.

WAR DIARY

OF

3/5th. Battn. Lancashire Fusiliers

February 1st. – February 13th.

Volume 12.

Army Form C. 2118.

WAR DIARY
3/5th Bn LANCASHIRE FUSILIERS
INTELLIGENCE SUMMARY.
(Erase heading not required.)

Instructions regarding War Diaries and Intelligence Summaries are contained in F. S. Regs., Part II. and the Staff Manual respectively. Title pages will be prepared in manuscript.

Place	Date	Hour	Summary of Events and Information	Remarks and references to Appendices
	1918			
MILITARY CAMP Pd		1	Lt. Col. T.J. BIDDULPH (2/8 Bn L.A.F.W.) assumed command of Battalion on from 6.1.18.	O.R. 637
Line		3	Relieved the 2/4th Bn EAST LANCS. Regt. in the line - Right Brigade.	
			Battalion Right Brigade. Details of Battalion moved at Stacks Corps.	
		4?	Battalion in line.	
		8	Battalion relieved in line. See Narrative our 638	O.O. G 38
			Strength - Decrease	
			@ Lieut. P.D. UREN "A" Coy	
			29.1.18	
			Duty: Lieut J.A. HOLDSWORTH M.C. from course of Instruction 3.2.18.	
			2/Lt W. HALL from course of Instruction 6.2.18	
		9	Battalion moved to ST-JANS-TER-BIEZEN	O.O. G 39
ST-JANS-TER-BIEZEN		11	Duty:- Capt. R.S. MORLEY "A" Coy Assumes Promotion at 2nd ARMY CENTRAL SCHOOL	
			2/Lt. H.P. SMITH "D" Coy from R.A.M.C. 66th Division.	
do			Battalion disbanded (out: 66th DIVISIONAL LETTER No 365/A 44 (A44))	
		13	Before being disbanded the G.O.C. 66th Division addressed the Battalion	

WAR DIARY
INTELLIGENCE SUMMARY.

Army Form C. 2118.

3/5th Bn LANCASHIRE FUSILIERS

Place	Date	Hour	Summary of Events and Information	Remarks and references to Appendices
ST JANVIER-BIZOT	19th Jan	13	in the presence of all other units of the 197 & 198 Bdes. He said that it was very unfortunate that such a good Battalion should be broken up, but owing to the question of man-power it was necessary to absorb a large number of Battalions. He welcomed the remnants of the Battalion (20 Offrs and 480 O.Rs) to other units of the 198th Brigade (14 Offrs and 200 O.Rs to the 3/8th Battalion Lon. Fus. and 10 Offrs and 250 O.Rs to the 2/7 Battalion Lon. Fus.) Unfortunately 9 Officers and 190 O.Rs were leaving to Brienne and proceeding to the 19th Bn. Lon. Fus. The ceremony of disbandment was carried out as follows:- The coys detailed for the 2/7 Lon. Fus and 2/8th Lon. Fus. formed farm in turn to the 2/7 Lon. Fus. & 2/8th Lon. Fus. respectively to salute returning to conforming the Company for the 19th Lon. Fus. then marched along the Brigade front and off the Parade.	

J.J. Birrell Lt. Col.
Comdg 3/5 Lanc. Fus.

SECRET   Copy No.

3/5th Bn. LANCASHIRE FUSILIERS

Operation Order G.37.

2.2.18.

Map reference   ZONNEBEKE   1/10,000 Ed. 9a.
Sheet 28   1/40,000

1. The 197th Infantry Brigade will relieve the 198th Infantry Brigade in the Right Sector on 3/4 February.
2. The Battalion will relieve the 2/4th East Lancs. Regt in the Right Front Line of the Right Sector, and will be relieved in HALIFAX CAMP by the 2/9th MANCHESTER Regt.
3. INSTRUCTIONS.
    (a) The Battalion will entrain at VANCOUVER at 1.0 pm 3/2/18 and detrain at BIRR CROSS ROADS at 2.30 p.m 3/2/18. It will move from BIRR CROSS ROADS in the following order - B.H.Q. - Reserve Coy - Left Front Coy - Right Front Coy - Support Coy.
    (b) Companies will relieve Companies of 2/4th EAST LANCS. in the line as follows ; "A" Coy will relieve the Right Front Coy.
                                 "B" ..   ..   ..   Left   ..   ..
                                 "C" ..   ..   ..   Support Coy.
                                 "D" ..   ..   ..   Reserve Coy.
    Strength of Coys in the line will be as follows.
    Two Front line Coys ("A" & "B") 85 O.Rs each. Support & Reserve Coys ("C" & "D") 80 O.Rs each
    (c) Guides at rate of 1 per post, 1 per Coy H.Q. and 1 per Bn. H.Q. will meet Coys at junction of MOLE TRACK and Corduroy Road as under:-
              Reserve Coy & B.H.Q.   at 4.0 p.m.
              2 Front Line Coys   5.0 p.m.
              Support Coy   5.15pm.
    (d) Immediately on arrival at BIRR CROSS ROADS the R.S.M. and C.S.Ms of C & D Coys will proceed forward and report to their respective Hdqrs for the purpose of taking over stores, etc., in daylight.
    (e) Rations will be sent up by Transport as before - carrying parties from Reserve Coy, as called for. Transport will not arrive at JABBER HOUSE tomorrow before 8.0 pm
    (f) All maps, air photos, Defence Schemes, Trench Stores etc., will be taken over and receipts in duplicate sent to this Office by 9.0 am 4.2.18.
    (g) The Camp will be handed over by O i/c Details in a clean & sanitary condition. O. i/c Details will obtain "Clean" certificates etc., from the incoming unit. All Defence Schemes etc., will be handed over and receipts in duplicate obtained and filed.
4. All working parties at present found by the 2/4th E.Lancs Regt in the line will be taken over and found by the Battn from 4th Feb. incl. Working parties found by Batt. at present will be handed over to incoming unit and details explained.
5. Transport & Details Camp will not move.
6. The T.O. will establish PACK TRANSPORT LINES at the Ecole I.9.c.5.2.
7. Any gum boots required in the line will be drawn from 198th Inf.Bde Stores at YPRES BARRACKS on 2.2.18 They will NOT be taken over in the line.
8. All stored reserve rations will be checked and taken over by an officer.
9. Completion of relief will be notified by telephoning the numeral "18"
10. ACKNOWLEDGE.

(sgd) J. ROUSE. Captn & Adjt
Issued at 9.45 pm   3/5th Battn. Lan. Fus.,

DISTRIBUTION

Copy No.1. C.O.   2. Second in Commd   3. "A" Coy
       4. "B" Coy   5. "C" Coy   6. "D" ..
       7. H.Q. ..   8. T.O.   9. Q.M.
      10. Adjt & File 11. War Diary   12. War Diary

SECRET

3/5th Bn. LANCASHIRE FUSILIERS
Operation Order No. 38

Copy No

Map reference:-
    ZONNEBEKE, 1/10,000 Ed.9A
    Sheet 28, 1/40,000

7.2.18.

1. The 197th Infantry Brigade will be relieved in the line as far as D.23.d.1.7. on 8th/9th February by 1st New Zealand Infantry Brigade.

2. The 3/5th Bn. Lan. Fus., will be relieved as follows:-
    (i) Front Line - Nos. 1 & 2 posts)
        Support Line - No.1. post   ) By 2nd WELLINGTN REGT.

    (ii) Front Line - Nos.3,4,5,6,7,9,)
                    10,11,14,15 & 16)
                    Posts   ) By 1st AUCKLAND REGT.
        Support Line - Nos. 2,3 & 4 posts)

3. On relief the Bn. will withdraw to HALIFAX CAMP.

4. INSTRUCTIONS:-
    (a) Nos. 1 & 2, Front Line posts will be relieved as arranged between the C.O.- Capt. HASTINGS & 2/Lt. DUNN (Dictated 10.30 am 7/2/18)
    (b) No.1. Post - Support line will be relieved as arranged.
    (c) Remainder of posts as given in para.2 & Reserve Coy will be relieved as follows:-
        Support Line Posts by 3.30 p.m.
        Reserve Coy   - 3.30 p.m.
        Front line posts commence at dusk.
    (d) All lists of position calls, air photos, which may be of use to incoming Units, Defence Schemes, Log books, Trench Stores, A.A. positions & Mountings, S.A.A., grenades and reserve rations, water etc., will be handed over and receipts in duplicate sent to this office by 9 a.m. 9.2.18.
    All out of date maps and documents will be burnt.
    (e) Guides at the rate of one per front line post will meet incoming units as under:-
    For posts 3,4,5,6,7,9,10 & 11 Junction of Mole Track and Jabber Track.
    For posts 14, 15 & 16 at H.Q. of Support Coy, Left Battn.
    (f) All work in progress and proposed will be handed over carefully.
    (g) Dugouts, pillboxes shelters etc., & ground in vicinity will be handed over in a clean condition, certificates (in duplicate) to this effect being obtained.
    (h) Trains leave BIRR CROSS ROADS as under for VANCOUVER.
        1st Train 5 p.m.   2nd Train 8 p.m.
    As many men as possible will travel by the first train. Tea will be provided at BIRR CROSS ROADS from 4.15 p.m to 5 p.m.
    O.C. Train - Capt. CROUCH.
    (i) Completion of relief will be wired to this office by code numeral - 24 O.C. "A" & "B" Coys will in addition call at these H.Q. when all men are clear and relief forward is complete.

5. To guard against possibilities of Trench feet due to a possible wait at entraining station, O.C. Coys will arrange where possible for an additional change of socks before leaving the Trenches.

6. ACKNOWLEDGE.

(sgd) J. ROUSE, Captn & Adjt
3/5th Lan. Fus.,

Issued at 7 a.m.   DISTRIBUTION
    Copy No.1. C.O.   2. 1st Auckland Regt
        3. O.C. "A"   4. O.C. "B" Coy
        5. O.C. "C"   6. O.C. "D" Coy
        7. Major Gowland, O i/c Details, T.O. & Q.M.
        8. War Diary
        9 ..   .. 10. H.Q. Coy & File.

SECRET   3/5th BATTN. LANCASHIRE FUSILIERS   Copy No. 9

OPERATION ORDER G.39.   9th Feby. 1918.

Map reference.
   Sheet 28 - 1/40,000.
   .. 27 - 1/40,000.

1. The 197th Infantry Brigade Group will move on 10th February to ROAD CAMP F.25.c. (ST-JAN-TER-BIEZEN Area) by march route.
2. The Battalion will move to ROAD CAMP, F.25.c. by march route.
3. INSTRUCTIONS:-
   (a) Order of march - - "H.Q" - "A" - "B" - "C" - "D" - Transport.
   (b) Route - - - - - - Road-junction, H.13.d.9.2. - Crossroads BRANDHOEK, G.6.d.5.3. - BRANDHOEK SWITCH ROAD N. of Poperinghe - ST-JAN-TER-BIEZEN.
       N.B. The Battn. must clear Brigade Starting Point before halting (X rds G.6.d.5.3)
   (c) Starting Point - - Road junction, H.13.d.9.2.
   (d) Time - - - - - - - 7-25 AM
   (e) All Officers valises, etc., and blankets (rolled in bundles of 9 with a tenth wrapped round them) will be stacked at Q.M. Stores by 6.00 a.m.
   (f) A loading party of 3 men per Company will be detailed to report To Q.M. at Q.M. Stores at 6.15 a.m. 10.2.18 The Company on duty will detail 1 NCO in addition to be in charge.
4. TRANSPORT:-
   Baggage wagons will report this evening.
   One lorry(to make 2 journeys, under arrangements to be made by the Q.M.) will report in the morning. A guide for this lorry (to be detailed by Q.M.) will report to Orderly Room at 7.30 a.m. 10.2.18. and report to Brigade Hdqrs at 8.00 a.m.
   The T.O. will arrange to be ready to follow the Battalion in time. All Transport will be packed and ready to-night with the exception of Officers valises, blankets, &c, &c., and any equipment to be sent on lorry (2 journeys). Transport will be limited and officers kits will be reduced to the authorised scale at once.
5. The strictest march discipline will be observed on the road. Fourth Army G.S. 148 d/d 15.12.17 (copy in possession of Coys) will be complied with in every particular, with the exception of para.4(e).
6. Captn. THOMPSON and 5 men per Company will remain behind to clean up the Camp. O.C. "A" Coy will also provide a NCO to assist Captn. THOMPSON. Particular attention to be paid to the incineration of all refuse.
   Captn. THOMPSON will, before leaving, obtain receipts from Area Commandant for all Area stores, &c., handed over. He will 2/6 MANCH REGT (relieving Unit) or also obtain a clean certificate for both camps and Transport Lines.
   Company Commanders will render a certificate to B.H.Q. by noon 11th inst., that no stores of any kind have been taken from the area except such stores as are allowed in War Establishment and amending GRO's.
7. ACKNOWLEDGE.

Issued at 5.30 PM.

Adjutant, 3/5th Battn. LAN. FUS., Captn,

DISTRIBUTION

Copy No.1.	C.O.	Copy No.2.	Second in Command.
3.	O.C. "A" Coy	4.	O.C. "B" Coy.
5.	O.C. "C" Coy	6.	O.C. "D" Coy.
7.	Q.M.	8.	T.O.
9.	War Diary	10.	War Diary
11.	File	12.	Spare.

www.ingramcontent.com/pod-product-compliance
Lightning Source LLC
Chambersburg PA
CBHW080906230426
43664CB00016B/2740